Birds in Literature

University Press of Florida

Gainesville Tallahassee Tampa Boca Raton Pensacola Orlando Miami Jacksonville

Birds in Literature

Leonard Lutwack

Copyright 1994 by the Board of Regents of
the State of Florida
Printed in the United States of America on
acid-free paper
99 98 97 96 95 94   6 5 4 3 2 1

Copyright acknowledgment appear on the
last printed pages of this book.

Library of Congress
Cataloging-in-Publication Data
Lutwack, Leonard, 1917–
Birds in literature/Leonard Lutwack.
p.   cm.
Includes bibliographical references and
index.
ISBN 0-8130-1254-6
1. Birds in literature.   2. Birds—Folklore.
I. Title.
PN56.B56L88   1994
809'.9336—dc20   93-30647

The University Press of Florida is the
scholarly publishing agency for the State
University System of Florida, comprised of
Florida A & M University, Florida Atlantic
University, Florida International Univer-
sity, Florida State University, University
of Central Florida, University of Florida,
University of North Florida, University
of South Florida, and University of West
Florida.

University Press of Florida
15 Northwest 15th Street
Gainesville, FL 32611

Best gems of Nature's cabinet,
With dews of tropic morning wet,
Beloved of children, bards and Spring,
O birds, your perfect virtues bring,
Your song, your forms, your rhythmic flight,
Your manners for the heart's delight.

Ralph Waldo Emerson, "May-Day"

c o n t e n t s

Animals must have evoked from primitive human beings a more immediate and telling response than any other feature of their natural surroundings simply because animals were perceived to be so nearly like humans and in many ways superior to humans. As the earliest inhabitants spread out from the limited locales that favored their earliest evolution, they moved into places where they found already well-established animal inhabitants. To struggling humanity the capability and beauty of the animal, a result of its perfect adaptation to environment and its single-minded effort to survive, must have been especially impressive, inspiring early humans to acquire the same powers by emulation or magic. The wild animal, then the tamed animal such as the horse and the falcon, and eventually the domesticated animal represented the most comprehensible link between man and nature. Like humans yet different, seeming to be both in and beyond nature, the animal was venerated because it appeared to have special powers that made it conversant with the more elusive forces of nature that governed the return of the sun each day, the miracle of reproduction and growth, the mystery of death. If not gods themselves animals were the familiars of the gods, served as their emissaries or agents, and therefore knew their secrets.

Of all wild animals the bird has always been closest to human-kind because so much of its life can be readily observed and appreciated. Flight and song make birds exceptionally noticeable in every sort of environment. Because they are able to avoid capture rather easily, birds are not nearly as furtive as other animals, and some wild species are even willing to set aside natural caution in order to accept food and nesting sites from humans. Indeed, many species often carry on the vital functions of their existence in the presence of people—feeding, mating, nest building, and caring for the young. Birds, as John Ruskin puts it, are "sociable to man extremely, building and nestling and rustling about him,—prying and speculating, curiously watchful of him at his work, if likely to be profitable to themselves." Henry David Thoreau seems to imply that there can even be a personal relationship between man and bird: "Sometimes when I am going through the Deep Cut, I look up and see half a dozen black crows flitting silently across in front and ominously eying down; passing from one wood to another, yet as if their passage had reference to me." Loren Eiseley recounts a similar experience with a crow that suddenly came upon him "at about the level of my eyes in a dense fog" and therefore "experienced the human world from an unlikely perspective. He and I share a viewpoint in common: our worlds have interpenetrated, and we both have faith in the miraculous."[1]

Thriving in a wide variety of habitats—human settlements as well as wilderness, field and garden as well as forest, marsh and mountain, pond, river, and sea—birds are unquestionably the wild animal most frequently encountered by people. The worldwide distribution of many avian species and families enables people all over the world to share a common body of knowledge concerning birds. Because of their migratory habit, wood warblers and water-fowl, for example, are known to both North and South Americans, the white stork and Scandinavian crane to both Europeans and Africans. In all of their activities there is such an extraordinary degree of intensity and animation that it is almost impossible not to notice birds. The "most ardent for life of all our blood kin," writes Saint-John Perse, "the bird is he who bears hidden in himself, to nourish his passion, the highest fever of the blood. His grace is that burning. Nothing symbolic about this: it is simple biological fact."

Birds have twice the amount of sugar in their blood as mammals, with the result that "few other creatures seem so alive in every fibre . . . so fully given to the action, whether in song, in motion or in display. Even in quiescence they are concentrations of vitality."[2] Yet there is nothing precipitous in their behavior; birds are profoundly deliberate in every move they make. Performing the same functions year after year, never appearing to change, birds present to humans enviable examples of self-possession, permanence, and changelessness.

For all their familiarity, however, except for a few tamable species, birds remain wild, unpossessed, living "beside us, but alone," as Matthew Arnold observes. The very attributes that make them familiar to us, flight and song, still retain an air of mystery that sets birds apart from other animals, which seem by comparison to be gross and earthbound. Flight makes birds highly visible, yet elusive—"apparitional" as Hart Crane describes gulls in "To Brooklyn Bridge." To the human ear bird song sounds almost like speech, even expressive of human feelings, and yet it is a communication stranger than speech and not quite the same as music. Arcane utterance and the freedom to escape earth seem to suggest a relationship with the supernatural in both its cosmic and minute forms. Emily Dickinson wonders whether perhaps the bird in the yard speaks the language of the gods:

> To hear an Oriole sing
> May be a common thing—
> Or only a divine,

and Izaak Walton's defender of birds in *The Compleat Angler* is certain that when his soaring hawks were "lost in the sight of men, then they attend upon and converse with the gods."[3] Birds are the envy of humankind because they appear to exist happily and effortlessly in a state of mixed animal and spiritual being that humans long to attain; they are perfectly adapted to the harsh conditions of life in nature and yet seem to enjoy a kind of freedom from necessity.

Familiarity and transcendence have given birds a wider range of meaning and symbol in literature than any other animal. The resemblance of their activities to common patterns of human family behavior—"the feathered parallel," in Robert Browning's phrase—makes them exceptionally suitable for anthropomorphic imagery that links man to the common forms of nature. The element of mystery in their behavior, on the other hand, furnishes material for symbolical meanings of a supernatural order. From both sources, from intimate knowledge and remote significance, there has accumulated an immense store of folklore and myth available to writers from the earliest beginnings of literature to the present.

Birds are used more frequently in poetry than in any other genre because they can be incorporated more easily in the minute imagery that makes up the basic stuff of poetry than in the broader elements of plot and character upon which drama and fiction depend. There are few novels in which a bird is the center of action and meaning, and few novelists make as much use of birds as does D. H. Lawrence, for example. Few poets, on the other hand, fail to respond to birds, and some, like Thomas Hardy and Emily Dickinson, make birds a prominent feature of their writing. Almost half of the animal imagery in Milton has to do with birds; in the works of Shakespeare, Caroline Spurgeon estimates that "images from birds form by far the largest section drawn from any single class of objects" except the human body. It was the poet, however, rather than the dramatist in Shakespeare who responded so frequently to birds with a power of imagination, as defined by Samuel Taylor Coleridge in his Shakespeare lectures, that "acts by impressing the stamp of humanity, and of human feelings, on inanimate or mere natural objects."[4] Coleridge chose a passage from Shakespeare's *Venus and Adonis* to illustrate his point:

> Lo! here the gentle lark, weary of rest,
> From his moist cabinet mounts up on high,
> And wakes the morning, from whose silver breast
> The sun ariseth in his majesty.
> (lines 853–56)

John Ruskin was also interested in the exercise of the imagination on natural objects, or showing how natural objects are connected with art and literature, something that science could not do. "Man is intended to *observe* with his eyes, and mind," he wrote to a friend, "not with microscope and knife" (25:xvi). Going beyond Coleridge, he believed that the first step in getting at the "natural history of anything, or of any creature" must be "to know the poetry of it—i.e. what it has been to man, or what man has made of it . . . what the effect of its existence has hitherto been on the minds of men" (22:244–45). The natural objects he proposed to study in this connection were birds, flowers, and minerals, and at Oxford in 1872 and 1873 he actually delivered two series of lectures on the relation of birds to art. But he could not hold himself to his task, and we are left only with some disconnected and random discussions that have any reference to his massive subject.

Even though I shall concentrate on but one of Ruskin's three kinds of natural objects, my field of study is still broad enough and will require limiting my attention to creative writing in which natural fact, literary art, and human significance are appropriately balanced. I do not propose, of course, to do a history of the immense volume of literature dealing with birds but rather to demonstrate how writers have adapted that tradition for the significance it may have for our times. The greatest part of my source material is the poetry and prose fiction of American and British writers of the nineteenth and twentieth centuries.

Of one of the characters in Salman Rushdie's *Satanic Verses* it is said that "he'd assembled in lighter days" an "Allegorical Aviary," a mere collection of "winged metaphors."[5] I hope that the same will not have to be said of my attempt to continue the discussion of what Coleridge and Ruskin called the poetry of natural objects.

In order to complete the picture of the ongoing tradition of making literary use of birds in the texts I discuss, I have drawn on several learned compilations of the folklore, mythology, and literature of birds, ranging from antiquity, through classical and early Christian times, to the Middle Ages and the Renaissance. I am particularly indebted to the folowing scholars: Beryl Rowland, *Birds with Human Souls: A Guide to Bird Symbolism* (Knoxville: University of Tennessee Press, 1978); Ernest Ingersoll, *Birds in Legend and Folklore* (Detroit: Singing Tree, 1968); and Edward A. Armstrong, *The Folklore of Birds* (New York: Dover, 1970) and *The Life and Lore of the Bird* (New York: Crown, 1975). I am also indebted to a second group of authors who combine an expert knowledge of ornithology with a deep appreciation of the values birds have for the literary artist. These include Charlton Ogburn, *The Adventure of Birds* (New York: Morrow, 1980); Grundy Steiner, "Of Men and Birds," introduction to James Edmund Harting, *The Birds of Shakespeare* (Chicago: Argonaut, 1965); and two bird dictionary makers: Sir A. Landsborough Thomson, entries for birds in poetry, Shakespeare, and the Bible in *A New Dictionary of Birds* (New York: McGraw-Hill, 1964); and Christopher Leahy, entries titled "Birds in Human Culture" and "Birds in Imagination," in *The Birdwatcher's Companion* (New York: Hill & Wang, 1982). A third group consists of those who have studied the use of birds in the works of some particular writer; these will be noted at the appropriate places in my text where their work has helped my discussions.

Birds, Poetry, and the Poet

Yours is of another order of being,
and wholly it compels.
William Everson, "A Canticle of Waterbirds"

o n e . Bird Song: The Nightingale

The ancient Greeks had a story about a king named Tereus who, having conceived a passion for his sister-in-law, Philomela, entices the girl away from home, rapes her, cuts out her tongue so that she cannot tell what has befallen, and holds her prisoner. Philomela nevertheless manages to communicate by weaving her sad story into the design of a tapestry and getting it into the hands of her sister Procne. The two women then perpetrate a horrible revenge against the man who has wronged them: they kill his son Itys and serve up the pieces of the body to the unsuspecting father at a banquet. As soon as he discovers the cruel trick, Tereus rushes at the sisters with his sword and is about to kill them when the gods change all the principals into birds. Procne becomes a nightingale, Philomela a swallow, Tereus a hoopoe, and poor Itys, reassembled, a pheasant. The grieving father of the two girls, Pandion, is turned into an osprey. In the transition from Greek to Roman versions of the story, Philomela somehow becomes the nightingale and Procne the swallow. Although it makes less sense this way because the tongueless Philomela is hardly fit to sing the elaborate song of the nightingale, the Roman version has prevailed in Western literature since the Renaissance.

An earlier story about the nightingale has to do with Aedon, a Greek matron who is moved by envy to kill the eldest son of her sister-in-law Niobe's twelve children but mistakenly kills her own son Itylus instead. The misery of the grief-stricken mother is eased when Zeus turns her into a nightingale. Homer alludes to the story in book 19 of the *Odyssey* when Penelope, anxious about the safety of her only son, recalls the fate of Aedon and mentions several details that have ever since remained in the poetic history of the nightingale: the bird sings in the early spring, it sings from a grove of trees sacred to the dead, and its song is a tragic lament. Sophocles makes good use of Homer in his description of the sacred grove, which like paradise knows no seasons or time, where the wandering, homeless Oedipus finds rest and final absolution for his sins of murder and incest, a place where "the sweet, sojourning nightingale / Murmurs all day long."[1]

Although the primary interest of the stories of Philomela, Aedon, and others like them is their tragic significance for human beings, they may have had their origin as simple folktales devised to explain why the song of the nightingale is so sad and why the swallow has no song at all. The stories also incorporate the primitive belief that after death the soul starts a new life in the body of an animal with which it shares some physical feature. The Pythagoreans later made the transmigration of souls a philosophical principle, but there is nothing exclusively Greek in this combination of etiology and metempsychosis. Among the Neskapi Indians of Labrador, the robin's red breast is explained by a folktale in which a woman who is pushed into the fire by her angry husband returns to life in the form of a bird.[2] To the primitive mind the passage from human to animal form would not have appeared at all implausible, so close at one time was the relation of human to animal. In the Greek story divine intervention is invoked to explain the transformation of the unfortunate family. At the very moment when the enraged Tereus is about to plunge his family into even deeper tragedy, the pitying gods lift all of the savage participants into the purer realm of innocent animal existence where time is always the present and revenge no longer matters. Now Philomela may tell her sad story in song for all to hear, may sing "with inviolable voice," as T. S. Eliot describes her in *The Waste Land.* Now Tereus, bearing the crest of a hoopoe as though it were the crown of a warrior king, may pursue his enemies with his spearlike beak and foul his nest, as the hoopoe was believed to do, without harming anyone.

As though the suffering of poor Philomela were not already enough, Renaissance poets added to the earlier versions of the Philomela story a colorful image of the disconsolate bird leaning its breast against a thorn, either to accentuate its grief or relieve its deeper woe by adding a lesser pain. This detail may have originated in a piece of symbolism commonly found in medieval Persian poetry. As early as the twelfth century, Persian love poetry represented the woman as a rose and her admirer as a bulbul, a songbird that European translators took to be the nightingale. Just as the bird is wounded by the thorns of the rosebush as it feeds on the nectar of the flower, so the lover suffers pain in his courtship of the woman he loves. We read in the odes of Hafiz that "drops of his heart's blood" go to nourish the rose and dye its petals red. A passage in the thirteenth-century *Roman de la Rose*, translated by Chaucer in 1386, seems to suggest that the thorn among the roses is an alternative metaphor for Cupid's arrows. The lover seeks his lady, or the love of his lady, symbolized by a rose, in a garden where many birds, including a nightingale, sing "layes of love." He avoids the "netles, thornes, and hokede breres," only to be wounded by the God of Love's "arowe full sharply whet" (lines 1,710–23). In "A Seying of the Nightingale," John Lydgate, a younger contemporary of Chaucer, speaks of the "sharpe thorne / Which pricketh his brest with fyry remembraunce." Sir Thomas Browne offers what he considers a natural explanation of the association of the nightingale with the thorn when he writes in *Vulgar Errors* that the bird "roosteth in thorny and prickly places, where serpents may least approach him."[3]

By the close of the sixteenth century the thorn was well established in the references to the story of Philomela in English literature. Typical are these lines from Richard Barnefield in "An Ode," once ascribed to Shakespeare:

> She, poor bird, as all forlorn,
> Leaned her breast up-till a thorn
> And there sung the doleful'st ditty,

That to hear it was great pity.
Fie, fie, fie, now she would cry,
Teru, teru, by and by.[4]

In *The Rape of Lucrece* Shakespeare does indeed adopt the imagery of the thorn in his most telling use of the Philomela legend. After being raped by Tarquin, Lucrece compares herself to the Greek maiden:

Come, Philomel; that sing'st of ravishment,
Make thy sad grove in my disheveled hair.

. . . .

And whiles against a thorn thou bear'st thy part,
To keep thy sharp woes waking, wretched I,
To imitate thee well, against my heart
Will fix a sharp knife to affright mine eye.

Then comes an explanation of the nightingale's singing at night:

And for, poor bird, thou sing'st not in the day,
As shaming any eye should thee behold,
Some dark deep desert, seated from the way,
That knows not parching heat nor freezing cold,
Will we find out; and there we will unfold
    To creatures stern sad tunes, to change their kinds.
    Since men prove beasts, let beasts bear gentle minds.

(lines 1128–48)

The irony Shakespeare introduces in the last line perfectly supplements the catharsis achieved by the transformation of humans into birds in Greek myths.

From a literary point of view the grafting of birds onto an otherwise human-oriented plot gives a special meaning to the story of Philomela. Transforming the principals into birds resolves nothing, as a deus ex machina might, but instantly stops the almost unbearable chain of horrible events and fixes all in the unchangeable state of animal existence that resembles the human condition but has no tragic consequences. The unself-consciousness of animals and their perfect adaptation to all conditions of life seem to place them in an order of being superior to human turbulence and torment. When the story devolves on them, violent action yields to symbol and the incident passes into the realm of timeless and transcendent beauty. The disturbing events, as Wallace Stevens might have said of them, are "placed, so, beyond the compass of change, / Perceived in a final atmosphere."[5]

The legend of Philomela has been a favorite poetic subject for almost three thousand years, making the nightingale the most famous bird in literature and its song the most moving of all bird song. Both the bird and the song are ignored, however, in one of the earliest and best-known versions of the story, the one Ovid included in his *Metamorphoses* in the first century A.D.[6] Allusions to birds are artfully woven into the narrative—an owl at the wedding of Tereus and Procne presages disaster, Tereus is compared to a rapacious eagle of Zeus, Philomela to a helpless pigeon—but bird song does not figure in the story, and the transformation of Philomela and Procne is left a little vague, one bird, presumably the nightingale, flying off to the woods and the other, the swallow, perching on the roof of a house. The breasts of both are spotted with blood, a detail that seems to place more blame on the sisters than on Tereus. Perhaps Ovid was following a version of the story that offered an explanation of plumage instead of song. In any event it is evident that Ovid was intent only on the human aspects of the story, particularly the horror and the passion, which in many ways resemble the bloody exchange between Jason and Medea, another story related in *Metamorphoses* and adapted by Ovid for the stage.

Ovid's concentration on the violent action of the story led to some unfortunate literary results. In *Titus Andronicus,* one of Shakespeare's least-admired plays, the horror of events exceeds even those related by Ovid. The unfortunate daughter of Titus, Lavinia, is raped by two brothers, who cut off her hands as well as her tongue. Holding a staff between her teeth, she writes the names of her violators in the sand, and when her avenging father cuts their throats she catches the blood with a basin held between the two stumps. She is herself killed by her noble father so that she will not "survive her shame." In the last speech of the play scavenger birds—vultures, it appears—are ironically associated with the person most responsible for starting all the trouble, Tamora, queen of the Goths.

> No mournful bell shall ring her burial;
> But throw her forth to beasts and birds to prey.
> Her life was beastly and devoid of pity,
> And being dead, let birds on her take pity.

The story of Philomela has survived more in brief allusions than in complete retellings such as Ovid's. Its plot has commanded less attention over the ages than the report of the nightingale's song lamenting the tragic result of wrongful love. Perhaps the case would have been different if *Tereus*, a tragedy written by Sophocles, had survived, though it is hard to see how a dramatic production could have successfully carried off the transformation of humans into animals. The story owes its unique place in the history of literature to the centuries-old accumulation of poetic feeling around the song of a bird representing the sad state of a human being. Tragedy in this case is mitigated by a lyrical cry of intense sorrow instead of a dramatic plot, as Aristotle would have required. Lyricism reflects a more primitive stage of literary expression than drama, being a brief exclamation of feeling and in its origin probably owing much to the sounds made by animals, especially birds with their extensive repertoire of musical calls and songs. It is in the song of the bird, ultimately in the voice of poetry, that the passions of intense sorrow and joy meet and are resolved. As Tennyson says of the nightingale,

> fierce extremes employ
> Thy spirits in the darkening leaf,
> And in the midmost heart of grief
> Thy passion clasps a secret joy.
> (*In Memoriam*, no. 88)

In *The Birds*, Aristophanes shows his appreciation of the nightingale's song and spurns the story of Philomela, retaining only the names Tereus, a hoopoe now living happily with his wife Procne, a nightingale. Produced in 414 B.C., the play is one of the earliest texts of any description to make extensive literary use of birds.

Although the birds are merely actors in masks and elaborate costumes, the play is of ornithological interest because about eighty avian species are mentioned, often with details proving the accuracy of at least some ancient bird lore.[7] That the playwright could count on his audience to recognize and appreciate so many allusions speaks well for the general knowledge of birds among Athenians of the fifth century B.C. Of course, Aristophanes employs birds primarily to create an amusing stage spectacle of a kingdom of birds, Cloudcuckooland, and by means of this fantasy to ridicule the follies of the politicians and citizens of the Athenian state. Even so, in spite of his comic and satirical purposes, the playwright was sensitive enough to appreciate the beauty of the nightingale's song and skillful enough as a poet to express it in lyrical speeches of the Chorus, beginning with these lines:

> Tawnythroat, Partner
> In song, dark
> Muse, dearest of Birds:
> Come, let the curving long
> Line of your fluting
> Fall, sparkling
> Undersong to our words.
>
> .   .   .   .
>
> Woodland Muse
>   *tiotiotinx*
>   Lucency
> Darting voice
>   Valley
> Wanderer, circling flight
>   *tiotinx tiotiotinx*
>   on the bright hills:
>   My singing
> Spills
>   duskiness into the light.[8]

John Ruskin found fault with the passage because Aristophanes renders the nightingale's song "simply as beautiful sound" and misses the "association of the bird-voice with deeply pathetic circumstances" (25: 42–43). We can be grateful, however, to have lines that constitute one of the earliest attempts to represent bird song in language. To accomplish this purpose Aristophanes employs two methods that have been standard practice for writers: he describes the song in words arranged in rhythmic patterns that imitate the musical pattern of the song itself, and he also supplies phonetic equivalents of the sounds made by the bird. Although onomatopoeia is hardly musical notation and at best is a highly variable tool to represent sounds, especially the sounds made by animals, it is about all that language can do in this respect. Its limitations may be seen in a sixteenth-century English version of Ovid's work, *The Complaynt of Phylomene,* in which George Gascoigne offers "an exposition of al such notes as the nightingale doth commonly use to sing." But only four are delivered: *Tereu, Tereu,* "the name of that false Thracian king"; *fye,* "which worde declares disdaine" for all the terrible things Tereus and the sisters had done; *Nemesis,* "the goddesse of al just revenge" against those who sin; and *Jug, Jug, Jug,* which Gascoigne professes he cannot fathom and leaves to the "latynists by learning to expresse." Of these, "Tereu" and "jug-jug-jug" are fair Elizabethan equivalents of what we might today hear as "tiou-tiou-tiou" and "chook-chook-chook" in the nightingale's song.[9] Gascoigne's suggestions appeared quite often in British dramas, as in this verse from John Lyly's *Alexander and Campaspe* (1584):

> What bird so sings, yet does so wail?
> Oh, 'tis the ravished nightingale.
> Jug, jug, jug, jug, tereus, she cries,
> And still her woes at midnight rise.
>   (Hebel and Hudson, 383)

Another method to render bird song is merely to describe its musical qualities from an objective point of view. The Roman writer Pliny the Elder tried this in his *Natural History:*

In the first place there is so loud a voice and so persistent a supply of breath in such a tiny little body; then there is the consummate knowledge of music in a single bird: the sound is given out with modulations, and now is drawn out into a long note with one continuous breath, now varied by managing the breath, now made staccato by checking it, or linked together by prolonging it, or carried on by holding it back; or it is suddenly lowered, and at times sinks into a mere murmur, loud, low, bass, treble, with trills, with long notes, modulated when this seems good— soprano, mezzo, baritone; and briefly all the devices in that tiny throat which human science has devised with all the elaborate mechanism of the flute.

Pliny's wonderment over the volume of sound issuing from such a tiny throat and the remarkable modulations in the nightingale's song has been a model for a number of followers. Izaak Walton in *The Compleat Angler* remarks how the nightingale "breathes such sweet, loud music out of her little instrumental throat that it might make mankind to think miracles are not ceased. . . . the clear airs, the sweet descants, the natural rising and falling, the doubling and redoubling of her voice." Pliny is echoed again in Richard Crashaw's "Music's Duel" (1648), an expanded transla- tion of a 1617 Latin poem by Famianus Strada in which a lutist engages in a musical contest with a nightingale:

> She measures every measure, everywhere
> Meets art with art; sometimes as if in doubt
> Not perfect yet, and fearing to be out,
> Trails her plain ditty in one long-spun note,
> Through the sleek passage of her open throat,
> A clear unwrinkled song.
>
> . . . .
>
> . . . He amazed
> That from so small a channel could be raised
> The torrent of a voice whose melody
> Could melt into such sweet variety.
>   (Hebel and Hudson, 760)

Finally exhausted, the bird falls dead on the musician's lute. The story is told again in John Ford's play *The Lover's Melancholy* (1623) and in William Cowper's "Strada's Nightingale." A late echo of Crashaw's version is to be found in Gerard Manley Hop- kins's "The Nightingale":

I thought the air must cut and strain
The windpipe when he sucked his breath
And when he turned it back again
    The music must be death.[10]

The musical contest with the nightingale goes as far back as the Homeric "Hymn to Pan":

In song he could even outdo
that bird which sits among the leaves
    at flower-rich springtime
and, pouring forth its dirge, trills honey-voiced tunes.[11]

Pliny reports that wealthy Romans spent huge sums on songbirds to be entered in singing contests. It was said of Saint Francis of Assisi that he spent a whole night singing alternately with a nightingale and finally conceded victory to the bird.

Obviously poets have committed some offenses against ornithology in their treatment of the nightingale's song, but there are also some good explanations of the origins of those errors. In England the nightingale (*Luscinia megarhynchos*) sings on breeding locations between April 15 and June 15, with such a high concentration of song in the few weeks between migration and the hatching of eggs that it is bound to attract attention. Pliny was not far off the mark when he observed that nightingales "pour out a ceaseless gush of song for fifteen days and nights on end when the buds of the leaves are swelling" (10.81). Before it was known that only a few female birds are able to sing, it was only natural to assume that the female nightingale sings, since there is no difference between the plumage of males and females and only close anatomical examination can determine the sex of the bird. Scientific field study has only recently found that bird song is used primarily to establish a territory suitable for feeding and nesting, an advantage that gives the male a better chance to attract a mate. To discourage potential rivals, the male may sing at night as well as day. Since nighttime bird song is more noticeable than daytime singing, when many different birds compete for attention, the nightingale was thought to be a nighttime singer only and consequently made a deeper impression on listeners, as Shakespeare points out in *The Merchant of Venice:*

> The nightingale, if she should sing by day
> When every goose is cackling, would be thought
> No better musician than the wren.
>
> (5.1.104–6)

The reputation of the nightingale in literature has served to re-inforce the favorable impressions of its song and has led people to confuse the nightingale with other birds. "Londoners fancy every bird they hear after sunset a Nightingale," observes John Clare, the English countryman poet.[12]

Even though the nightingale does have some ugly croaking sounds in its repertoire, like that represented by "jug," there is no question that it is among the best songsters of the bird world. In his study of bird song Charles Hartshorne finds aesthetic qualities in the nightingale's song even though "it is not highly melodic or tuneful, relying heavily as it does on reiteration of single notes, and employing some noisy sounds. . . . What makes the song outstanding, in spite of these limitations, is the large number of complex phrases (up to 24), and their neatness and dynamic power." Hartshorne is of the opinion that the more elaborate the song the more chance there is of its attracting a female, since complex song is more stimulating than a simpler song would be; and it has been scientifically established that birds who have not yet found a mate continue to sing at least more frequently and vigorously, and perhaps more beautifully. William H. Thorpe believes that there is "something approaching aesthetic appreciation" in the female's reaction to a more highly developed song. Louis J. Halle goes so far as to claim that the nightingale has a "creative impulse" like the poet's, "a drive in all life toward the progressive realization of an idea of perfection."[13] The perfect song is thus part of an elaborate strategy for survival. Some ornithologists are even willing to concede that songs emitted during flight may be purely emotional acts. Plutarch was not far from this point of view in his essay "The Cleverness of Animals" when he wrote that birds cherished the beauty of their own singing. It is now well known that there are individual as well as regional variations in the songs of the same species. Whatever its function may be, bird song has a strong appeal to the poet, who hears in it a kind of incipient communication on the verge of breaking into words. Poets recognize in the song of a bird their own struggle to express meanings and feelings.

All bird song is open to a variety of human interpretations, of course. In "The Spring Call" Thomas Hardy amusingly records variations in the sounds people from different regions hear in the song of the English blackbird:

> Down Wessex way, when spring's a-shine,
>   The blackbird's "pret-ty de-urr!"
> In Wessex accents marked as mine
>   Is heard afar and near.
>
> . . . .
>
> Yet they pipe "prattie deerh!" I glean,
>   Beneath a Scottish sky,
> And "pehty de-aw!" amid the treen
>   Of Middlesex or nigh.

E. B. White, in "A Listener's Guide to the Birds," makes the same sort of observation about American inconsistencies:

> Let us suppose you hear a bird say, "Fitz-bew,"
> The things you can be sure of are two:
> First, the bird is an alder
>   flycatcher (*Empidonax traillii traillii*):
> Second, you are standing in Ohio—or, as
>   some people call it, O-hee-o—
> Because, although it may come as a surprise to you,
> The alder flycatcher, in New York or New England,
>   does not say, "Fitz-bew,"
> It says, "Wee-be-o." [14]

New Englanders hear the white-throated sparrow say "Old Sam Peabody, Peabody, Peabody," while Canadians are just as certain that it says, "Oh sweet Canada, Canada, Canada."

It is not surprising that many listeners have found the long, drawn-out notes of the nightingale to be sad even though the bird is also capable of uttering other sounds that may seem joyful. In his essay on the nightingale in English poetry, H. W. Garrod holds that the "merry" nightingale of the native English tradition has been the source of better poetry than the classical bird of "mythical connexions." He commends Coleridge for having challenged the ancient tradition and restored the proper point of view in "The Nightingale" when he wrote that only someone suffering from a wrong, a disease, or "neglected love" could find the nightingale's song to be sad: "A melancholy bird? Oh! idle thought! / In nature there is nothing melancholy." In a poem entitled "Song" Hartley Coleridge appears to disagree with his father: "Ne'er on earth was sound of mirth / So like to melancholy." John Keats in his famous "Ode to a Nightingale" would have it both ways: it is at first a happy bird, a "light-winged Dryad of the trees," yet later its "plaintive anthem" inspires in him a melancholy mood because he envies the bird its freedom from worldly cares and the "full-throated ease" with which it sings. D. H. Lawrence found no "sobbing" in the song of the nightingales he heard in Tuscany but rather a "pure, angel-keen, demon-keen assertion of true self"; the bird is merely saying "Lo! It is I!"—an explanation that ornithologists would accept. Further, he points out that "the ear is much less cunning than the eye. . . . The ear is so stupid it will accept any amount of false money in words." Coleridge and Lawrence could have called to their support no less an authority than Plato, in whose *Phaedo* Socrates, by way of explaining his lack of fear over his impending death, claims that neither swans nor nightingales can be said to sing sad songs: "Men, because they are themselves afraid of death, slanderously affirm of the swans that they sing a lament at the last, not considering that no bird sings when cold, or hungry, or in pain, not even the nightingale, nor the swallow, nor yet the hoopoe." Medieval Latin and Provençal poetry featured the nightingale as singing joyously in springtime, and in the poetry of clerics the nightingale sang joyful praises of God, as in Alcuin's "De Luscinia." [15] Nightingales in *The Arabian Nights' Entertainment* do the same for Allah.

Except the scientist at his work, everyone has the right to respond freely to appearances in nature, and responses are inevitably colored by the emotional condition of the observer. "The *cheerful* man hears the lark in the morning," Dr. Johnson says in his essay on Milton, "the *pensive* man hears the nightingale in the evening."

It is the "fashion of the ear," Emily Dickinson thought, that makes the song of the oriole either "dun or fair":

> So whether it be Rune,
> Or whether it be none
> Is of within.
>   (no. 526)

And Ralph Waldo Emerson said, "When that bird sang, I gave the theme." In "All These Birds" Richard Wilbur grants

> That nothing is so worn
> As Philomel's bosom-thorn,
> That it is, in fact, the male
> Nightingale which sings—

but he insists that one should not on that account restrict the right of poets to exercise their imagination when writing about birds as long as the effort creates something "so fresh, so pure, so rare / As to possess the air." Of bird song John Ciardi says that it is

> a code no different from the wolf howl, warthog grunt
> porpoise twitter. It is a way of placing
> the cardinal in its sconce, of calling its hen,
> of warning off others. *That* code. We hear it
> and re-code it: it sounds like something
> we might like to try. Who cares how it sounds
> to another bird? We take what we need from nature,
> not what is there. We can only guess what is there.

This is in agreement with Wallace Stevens's statement that a bird

> Sings in the palm, without human meaning,
> Without human feeling, a foreign song.

> You know then that it is not the reason
> That makes us happy or unhappy.

Ciardi is again helpful:

> Birds have nothing to say. Yet not to listen
> to that sung nothing is the death of rapture.
> Rapture or loneliness?—the difference is in

what one is reminded of, listening. Only after
reminders can one hear the first, last, and first
again sweet scald of nothing in the bird-burst.[16]

Among animals the bird is the most productive of "reminders"
and associations. Somehow sighting a bird or hearing a bird's song
evokes the memory of other occasions when the bird was seen or
heard and the feelings associated with those occasions. And each
new encounter makes the next one richer and more meaningful.
"If we have no associations with these sounds, they will mean very
little to us," John Burroughs writes. "Their merit as musical performance is very slight. . . . The nightingale's song, like the lark's,
needs all the accessories of time and place, the song is not all in
the singing, any more than wit is all in the saying. It is in the
occasion, the surroundings, the spirit of which it is the expression." The association may also be with a myth or literary work in
which the bird figures. Although placing most emphasis on what
he could actually observe in the field, Louis Halle admits the importance of literary associations in the fullest appreciation of birds:
"I have never seen an upland plover, or heard its cry, but the experience when it comes will be more meaningful for me because I
shall recall that description of the bird as [W. H.] Hudson knew it,
flying over the pampas on its long migration to North America."
Swallows flying about in a barn reminded Whitman of book 22 of
the *Odyssey*, in which "Ulysses slays the suitors . . . and Minerva,
swallow-bodied, darts up through the spaces of the hall, sits high
on a beam, looks complacently on the show of slaughter, and feels
in her element, exulting, joyous." [17]

The legend of Philomela has been most productive of associations in which distance and time are bridged by the song of a bird.
A stanza in Keats's "Ode" beautifully captures the wide range of
associations aroused by the song of the nightingale:

Thou wast not born for death, immortal bird!
  No hungry generations tread thee down;
The voice I hear this passing night was heard
  In ancient days by emperor and clown:
Perhaps the self-same song that found a path
  Through the sad heart of Ruth, when, sick for home,

She stood in tears amid the alien corn;
The same that oft-times hath
Charm'd magic casements, opening on the foam
Of perilous seas, in faery seas forlorn.
(lines 61–70)

Here Philomela is the prototype of the woman who has been taken from her homeland and faces the prospect of becoming the mate of a man in a foreign land. Such is the heroine of the Book of Ruth as well as the daughters of Danaus, refugees in Argos, who hear the piteous wail of the nightingale in *The Suppliants* of Aeschylus (lines 60–66). In "Philomela" Matthew Arnold ponders another instance of the plight of the displaced bird-maiden:

O wanderer from a Grecian shore,
Still, after many years, in distant lands,
Still nourishing in thy bewildered brain
That wild, unquenched, deep-sunken, old-world pain—
Say, will it never heal?
And can this fragrant lawn
With its cool trees, and night,
And the sweet, tranquil Thames,
And moonshine, and the dew,
To thy racked heart and brain
Afford no balm?

For Arnold the nightingale represents the endurance of the spirit of classical tragedy in modern times, an important element in his conservative point of view. In his better known "Dover Beach" it is the roar of the surf on an English shore, rather than the song of a bird, that links the ancient past with the present. In "Ornithology in a World of Flux" Robert Penn Warren implies that the converse of this phenomenon holds true, that even *failing* to hear a once-heard birdcall and the stillness surrounding it can have the same effect as hearing it again:

Years pass, all places and faces fade, some people have died,
And I stand in a far land, the evening still,
    and am at last sure

That I miss more that stillness at bird-call than some things
  that were to fail later.[18]

The traditional response of poets to the song of the nightingale is an example of the remarkable association that literature
is able to create between animal life and the deepest concerns
of humankind. In trying to account for the haunting song of the
nightingale, an ancient storyteller links the song with the grief of a
tragic maiden, and then that association, with its set of images and
feelings, becomes available to generations of writers. This kind
of imaginative aggrandizement is applied to many other birds as
well as the nightingale. The store of symbols is enriched by the
appropriation of details from nature, and the natural world, no
matter how imperfectly or unscientifically observed, is poeticized
or given human significance. This process of assimilating the animal to human thought and feeling is of crucial importance in our
continuing need to maintain a meaningful relation to the natural
environment of which we are part.

two. From Fact to Symbol

> *My heart in hiding*
> *Stirred for a bird,—the achieve of, the mastery of the thing!*
> Gerard Manley Hopkins, "The Windhover"

The influence of birds on the human imagination undoubtedly
began with simpler reactions than the melancholy feelings inspired by the nightingale. Before complex associations could have
developed, the presence of birds in their concreteness must have
been perceived, the actual songs heard, the movements seen, the
typical surroundings noted. Such immediate observations then became part of a poetic tradition that poets in later ages adopted,
some merely copying from predecessors and others confirming details by making their own observations.

Even though birds are more readily observed than any other
wild animal, the range of observation has never been great. It must
be remembered that only a few of many thousand species ever get
noticed in literature—large birds that are conspicuous on land or

in flight and only those small birds that can be heard or seen near human dwellings and workplaces. Wood warblers, for example, are among the most beautifully colored birds in North America, but they seldom appear in literature because they are almost impossible to see without the aid of binoculars and their songs are issued during a very brief period during spring migration. Emerson's pine warbler in "Dirge" is rare for the literature of his time, and Wallace Stevens's "wild warblers" in "Meditation Celestial and Terrestrial" are heard only and not identified. Although binoculars and informative guidebooks are now available to bird lovers, they do not seem to have made much difference in the literary treatment of birds. It is not the minute but the salient characteristics of form and activity that capture the imagination, and once these are established in the oral and written tradition, they persist in spite of the new knowledge that science or improved methods of observation may afford. Whereas science forever abandons propositions that facts no longer support, literary traditions never quite die as long as they serve some expressive purpose. The nightingale still sings only at night, the eagle still "stares into the sun" for Elinor Wylie in "The Eagle and the Mole," and the "plangent wings" of a bird "disappear into the waning moon" for Theodore Roethke in "Meditations of an Old Woman." And yet, in spite of the pull of customary imagery, creative writers over the centuries have accumulated a fairly respectable amount of factual material about the behavior of birds, enough for the claim to be made that poetry was one of the few sources of information on the subject before ornithology became a science.

Ancient Egyptian drawings of birds incorporated realistic details as well as esoteric symbolical meanings. The primitive singer, whether he was simply celebrating a totem animal or performing the prophetic role of a shaman, was "able to combine his belief in unseen powers with a practical knowledge of the visible world. His sense of their presence and their influence makes his accounts of it more lively, and at no point do we feel that his interest in the supernatural background dims or distorts his physical vision." Similarly, no one has a better right to subjective reactions than creative artists who are able to fashion a painting, sculpture, or poem without seriously compromising the bits of reality they use

for inspiration and material. The freedom of the poet in these matters, particularly as they concern birds, is stated by Oscar Wilde in
response to a reviewer who pointed out his mistake in locating a
nightingale's nest in a holm oak tree: "Any imaginative or fanciful
writer can make nightingales build in any tree under heaven, or
in any tree that heaven knows not, for that matter." This goes too
far, but so do critics, Wilde insists, who "gravely censure the teller
of fairy-tales for his defective knowledge of natural history, who
will measure imaginative work by their own lack of any imaginative faculty." Good poetry, if not the fairy tale and folktale, usually
respects the facts of natural history when they are available to
the general public. In "Nature and the Poet" John Burroughs lays
down the principle succinctly: "It is the lesser poets who trip most
over their facts. . . . We expect [poets] to see the fact through their
imagination, but it must still remain a fact; the medium must not
distort it into a lie." Before careful field observations proved otherwise, poets could hardly be blamed for going along with the common belief that a bird's nest is a permanent dwelling place rather
than a purely temporary shelter, which is abandoned as soon as
the young are able to fly. Ornithologists also err: since Darwin's
time they believed that birds are monogamous in order to share
the burden of raising offspring, whereas now it appears that the
females of many species are promiscuous in order to ensure the
best genetic strain for survival.[19]

The most we can expect of poets is that they will do their best to
"combine both the naturalist's practical observation and the poet's
illuminated imagination," in the words of Sir A. Landsborough
Thomson, the distinguished British ornithologist. Such a formulation will serve as long as it is conceded that not all facts can be
dealt with imaginatively; poets would be hard put to find in the
articles of a professional ornithological journal much material that
they could use in their writing. Scientists must not expect that all
of their findings will be useful for those who make a different approach to reality. "You must not know too much, or be too precise
or scientific about birds and trees and flowers," cautions Whitman
in *Specimen Days*.[20] It must be remembered, too, that the poet's
imagination is more insistently illuminated by literary precedents
and by analogous images than by facts. What Shakespeare may

have written about the swan—"And now this pale swan in her watery nest, / Begins the sad dirge of her certain ending" (*The Rape of Lucrece*, 1611–12)—will count for more among readers of poetry than the fact that swans do not occupy a nest after the cygnets are able to swim (within twenty-four hours after hatching) and that there is no foundation for the ancient belief that swans sing before they die.

Ezra Pound enunciates the principle that good writing never loses sight of the factual side of metaphor in terms appropriate for our purpose here: "I believe that the proper and perfect symbol is the natural object, that if a man uses 'symbols' he must so use them that their symbolic function does not obtrude; so that *a* sense, and the poetic quality of the passage, is not lost to those who do not understand the symbol as such, to whom, for instance, a hawk is a hawk." A vulture is a vulture before it is a symbol in Ernest Hemingway's "Snows of Kilimanjaro." Even though he is on his deathbed, Harry, the dying writer, intently observes the way three vultures, attracted by his gangrened leg, have landed near his cot on a plain in Africa: "I watched the way they sailed very carefully at first in case I ever wanted to use them in a story." The scavengers are given symbolical significance, of course, but not until the pertinent facts are noted: "He looked over to where the huge, filthy birds sat, their naked heads sunk in the hunched feathers. A fourth planed down, to run quick-legged and then waddle slowly toward the others."[21]

Landing is a crucial transition from being a creature in air to one on land. John Ciardi devotes a whole poem to a description of the way gulls land:

> Spread back across the air, wings wide,
>   legs out, the wind delicately
> dumped in balance, the gulls ride
>   down, down, hang, and exactly
> touch, folding not quite at once
>   into their gangling weight, but
> taking one step, two, wings still askance,
>   reluctantly, at last, shut,

> twitch one look around
>   and are aground.
> ("Gulls Land and Cease to Be," *Selected Poems*, 45)

Here an accurate observation of animal behavior stands by itself
without pointed reference to something of human significance. In
"Birds, Like Thoughts," however, Ciardi allows himself to draw a
metaphorical inference from the observations he has made of the
way various birds perform their landings:

> Whatever is hatched
> to wings has its own way with them. But I'm
> sure of one thing: the more weight you take to air,
> the more space you need to get down
> the more slowly. Birds are like thoughts: they're
> more instant as they stay light. Both come and gone.
>   (*Selected Poems*, 45)

In the ironically titled "Sunset Scrupulously Observed," Robert
Penn Warren is himself quite scrupulous in his description of a
perching bird at sunset:

> A flycatcher, small, species not identified, is perched
> Unmoving but for tiny turning and scanning
> Twist of head, on the topmost twig, dead,
> Of the tall, scant-leafed and dying poplar. It
> Is a black point against the cloud-curdled drama
> Of sunset over dark heave
> Of the mountains.[22]

John Clare, early nineteenth-century English poet and amateur
field naturalist, is notable for having written an extensive body
of nature poetry with the barest minimum of metaphor. He con-
tented himself with the minutest observations of birds and only
occasionally allowed himself to express the simple feelings that his
careful descriptions so well earned. Here is his description of a
kingfisher hunting:

> In coat of orange green and blue
> Now on a willow branch I view

Grey waving to the sunny gleam
King fishers watch the ripple stream
For little fish that nimble bye
And in the gravel shallows lie.

The lightest metaphorical touch is given in "coat." Theodore Roethke's feeding heron is remarkably like Clare's kingfisher:

The heron stands in water where the swamp
Has deepened to the blackness of a pool,
Or balances with one leg on a hump
Of marsh grass heaped above a musk-rat hole.

He walks the shallow with an antic grace.
The great feet break the ridges of the sand,
The long eye notes the minnow's hiding place.
His beak is quicker than a human hand.

He jerks the frog across his bony lip,
Then points his bill above the wood.
The wide wings flap but once to lift him up,
A single ripple starts from where he stood.

T. S. Eliot limits himself to but three figurative expressions in ten lines of verse describing his favorite birds in "Cape Ann":

O quick quick quick, quick hear the song-sparrow,
The swamp sparrow, fox-sparrow, vesper sparrow
At dawn and dusk. Follow the dance
Of the goldfinch at noon. Leave to chance
The Blackburnian warbler, the shy one. Hail
With shrill whistle the note of the quail, the bob-white
Dodging by bay-bush. Follow the feet
Of the walker, the water-thrush. Follow the flight
Of the dancing arrow, the purple martin. Greet
In silence the bullbat. All are delectable. Sweet sweet sweet.

The human significance of all this is enforced by the series of verbs that command us to appreciate some salient detail in the typical behavior of a number of birds. The complex verse patterns used by Marianne Moore are nonetheless vehicles of precise description of the flight of the magnificent frigate bird in "The Pelican Frigate" or the feeding of young mockingbirds in "Bird-Witted." In "No Swan So Fine," a beautiful porcelain swan outlasts the king who ordered it made:

> No water so still as the
>   dead fountains of Versailles. No swan,
> with swart blind look askance and gondoliering legs, so fine
>   as the chintz china one with fawn—
> brown eyes and toothed gold collar to show whose bird it was.
> Lodged in the Louis Fifteenth
>   candelabrum-tree of cockscomb-
> tinted button, dahlias, sea-urchins, and everlastings,
>   it perches on the branching foam
> of polished sculptured
> flowers—at ease
>   and tall. The king is dead.

Both the sculpture and the poem describing it are exquisitely artful yet still true to the physical details of a swan—the "swart blind look askance," the color of the eyes, the legs set far back on the body like the gondolier's oars near the stern of the boat.[23]

The primary impression birds made on humans from earliest times was probably their role as harbingers of the times of day and the seasons of the year. Birds are most active at sunrise and dusk, spring and fall. Their singing at dawn and nightfall was quite naturally heard as marking, if not actually causing, the start and close of day; their burst of activity in the spring and their disappearance in the fall were taken as signs of the beginning and end of the year. Being closer to nature, birds were accounted more dependable than humans in these matters. As the prophet Jeremiah writes,

> Yea, the stork in the heaven
> knoweth her appointed times;
> and the turtle [dove] and the crane and the swallow
> observe the time of their coming.
>   (8.7)

Because birds are "intelligent of seasons," as Milton writes in *Paradise Lost* (7.427), most references to birds in literature, as well as in ordinary converse, have to do with their utilitarian role as season markers. Homer and Aristophanes note that farmers are warned of the approach of winter by migrating cranes; in *Works and Days* Hesiod advises that their return is "the signal for ploughing." Virgil, in book 1 of *Georgics*, lists four species of birds that signal the approach of storms and four that foretell their passing. Classical literary traditions of this sort lasted well into the Renaissance, as evidenced by one of the popular items in emblem books of the sixteenth century, such as this from Geffrey Whitney's collection in 1586:

> By swallowes note, the Springe wee understande,
> The Cuckowe comes, ere Sommer doth beginne:
> The vinefinch showes, that haruest is at hande:
> The Chaffinche singes, when winter commeth in:
> Which times they keepe, that man therebie maie knowe,
> Howe Seasons chaunge, and tymes do come and goe.[24]

Whoever wrote "The Cuckoo Song," one of the earliest lyrics in English literature (c. 1300), probably needed no guiding tradition.

> Sumer is icumen in;
> Lhude sing, cuccu!
> Groweth sed, and bloweth med,
> And springth the wude nu.
> Sing, cuccu!

From many such elemental field observations there originated sets of complex feelings and symbolical meanings in which bird song at dawn and increased activity in springtime became the tokens of joy, love, and rebirth; bird song at dusk and the departure of birds in the fall, sorrow and death. Few images in literature have been honored so long or enjoyed such a consensus of interpretive meaning as these. The unfailing rhythms of migration, song and silence, nesting and fledging, have supplied poets with easily comprehended symbols of the cycle of life and death that all nature seems to suggest.

A rich store of poetry celebrates the dawn chorus of birds in the

spring since birds are most active at the time of the vernal equinox.
As Robert Frost writes in "Our Singing Strength,"

> In spring more mortal singers than belong
> To any one place cover us with song.
> Thrush, bluebird, blackbird, sparrow, and robin throng;

and in "Birds Waking" W. S. Merwin stands in awe of

> Such uncontainable tempest of whirled
> Singing flung upward and upward into the new light.
>
> . . . .
>
> I thought I had never known the wind
> Of joy to be so shrill, so unanswerable,
> With such clouds of winged song.[25]

No poet has offered a more detailed account of the springtime
activity of birds than James Thomson in *The Seasons*. His grand
theme in the section of his poem called "Spring" is the wonderful
harmony of nature, which begins with the renewal of vegetation,
"ascends" to birds, and finally strikes the highest note in the "effu-
sive force of Spring on man." The treatment of birds is devoted to
"the passion of the groves," or the love that underlies the process
by which birds reproduce their kind. Song is the first step male
birds use to attract a mate:

> 'Tis love creates their melody, and all
> This waste of music is the voice of love,
> That even to birds and beasts the tender arts
> Of pleasing teaches.

Then comes the courtship display performed by the males:

> First, wide around,
> With distant awe, in airy rings they rove,
> Endeavoring by a thousand tricks to catch
> The cunning, conscious, half-averted glance
> Of their regardless charmer. Should she seem
> Softening the least approvance to bestow,
> Their colours burnish, and, by hope inspired,
> They brisk advance; then, on a sudden struck,

> Retire disordered; then again approach,
> In fond rotation spread the spotted wing,
> And shiver every feather with desire.

Nesting follows and the feeding and training of the young until they are ready to fend for themselves:

> Till, vanished every fear, and every power
> Roused into life and action, light in air
> The acquitted parents see their soaring race,
> And, once rejoicing, never know them more.[26]

As in Chaucer's *Parliament of Fowls*, the poet selects the life history of birds as a model for human beings to follow in order to preserve the delicate balance of nature.

Emily Dickinson was one who resisted the universal custom to respond with joy to the return of birds in the spring. She can write that "Hope is the thing with feathers— / That perches in the soul," that springtime bird song is "music numerous as space," and yet she is not at all assured of the return of life after winter. She is too well aware of her own mortality—

> If I shouldn't be alive
> When the Robins come,
> Give the one in Red Cravat,
> A Memorial Crumb—
>   (no. 182)

and doubtful even of the return of spring from one year to the next:

> When they begin, if Robins may,
> I always had a fear
> I did not tell, it was their last Experiment
> Last Year.
>
> When it is May, if May return,
> Had nobody a pang
> Lest in a Face so beautiful
> He might not look again?
>   (no. 1080)

Calling herself "the Queen of Calvary" because of her persistent sadness, she considers herself not in tune with spring and must steel herself against it:

> I dreaded that first Robin, so,
> But He is mastered, now,
> I'm some accustomed to Him grown,
> He hurts a little, though—
>
> (no. 348)

The Calvary figure is repeated in another poem:

> The Morning after Woe . . .
> The Birds declaim their Tunes—
> Pronouncing every word
> Like Hammers—Did they know they fell
> Like Litanies of Lead—
> On here and there—a creature—
> They'd modify the Glee
> To fit some Crucifixal Clef—
> Some Key of Calvary—
>
> (no. 364)

Nature plays cruel tricks: the dawn chorus stabs her spirit with "Dirks of Melody," and the "saddest noise" is the burst of song at "night's delicious close" in the spring:

> It makes us think of all the dead
>   That sauntered with us here,
> By separation's sorcery
>   Made cruelly more dear.
>
> It makes us think of what we had,
>   And what we now deplore,
> We almost wish those siren throats
>   Would go and sing no more.
>
> (no. 1764)

Tennyson for a moment has the same feeling when he asks in *In Memoriam* whether grief over the loss of a dear one is "keenlier in sweet April," but he quickly recovers when the songs of birds "cry through the sense to hearten trust / In that which made the world so fair" (no. 116). But not Dickinson, who insists that "a Pang is more conspicuous in the Spring / In contrast with the things that sing" (no. 1530). In all this she anticipates Eliot's painful paradox of April being the "cruellest month" and Edna St. Vincent Millay's "Spring," in which April may come "strewing flowers" but "can no longer quiet me with redness / Of leaves opening stickily."[27] The modern mood finds us at the opposite pole from Chaucer's happy April when "smale foweles maken melodye."

In summer, after breeding and fledging, birds are relatively quiescent and human interest in them flags. It resumes in the fall when a new set of feelings comes into play. Fall is the time when migratory birds depart and bird song ceases; winter is the time of failing light, food, and protection from the elements for birds that remain. The departure of migrants and the suffering of resident birds supply metaphors for the melancholy sense of change and impending death that humans begin to feel with the onset of darker days and unpleasant weather. The migration of birds is one of the most impressive wonders of nature. The shock of its suddenness and mystery is beautifully described by A. R. Ammons in "Saliences":

> what change in
> a day's doing!
> desertions of swallows
>   that yesterday
> ravaged air, bush, reed, attention
> in gatherings as wide as this neck of dunes:
> now, not a sound
> or shadow, no trace of memory, no remnant
> explanation:
> summations of permanence![28]

After migration the image of trees stripped of both birds and leaves comes into play, as in Shakespeare's well-known line from Sonnet 73 having to do with old age: "Bare ruined choirs where late the sweet birds sang." Presumably these are migrant birds, while those from Thomson's *The Seasons* are resident birds: "Robbed of their tuneful souls, now shivering sit / On the dead tree, a dull despondent flock ("Autumn," 979–80). In "Looking for a Sunset Bird in Winter" Robert Frost comes close to Shakespeare's image of mutability:

> In summer when I passed the place
> I had to stop and lift my face;
> A bird with an angelic gift
> Was singing in it sweet and swift.
>
> No bird was singing in it now,
> A single leaf was on a bough,
> And that was all there was to see
> In going twice around the tree.
>
> (287)

Add snow to the scene and the desolation of winter is even greater, as in Shakespeare's "birds sit brooding in the snow," or William Carlos Williams's image of old age as

> a flight of small
> cheeping birds
> skimming
> bare trees
> above a snow glaze.[29]

A blackbird or crow in a tree in winter seems to appeal to many poets as an image of forlornness. It is an emblem of death in Wallace Stevens's "Thirteen Ways of Looking at a Blackbird," which begins

> Among twenty snowy mountains
> The only moving thing
> Was the eye of the blackbird—

and closes with

> It was evening all afternoon.
> It was snowing
> And it was going to snow.

The blackbird sat
In the cedar-limbs.
(92, 95)

The crow presides over an even more desolate scene in Stevens's "No Possum, No Sop, No Taters," in which the only sound that can be heard in "deep January" is the short note of the crow:

It is in this solitude, a syllable,
Out of these gawky flitterings,

Intones its single emptiness,
The savagest hollow of winter-sound.

It is here, in this bad, that we reach
The last purity of the knowledge of good.

The crow looks rusty as he rises up.
Bright is the malice in his eye . . .

One joins him there for company,
But at a distance in another tree.
(294)

The crow and the necessary "bad" of winter also appear in T. S. Eliot's *Murder in the Cathedral:*

The starved crow sits in the field, attentive; and in the wood
The owl rehearses the hollow note of death.
. . . .
And the world must be cleaned in the
    winter, or we shall have only
A sour spring, a parched summer, an empty harvest.
(201)

A Darwinian explanation of nature's seeming indifference to its offspring is offered by George Meredith in "Hard Weather": nature "winnows, winnows roughly" in order to develop a "stouter stock," and the end result is man, "her noblest born, / The station for the flight of soul." The longtime survival of humankind is still in doubt, but Meredith is right concerning birds. The genes of individuals that survived the perils of migration and the rigors

of winter have gone to preserve a species for almost two hundred
million years. It is a moral rather than a genetic lesson, however,
that poets have learned from the survival of birds in winter, namely
that the persistent affirmation of life in the face of terrible odds
can be an inspiring example. Thus, for Emerson, a lively chickadee
on a bitter cold day, when the poet is almost ready to surrender to
the "frost-king," becomes an example of stoicism, an "antidote of
fear" that the poet prizes more than "all that mass and minister"
can do for him:

> Here was this atom in full breath,
> Hurling defiance at vast death;
> This scrap of valor just for play,
> Fronts the north-wind in waistcoat gray,
> As if to shame my weak behavior.[30]

A close reader of Emerson, Emily Dickinson borrows the sentiment but chooses the bluejay for her "tonic" on a day in February:

> The Snow and he are intimate—
> I've often seen them play
> When Heaven looked upon us all
> With such severity
> I felt apology were due
> To an insulted sky
> Whose pompous frown was Nutriment
> To their Temerity—
> (no. 1561)

To Robert Frost the mere gesture of a crow in a tree brings comfort
in the well-known "Dust of Snow":

> The way a crow
> Shook down on me
> The dust of snow
> From a hemlock tree
>
> Has given my heart
> A change of mood
> And saved some part
> Of a day I had rued.
> (270)

In "Black Rook in Rainy Weather" Sylvia Plath seems to be combining clues from Frost and two lines from James Russell Lowell's "The Vision of Sir Launfal" ("A single crow on the tree-top bleak / From his shining feathers shed off the cold sun"):

> I only know that a rook
> Ordering its black feathers can so shine
> As to seize my senses, haul
> My eyelids up, and grant
>
> A brief respite from fear
> Of total neutrality.[31]

No poet has ever been more deeply troubled by the hardships birds suffer in winter than Thomas Hardy. Together with the hard lot of caged birds, the trials of winter lend force to the naturalistic bent of his writing. "The cruel frost encrusts the cornland" in "Winter in Durnover Field"; there are no berries to be had in "Birds at Winter Nightfall," no warmth for blackbirds in "The Best She Could"; and in "The Reminder" the wintering thrush is reduced to feed on the very "Dregs of food by sharp distress." Mother Nature, he must conclude, as George Meredith had also,

> never shows endeavour
> To protect from warrings wild
> Bird or beast she calls her child.
> ("The Bullfinches")

But in spite of all this, in his best-known poem, "The Darkling Thrush," Hardy is able to rejoice in the song of a mistle thrush on a day "when all was spectre-gray," the very last day of the nineteenth century:

> At once a voice arose among
>   The bleak twigs overhead
> In a full-hearted evensong
>   Of joy illimited;
> An aged thrush, frail, gaunt, and small,
>   In blast-beruffled plume,
> Had chosen thus to fling his soul
>   Upon the growing gloom.

So little cause for carolings
    Of such ecstatic sound
Was written on terrestrial things
    Afar or nigh around,
That I could think there trembled through
    His happy good-night air
Some blessed Hope, whereof he knew
    And I was unaware.
          (150)

The poet is not so sure about the broader implication that there may be reason to have hope for humankind in the new century. He is more certain in the simpler hope that lies in the "ancient pulse of germ and birth," which he describes in another poem. "Proud Songsters" has to do with last year's young birds asserting themselves against the night after having survived the winter,

The thrushes sing as the sun is going,
And the finches whistle in ones and pairs,
And as it gets dark loud nightingales
    In bushes
Pipe, as they can when April wears,
    As if all Time were theirs.
These are brand-new birds of twelve-months' growing,
Which a year ago, or less than twain,
No finches were, nor nightingales,
    Nor thrushes,
But only particles of grain,
    And earth, and air, and rain.
          (835–36)

In a lighter vein, Hardy, like Frost after him, takes pleasure in a bird trying to stay perched during a snowstorm:

A sparrow enters a tree,
    Whereon immediately,
A snow-lump thrice his own slight size
Descends on him and showers his head and eyes,
    And overturns him,
    And near inurns him,

> And lights on a nether twig, when its brush
> Starts off a volley of other lodging lumps with a rush.
> ("Snow in the Suburbs," 732–33)

Both poets use birds to express the range of feelings from despair to humor and hope.

George Meredith also found hope in the song of the thrush:

> He sings me, out of Winter's throat,
> The young time with the life ahead;
> And my young time his leaping note
> Recalls to spirit-mirth from dead.
> ("The Thrush in February")

And D. H. Lawrence, who studied and wrote about Hardy, marveled at the resilient spirit with which birds faced hardship. Published just after World War I, "Whistling of Birds" is an essay celebrating the indomitable instinct to live as it is demonstrated by birds. For Lawrence the piece must have been an effort to restore his faith in life after the terrible devastation of the war. It has the tone and organization of poetry. The first paragraph is devoted entirely to the decimation of birds in winter: "The frost held for many weeks, until the birds were dying rapidly. Everywhere in the fields and under the hedges lay the ragged remains of lapwings, starlings, thrushes, redwings, innumerable ragged bloody cloaks of birds, whence the flesh was eaten by invisible beasts of prey." In each of the remaining seventeen paragraphs two notes are struck over and over again: the ravages of death followed by the unconquerable assertion of renewed life.

> Even whilst we stare at the ragged horror of the birds scattered broadcast, part-eaten, the soft, uneven cooing of the pigeon ripples from the outhouses, and there is a faint silver whistling in the bushes come twilight. No matter, we stand and stare at the torn and unsightly ruins of life, we watch the weary, mutilated columns of winter retreating under our eyes. Yet in our ears are the silver vivid bugles of a new creation advancing on us from behind, we hear the rolling of the soft and happy drums of the doves.
> (*Phoenix*, 3–4)

What appears to be the hard life of seabirds has inspired some of the finest writing about birds, perhaps because of the vivid impression made on seafarers by the few living things available for observation during a voyage and because of the inevitable comparison of sailors and seabirds experiencing the extreme severity of winter at sea. "Lonely and friendless and far from home," the eighth-century Anglo-Saxon sailor-poet of "The Seafarer" sees in the plight of seabirds a reflection of his own misery:

> In my ears no sound but the roar of the sea,
> The icy combers, the cry of the swan;
> In place of the mead-hall and laughter of men
> My only singing the sea-mew's call,
> The scream of the gannet, the shriek of the gull;
> Through the wail of the wild gale beating the bluffs
> The piercing cry of the ice-coated petrel,
> The storm-drenched eagle's echoing scream.[32]

Hardy uses pelagic birds to underscore the indifference of the natural world to the miserable life his heroine Tess faces in winter after having been abandoned by her husband:

> After this season of congealed dampness came a spell of dry frost, when strange birds from behind the North Pole began to arrive silently on the upland of Flintcombe-Ash; gaunt spectral creatures with tragical eyes—eyes which had witnessed scenes of cataclysmal horror in inaccessible polar regions of a magnitude such as no human being had ever conceived, in curdling temperatures that no man could endure; which had beheld the crash of icebergs and the slide of snowhills by the shooting light of the Aurora; been half blinded by the whirl of colossal storms and terraqueous distortions; and retained the expression of feature that such scenes had engendered. These nameless birds came quite near Tess and Marian, but of all they had seen which humanity would never see, they brought no account.[33]

Melville's seabirds are also spectral, especially the albatross in *Moby-Dick* and *The Encantadas*, "the snow-white ghost of the haunted Capes of Hope and Horn." It is at the extremities of the Southern Ocean, too, that Poe's voyager, A. Gordon Pym, is ushered behind the mysterious white veil by "many gigantic and pallidly white birds." The impending death of Eliot's little old man, "Gerontion," is signaled by similar imagery:

> Gull against the wind, in the windy straits
> Of Belle Isle, or running on the Horn,
> White feathers in the snow.
>
> (23)

Yet, for some poets, even the horror of sea and cold is countered by the example of hardy birds. "The sea-fowl takes the wintry blast for a cov'ring to her limbs," William Blake writes in a memorable line from "Visions of the Daughters of Albion."[34] And from General Adolphus Washington Greely's account of his exploration of Greenland in 1881, Walt Whitman finds a lesson for his declining years in the song of a snow bunting on the tundra:

> Of that blithe throat of thine from arctic bleak and blank,
> I'll mind the lesson, solitary bird—let me too welcome
>   chilling drifts,
> E'en the profoundest chill, as now—a torpid pulse,
>   a brain unnerv'd,
> Old age land-lock'd within its winter bay—(cold, cold, O cold!)
> These snowy hairs, my feeble arm, my frozen feet,
> For them thy faith, thy rule I take, and grave it to the last;
> Not summer's zones alone—not chants of youth,
>   or south's warm tides alone,
> But held by sluggish floes, pack'd in the northern ice,
>   the cumulus of years,
> These with gay heart I also sing.[35]

Variation in the amount of sunlight over the course of a day and year is one of the principal determinants of the sense of seasonal change for both man and beast. Ornithologists have recently proved what poets had long sensed, that changes in the intensity of light are important factors in the behavior of birds, that longer days, for example, stimulate the production of hormones needed for mating. Ancient mythmakers recognized the relation of birds to light. The phoenix was the legendary bird whose death and mi-

raculous resurrection signified the all-important regeneration of
the sun; and the preeminence of the eagle was based on its pur-
ported ability to look at the sun without being blinded—"kindling
her undazzled eyes at the full midday beam," as Milton has it in
Areopagitica; or, in flight, drawing "light from the fountain of the
setting sun," in Wordsworth's *Yarrow Revisited.* The cock was long
the familiar herald of light, succeeded by the lark in the writings
of English romantic poets.

If joyful outbursts of song welcome the return of light and life to
the world, the mournful tones of the nightingale and the owl mark
the subsidence of life at night. Some poets have been particularly
sensitive to the opposition of light and darkness in the life of birds
as it may apply to the varying moods of human beings. Robert
Penn Warren's high-flying birds are always associated with diminishing light in a darkening world. The bird in "Evening Hawk"
is described as riding "the last tumultuous avalanche of / Light
above pines and the guttural gorge." In "Mortal Limit" a hawk's
flight marks the "last scrawl of light," and in Warren's long poem
on John James Audubon one sees

> from the forest pond, already dark,
> the great trumpeter swan
> Rise, in clangor, and the fight up the steep air where,
> At the height of the last light, it glimmered like last flame.[36]

Throughout his poetry Wallace Stevens makes the recurrence of
light and dark in the life of birds an important theme. In "Meditation Celestial and Terrestrial" he takes the warbler as his light-
bringing bird:

> The wild warblers are warbling in the jungle
> Of life and spring and of the lustrous inundations,
> Flood on flood, of our returning sun.
> (123)

More traditional is the association Stevens makes in "Some
Friends from Pascagoula" between sunlight and an eagle aloft:

> Say how his heavy wings,
> Spread on the sun-bronzed air . . .

> Dropping in sovereign rings
> Out of his fiery lair.
> Speak of the dazzling wings.
>
> (127)

The time of death, on the other hand, is represented in Stevens by the flight of pigeons sinking into darkness at the end of "Sunday Morning" and the "cry against the twilight" of peacocks as they fly down from the hemlocks just before nightfall in "Domination of Black":

> Out of the window,
> I saw how the planets gathered
> Like the leaves themselves
> Turning in the wind.
> I saw how the night came,
> Came striding like the color of the heavy hemlocks,
> I felt afraid.
> And I remembered the cry of the peacocks.
>
> (9)

The last poem of his *Collected Poems*, "Not Ideas about the Thing but the Thing Itself," presents another cry, however, the "scrawny cry" of a bird in March announcing "at the earliest ending of winter" the sun's vernal equinox:

> That scrawny cry—it was
> A chorister whose c preceded the choir.
> It was part of the colossal sun,
>
> Surrounded by its choral rings,
> Still far away. It was like
> A new knowledge of reality.
>
> (534)

It is clear from these examples that the recurrent daily and seasonal activities of birds have aroused deep feelings in poets and supplied them with forceful symbols of moral and philosophical values. Drawing simple moral lessons from the behavior of birds began in animal folktales and developed into literary forms such as the bestiary, the emblem, and the learned debates conducted by birds in such medieval poems as *The Owl and the Nightingale* and Chaucer's Pardoner's Tale. The entry for the crow in a twelfth-century bestiary has this bit of moral edification for the reader: "Let men learn to love their children from the example and from the sense of duty of crows. They diligently follow their sons as an escort when they fly, and, fearing that the babies might possibly pass away, food is laid in, and they do not neglect this chore of feeding for a long time." There follows an imprecation against the practice of abortion by "the women of our own race" who "kill their own children in the belly, so that the inheritance may not be divided among many."[37] The stork supplies a similar lesson in Geffrey Whitney's sixteenth-century emblem book:

> See heare the storke prouides with tender care,
> And bringeth meate, unto her hatched broode:
> They like againe, for her they doe prepare,
> When shee is oulde, and can not get her foode:
> Which teacheth bothe, the parente and the childe,
> Theire duties heare, which eche to other owe;
> First, fathers must be prouident, and milde,
> Unto theire fruicte, till they of age doe growe:
>   And children, muste with dutie still proceede,
>   To reuerence them, and helpe them if they neede.
> (Emblemes, 73)

Because of their innocent state animals were presumed to practice naturally all the virtues that mankind came at only with the greatest difficulty. Ornithologists know now that monogamy is the exception rather than the rule among birds, though the general public may still believe with Plato that "when they have reached the proper time of life birds are coupled, male and female, and lovingly pair together, and live the rest of their lives in holiness and innocence, abiding firmly in their original compact" (*Laws*, 8.840).

Inevitably these lessons from nature took a simple two-part form, in which a description of natural fact is followed by a moral application, as in these two stanzas from Longfellow's *Song of Hiawatha:*

Never stoops the soaring vulture
On his quarry in the desert,
On the sick or wounded bison,
But another vulture, watching
From his high aerial lookout,
Sees the downward plunge, and follows;
And a third pursues the second,
Coming from the invisible ether,
First a speck, and then a vulture,
Till the air is thick with pinions.

So disasters come not singly;
But as if they watched and waited,
Scanning one another's motions,
When the first descends, the others
Follow, follow, gathering flock-wise
Round their victim, sick and wounded,
First a shadow, then a sorrow,
Till the air is dark with anguish.
                    (19, lines 1–18)

The details of the second stanza almost exactly duplicate the description of the vultures in the first stanza, only now, with the addition of but two words, "disasters" and "sorrow," the focus is shifted to human beings. William Cullen Bryant is more subtle in the way he distributes both observation and application throughout "To a Waterfowl," an immensely popular poem that ascribes the unerring spring migration flight of a bird to the guiding hand of God:

There is a Power whose care
Teaches thy way along that pathless coast—
The desert and illimitable air—
Lone wandering, but not lost.

Then the poet draws a lesson from the example of the bird:

He who, from zone to zone,
Guides through the boundless sky thy certain flight,
In the long way that I must tread alone,
Will lead my steps aright.

Some years after Bryant, the hero of Robert Browning's *Paracelsus* also finds in migrating birds confirmation of his faith that God will direct him aright in his pursuit of truth:

> I see my way as birds their trackless way,
> I shall arrive, what time, what circuit first,
> I ask not: but unless God send his hail
> Or blinding fireballs, sleet or stifling snow,
> In some time, his good time, I shall arrive:
> He guides me and the bird![38]

The best-known formulation of the all-encompassing power of providence for both bird and human occurs in Matthew 10.29: a sparrow "shall not fall to the ground without your Father." The idea is sharpened in *Hamlet:* "There is special providence in the fall of a sparrow" (5.2.221). In "Small Elegy" John Ciardi renews the ancient proverb; having found the remains of a dead bird "pasted to muck," the poet is left "guessing out first laws" by which all living things fall into the "mass of God":

> Think it and change! Oh, could I think
> this bird back to its weightlessness!
> Or that bird, soul! Then I could thank
> my father for a massive guess.
> And, myself lightened into flight,
> soar to some singing Infinite.[39]

An extensive marsh in Georgia, the "Vast of the Lord," is Sidney Lanier's symbol of creation in "The Marshes of Glynn." The animal he identifies with the place and with himself is the marsh hen, which he presents as an example of the perfect adaptation of living things to the order of existence that God has created.

> As the marsh-hen secretly builds on the watery sod,
> Behold I will build me a nest on the greatness of God:
> I will fly in the greatness of God as the marsh-hen flies
> In the freedom that fills all the space 'twixt the marsh
>   and the skies:
> By so many roots as the marsh-grass sends in the sod
> I will heartily lay me a-hold on the greatness of God:

Oh, like to the greatness of God is the greatness within
The range of the marshes, the liberal marshes of Glynn.

The adaptation of birds to the minute intricacy as well as to the vastness of habitats is reflected in William Everson's "A Canticle of Waterbirds." The Pacific coast is the world of the sixteen species of birds he names in this remarkable poem.

For you hold the heart of His mighty fastnesses,
And shape the life of His indeterminate realms.
You are everywhere on the lonesome shores
    of His wide creation.

   . . . .

You are His secretive charges and you serve His secretive ends,
In His clouded, mist-conditioned stations, in His murk,
Obscure in your matted nestings,
   immured in His limitless ranges.
He makes you penetrate through dark interstitial joinings
   of His thicketed kingdoms,
And keep your concourse in the deeps of His shadowed world.

Like Whitman, Everson commends animals for accepting whatever life requires of them:

But mostly it is your way you bear existence wholly within the
   context of His utter will and are untroubled.
Day upon day you do not reckon, nor scrutinize tomorrow,
   nor multiply the nightfalls with a rash concern,
But rather assume each instant as warrant sufficient of
   His final seal.
Wholly in Providence you spring, and when you die you look
   on death in clarity unflinched.

And after the observation comes the lesson:

Yet may you teach a man a necessary thing to know,
Which has to do of the strict conformity
   that creaturehood entails,
And constitutes the prime commitment all things share.

For God has given you the imponderable grace
    to *be* His verification,
Outside the mulled incertitude of our forensic choices;
That you, our lessers in the rich hegemony of Being,
May serve as testaments to what a creature is,
And what creation owes.[40]

Everson describes his poem as "a simple meditation of the mutual relation between birds and God and man."[41] It was written after his conversion to Catholicism and just prior to his becoming a Dominican lay brother (Brother Antoninus). In addition to the work of Bryant, Browning, and Lanier, Everson may have known another poem in the tradition that uses the exemplary behavior of birds to glorify a divine creator, "The Windhover," written by another convert and member of a holy order, Gerard Manley Hopkins. In this sonnet only one bird is described, a kestrel, in whose flight—"Brute beauty and valour and act, oh, air, pride, plume"— the poet sees reflected the infinitely greater glory of Christ's perfection.

Some poets, of course, stop short of seeing a divine presence in nature. In "This Lime-Tree Bower My Prison" Coleridge observes a rook beating "its straight path along the dusky air / Homewards." But whereas Bryant and Browning find religious significance in the phenomenon, Coleridge sees it as another illustration of the principle that there is no living thing without charm. Nor does Emerson insist on the presence of divinity in nature; spring, the "Daughter of Heaven and Earth," exists as an intermediary condition between God and man, and birds are the most lovingly detailed part of spring:

Best gems of Nature's cabinet,
With dews of tropic morning wet,
Beloved of children, bards and Spring,
O birds, your perfect virtues bring,
Your song, your forms, your rhythmic flight,
Your manners for the heart's delight,
Nestle in hedge, or barn, or roof,
Here weave your chamber weather-proof,

Forgive our harms, and condescend
To man, as to a lubber friend,
And, generous, teach his awkward race
Courage and probity and grace!
                ("May-Day," 155)

The lady in Wallace Stevens's "Sunday Morning" ponders the competing claims made upon her by religion—"the holy hush of ancient sacrifice"—and nature, such as the "green freedom of a cockatoo" and especially the dawn chorus of birds in the spring:

She says, "I am content when wakened birds,
Before they fly, test the reality
Of misty fields, by their sweet questionings;
But when the birds are gone, and their warm fields
Return no more, where, then, is paradise?"
                                    (68)

Nothing, "neither the golden underground" nor Heaven endures

As April's green endures; or will endure
Like her remembrance of awakened birds,
Or her desire for June and evening, tipped
By the consummation of the swallow's wings.
                                    (68)

A little like Emily Dickinson, who felt the "pang" of spring, Stevens's lady is left with the thought that there is no "imperishable bliss." Her search for paradise, both the earthly paradise and the paradise promised by religion, is emphatically ended with the knowledge that the only certainty is the cycle of life and death as it occurs in nature:

Deer walk upon our mountains, and the quail
Whistle about us their spontaneous cries;
Sweet berries ripen in the wilderness;
And, in the isolation of the sky,
At evening, casual flocks of pigeons make
Ambiguous undulations as they sink,
Downward to darkness, on extended wings.
                                    (70)

The philosophical statement Stevens makes in "Sunday Morning" owes much of its compelling beauty to his metaphorical use of birds. The last stanza of Theodore Roethke's "Meditations of an Old Woman: First Meditation" also makes use of birds to express a similar theme in a more explicit manner.

> There are still times, morning and evening;
> The cerulean, high in the elm,
> Thin and insistent as a cicada,
> And the far phoebe, singing,
> The long plaintive notes floating down,
> Drifting through leaves, oak and maple,
> Or the whippoorwill, along the smoky ridges,
> A single bird calling and calling;
> A fume reminds me, drifting across wet gravel;
> A cold wind comes over stones;
> A flame, intense, visible,
> Plays over the dry pods,
> Runs fitfully along the stubble,
> Moves over the field,
> Without burning.
>   In such times, lacking a god,
>   I am still happy.
>   (159–60)

three. Birds and the Poet's Vocation

Hail to Thee, far above the rest
In joy of voice and pinion!
Thou, Linnet! in thy green array,
Presiding Spirit here to-day,
Dost lead the revels of the May;
    And this is thy dominion.
William Wordsworth, "The Green Linnet"

It is only fitting that song and flight are the two qualities we most admire in birds, for it is to these powers that birds owe their remarkable survival in the vast and varied environment they inhabit. The ability of birds to fly has inspired both scientists and poets, scientists esteeming flight a physical triumph of the first order and poets seeing in flight a powerful symbol of the transcendence they wish to achieve in their writing. The song of birds is especially cherished by poets, probably because it is the only animal utterance with sound patterns just close enough to those made by people to tease us into the belief that bird song is like human language. On the simplest level we all know that the songs and calls of birds readily suggest words, and we even identify and name some bird species by the words they seem to say. On a deeper level, bird song shares with music and poetry aesthetic qualities that are capable of arousing powerful feelings.

The notion that bird song conveys meanings was first recognized by seers or shamans, whose influence among primitive peoples depended upon their professed ability to understand the language of animals.[42] This was tantamount to communicating with the gods, to have their knowledge of both present and future events, since animals, especially birds, were considered to be so close to the gods that they were privy to their secrets and wishes. The essential condition of the shaman's gift was his mystical identification with a wild animal. By inducing an ecstatic trance and simulating a bird's flight (Nascan Indians of Peru took hallucinogenic cactus to produce the illusion of flying), it was presumed that the shaman was able to conduct souls to their resting place and to acquire privileged knowledge from his travels throughout earth and heaven. His account of these unusual experiences was the stuff of poetry, the journey on land and sea constituting the essential narrative motif of the epic, the flight skyward the common motif of the lyric. Divine inspiration made shaman and poet one and the same person until the development of a more sophisticated culture separated the two and limited the role of divinity in human affairs. The flight and song of birds have remained as symbols of poetic inspiration, however. The bird is the poet's tutor, the report of bird song his poem. Thus, at the opening of *Paradise Lost*, John Milton invokes the Holy Spirit in the form of a dove to instruct him so that his poem will "soar / Above th'Aonian Mount"; he is not too far from the posture of the shaman when at the start of *Paradise Regained* he asks the Spirit to inspire

As thou art wont, my prompted Song, else mute,
And bear through height or depth of nature's bounds
With prosperous wing full summ'd to tell of deeds
Above Heroic, though in secret done.

(1.12–15)

(The "full summ'd" wings are the fully grown wings of a falcon.)
The unique power of the shaman is also implied by William Blake
in *Jerusalem:*

I see the Past, Present & Future existing all at once
Before me, O Divine Spirit, sustain me on thy wings,
That I may awake Albion from his long & cold repose.

(15.8–10)

Longfellow's Hiawatha learned the language of birds in his youth,
and the poet's *Song of Hiawatha* comes from the Indian "sweet
singer" Nawadaha, who had it from a number of "wild-fowl"—
the plover, loon, wild goose, blue heron, and grouse. Two of Walt
Whitman's most notable poems (to be examined later) depend
upon a shamanistic relation of the poet to birds.

The nightingale was long the favorite muse of the poet because
of its haunting song and its association with woman in both the
Philomela legend and Persian love poetry. *Aedon*, the Greek word
for nightingale, also means "song" and "singer." As early as the
fifth century B.C. the Chorus in *The Birds* of Aristophanes calls
the nightingale its "partner in song," although the playwright also
allows himself to take a comic view of the bird when later in
the play the poet Cinesias is made to look ridiculous because he
wants to become "a tuneful nightingale" and "gather songs in the
clouds." Five hundred years after Aristophanes, Pliny reports a
piece of information he probably garnered from an anthology of
Greek poetry, the *Garland of Meleager,* that the nightingale "made
music on the lips of the infant Stesichorus," a sixth-century B.C.
Greek poet (10.83). Hardly a generation has passed without sub-
scribing to the notion that the nightingale is the tutor of the poet.
It was the pain of tragic feeling that drew the poet to the nightingale, for suffering was thought to elicit the best poetry. Sorrow is

the source of the "sweetest melody," Shelley writes in "A Defence of Poetry," and the poet is a nightingale "who sits in darkness and sings to cheer its own solitude with sweet sounds." In "Ode to a Nightingale" Keats listens "darkling" to the song of the bird and contemplates death. Both Shelley and Keats revert to Milton's "wakeful Bird" that "sings darkling, in shadiest Covert hid" (*Paradise Lost*, 3.37–38). In Matthew Arnold's "Philomela" both the poet and the bird must endure a "racked heart and brain" in order to create a song bursting with passion and pain.

While the nightingale's song has been the preeminent symbol of poetic inspiration, many other birds have been associated with the poet—the swan and the eagle, of equal antiquity with the nightingale; the bulbul, inspiration of medieval Persian poets; the dove, muse for Christian poets such as Milton and Dante; the cuckoo and skylark, favorites of romantic poets; the mockingbird and hermit thrush of Whitman.

Two curious details in the folklore of swans may have led to the association of the swan with poets: one, that just before its death the swan somehow produces beautiful musical sounds—as Aristotle puts it in his *Historia Animalium*, the swan "sings chiefly at the approach of death"; another, that upon dying the swan ascends to heaven.[43] Both of these notions are to be found in Plato's *Phaedo* when Socrates uses the example of swans in his argument that death is not to be considered a misfortune: "They, when they perceive that they must die, having sung all their life long, do then sing more lustily than ever, rejoicing in the thought that they are about to go away to the god whose ministers they are" (85b). The god they served was Apollo, who gave swans the gift of prophecy. Homer was known as the Swan of Meander, and, according to a fable of Er that Plato tells in the *Republic*, the mythical poet Orpheus chose to be a swan in his second incarnation (10.620a). By the time these notions reached Rome, they were treated facetiously by Horace, who at age forty-two was beginning to feel the approach of death:

> E'en now rough scales invest each shin,
> My frame a bird's white form assumes

> Above, and back and arms begin
>> To be arrayed in fluffy plumes.

No need for his friends to mourn his death:

> A tuneful swan, on safer vanes
>> Than Icarus', I soon shall soar
> O'er Libyan deserts, Arctic plains,
>> And Bosporus' tumultuous shore.[44]

It was a commonplace of Renaissance poetry that the departing soul of a great poet becomes a swan and takes its place in heaven as a constellation, an image supported by the ancient denomination of one constellation as Cygnus the Swan. Ben Jonson makes more than polite use of this figure in the memorial poem he wrote for the first edition of Shakespeare's works:

> Sweet swan of Avon! what a sight it were
>> To see thee in our waters yet appear,
> And make those flights upon the banks of Thames
>> That so did take Eliza, and our James!
> But stay, I see thee in the hemisphere
>> Advanced, and made a constellation there!
>>>> (Hebel and Hudson, 513)

The epithet caught on, for a little later the editors of the folio edition of Beaumont and Fletcher refer to Shakespeare as the "expired sweet Swan of Avon." Edmund Spenser pays homage to Sir Philip Sidney in these lines:

> With loftie flight above the earth he bounded,
> And out of sight to highest heaven mounted:
> Where now he is become a heavenly signe;
> There now the joy is his, here sorrow mine.[45]

An anonymous seventeenth-century song uses the swan image to decry the low estate of poetry at that time:

> The silver swan, who living had no note,
> When death approached, unlocked her silent throat;
> Leaning her breast against the reedy shore,

Thus sung her first and last, and sung no more,
Farewell, all joys; O death, come close my eyes;
More geese than swans now live, more fools than wise.[46]
(Hebel and Hudson, 438–39)

The idea of the bird as tutor of the poet acquired a considerably deepened meaning with the important position given to nature in the aesthetic theory of the romantic movement. Exalting intuition over reason, romantic poets approached the shaman's ecstatic identification with birds as a revered method of discovering truth rather than a mere token obeisance to literary convention. The song of birds again became, as it had been for primitive peoples, a mysterious source of profound meanings and feelings. Thus the song of the cuckoo in William Wordsworth's 1802 poem on that bird recalls the "visionary hours" of the poet's childhood when the earth appeared in its primal glory:

And I can listen to thee yet;
Can lie upon the plain
And listen, till I do beget
That golden time again.

O blessed Bird! the earth we pace
Again appears to be
An unsubstantial faery place;
That is fit home for Thee![47]

The cuckoo is chosen, Wordsworth explains in the 1815 preface to *Lyrical Ballads,* because "the seeming ubiquity of the voice of the cuckoo . . . dispossesses the creature almost of a corporeal existence" (754). Although this leads poets to exercise their imagination more, Wordsworth is careful to warn that poets must still build their images on "properties and qualities the existence of which is inherent and obvious" in the object, in this case the bird's song. Wordsworth takes another step toward etherealization of the bird-tutor in his 1805 skylark poem when he places special emphasis on the flight of a bird as representing the ability of the poetic imagination to transcend the real world and move about freely in the world of ideal beauty:

I have walked through wildernesses dreary,
And to-day my heart is weary;
Had I now the wings of a Faery,
Up to thee would I fly.
There is madness about thee, and joy divine
In that song of thine;
Lift me, guide me, high and high
To thy banqueting place in the sky.
                         ("To a Skylark")

The poem was not published until 1807, and the following year the first part of Goethe's *Faust* appeared, in which images of flight occur frequently, as in this passage:

Alas, it is not easy for earthly wing
To fly on level terms with the wings of the mind.
Yet born with each of us is the instinct
That struggles upwards and away
When over our heads, lost in the blue,
The lark pours out her vibrant lay;
When over rugged pine-clad ranges
The eagle hangs on outspread wings
And over lake and over plain
We see the homeward-struggling crane.[48]

For English poets the skylark became more important than the nightingale. This change may be noted as early as 1804 in a passage from Blake's *Milton* in which the skylark takes precedence over the nightingale as the leader of the "Choir of Day":

Mounting upon the wings of light into the Great Expanse,
Reechoing against the lovely blue and shining heavenly Shell,
His little throat labours with inspiration; every feather
On throat & breast & wings vibrates with the effluence Divine.
                                         (31.32–35)

By 1825 in still another skylark poem Wordsworth was prepared to point up the essential difference between the skylark and the night- and earthbound nightingale: "Leave to the nightingale her shady wood; / A privacy of glorious light is thine." High flight gives the skylark access to light, or the truth sought by the poet, and the bird becomes less real, less apprehended by the senses and more "visionary," out of hearing for Shelley and out of sight for Wordsworth and for Tennyson, who includes the skylark in his description of a spring day:

> Now rings the woodland loud and long,
>   The distance takes a lovelier hue,
>   And drown'd in yonder living blue
> The lark becomes a sightless song.
>   (*In Memoriam*, 115)

In the best known treatment of the skylark, Shelley's "To a Skylark," the bird's flight is associated with light in one striking image after another:

> Higher still and higher
>   From earth thou springest,
> Like a cloud of fire. . . .
> In the golden light'ning
>   Of the sunken sun,
> O'er which clouds are bright'ning,
>   Thou dost float and run.
>   (lines 6–8, 11–14)

There are six stanzas of such imagery. The brilliant light, rendering the bird "unseen," is the element of truth in which the bird moves, and the empathizing poet, "hidden in the light of thought," may learn from the bird "things more true and deep / Than we mortals dream." The "harmonious madness" of the bird's song characterizes the style in which the poet would like to deliver these truths, in "profuse strains of unpremeditated art." Shelley's skylark poem aptly formulates the emotional spontaneity that romanticism favored over the carefully reasoned composition of classical art. The romantic emphasis on the tutelary skylark is a return to the primitive shamanistic identification with flying birds that enables human beings to make their escape from earth and move through space and time like gods.

Like so much romantic thought, the association of flight with the power of poetry to discover truth owes a good deal to Plato.

"The mind of the philosopher alone has wings," he writes in *Phaedrus,* that enable him in a preexistent state to follow God; in this life, however, "he is transported with the recollection of the true beauty; he would like to fly away, but he cannot; he is like a bird fluttering and looking upward and careless of the world below; and he is therefore thought to be mad" (249e). George Santayana echoes Plato and honors Shelley in a fine essay, "Skylarks." Of the poet he writes:

> His wings are his intelligence; not that they bring ultimate success to his animal will, which must end in failure, but that they lift his failure itself into an atmosphere of laughter and light, where is his proper happiness. He cannot take his fine flight, like the lark, in the morning, in mad youth, in some irresponsible burst of vitality, because life is impatient to begin: that sort of thing is the fluttering of a caged bird, a rebellion against circumstances and against commonness.

Both philosophers remind us that the freedom and "unbodied joy" of the skylark are but the poet's idealization. The lesson of Daedalus and Icarus still holds true, that the exercise of the imagination is not free like the flight of a bird, but uncertain and full of perils. A recent biographer of Coleridge finds that the poet was obsessed with "an image of the imagination at work: either flying freely, or else trapped and caged," and cites a passage in the Notebooks describing a flight of starlings that seemed to represent for him two aspects of the imagination, the promise of freedom and the threat of chaos:

> Starlings in vast flights drove along like smoke, mist, or anything misty without solution—now a circular area inclined in an Arc— now a Globe—now from complete Orb into an Elipse & Oblong— now a balloon with the car suspended, now a concave Semi- circle—& still it expands and condenses, some moments glim- mering & shivering, dim & shadowy, now thickening, deepening, blackening.[49]

Another hazard is the difficulty the poet has in practicing his highly spiritualized craft in the real world. The poet's despair over enjoying a bird's freedom to sing and fly free became a familiar romantic theme, best stated by John Keats in his "Ode to a Nightingale." While the bird is "light-winged" and sings "in full-throated ease," the poet is imprisoned in a world "where but to think is to be full of sorrow." He cannot forget the "weariness, the fever, and the fret" of the world and join the bird on "the viewless wings of Poesy." His "dull brain perplexes and retards," and finally he doubts whether the bird may be "a vision, or a waking dream." Keats could not muster the optimism about the poet's situation that Wordsworth had earlier expressed in his 1805 skylark poem, which closes with "hope for higher raptures, when life's day is done."

Edgar Allan Poe's "Romance" is a fine elaboration in avian imagery of the theme of his British predecessors, the predicament of the poet who is caught between his obligation to sordid, worldly cares and his indulgence in the exercise of his poetic gifts:

> Romance, who loves to nod and sing,
> With drowsy head and folded wing,
> Among the green leaves as they shake
> Far down within some shadowy lake,
> To me a painted paroquet
> Hath been—a most familiar bird—
> Taught me my alphabet to say,
> To lisp my very earliest word,
> While in the wild wood I did lie,
> A child—with a most knowing eye.

One would like to believe that the poet's mentor here is a native American bird, the Carolina parakeet (extinct since 1914), instead of an exotic imported parrot. In the second stanza the imagery of another bird is skillfully contrasted with the first:

> Of late, eternal Condor years
> So shake the very Heaven on high
> With tumult as they thunder by,
> I have no time for idle cares
> Through gazing on the unquiet sky.
> And when an hour with calmer wings
> Its down upon my spirit flings—
> That little time with lyre and rhyme

To while away—forbidden things!
My heart would feel to be a crime
Unless it trembled with the strings.

A variation of the theme in "Romance" is found in Poe's "Sonnet
—To Science" in which science is compared to a vulture "whose
wings are dull realities" and who preys upon the poet's heart. It
will be noted that sight and song are more significant for Poe than
flight, which he associates with the beating wings of scavengers.

Poe's French admirer and translator, Charles Baudelaire, in
"Élévation," uses the flight of skylarks as an image of escape from
the "miasmes morbides" of earth:

> Heureux celui qui peut d'une aile vigoreuse
> S'élancer vers les champs lumineux et screins!
> Celui dont les pensers, commes les alouettes,
> Vers les cieux le matin prennent un libre essor.[50]

The alienation of the poet from a workaday world is set forth again
in Baudelaire's "L'Albatros," in which the poet is compared to
an albatross, beautiful in flight but comical and ugly when it is
caught out of its element by sailors and made to walk on the deck
of a ship.

As the nineteenth century wore on and the effects of the Industrial Revolution became more apparent and disturbing to sensitive
observers, poetry had to change in order to meet the challenge of
realistic prose fiction, which seemed better able to respond to the
new order of things. The mystery and etherealism of the nightingale and skylark required toning down. Twenty years after his first
treatment of the skylark, Wordsworth had some second thoughts
about the kind of poetry represented by this bird. By this time he
had modified the theory of poetry so confidently announced in the
preface to the *Lyrical Ballads* in 1798, that "all good poetry is the
spontaneous overflow of powerful feelings." In his second skylark
poem, written in 1825, the bird is called an "ethereal minister" and
"pilgrim of the sky," yet it does not "despise the earth where cares
abound" and is happy to return to its ground nest: "Thy nest which
thou canst drop into at will, / Those quivering wings composed,
that music still!" This is hardly the "drunken lark" of the earlier

poem nor Shelley's "scorner of the ground" but rather the "type of the wise who soar, but never roam; / True to the kindred points of Heaven and Home" (166). This view of the skylark emphasizes Wordsworth's belief, also a part of his early pronouncements, that poetry must not fail to start from earth, from common things, if it is to be truly transcendent. He rejects the nightingale on this count, because its "fiery heart" makes it sing

> A song in mockery and despite
> Of shades, and dews, and silent night;
> And steady bliss, and all the loves
> Now sleeping in these peaceful groves.

The poet therefore prefers the "homely tale" of the stock dove or ring dove:

> He sang of love, with quiet blending,
> Slow to begin, and never ending;
> Of serious faith, and inward glee;
> That was the song—the song for me!
> (*Poems of the Imagination*, no. 9)

Later in the century George Meredith's skylark in "The Lark Ascending" resembles Wordsworth's revised earthbound bird even though his marvelous flight carries him to "the shining tops of day":

> For singing till his heaven fills,
> 'T is love of earth that he instils,
> And ever winging up and up,
> Our valley is his golden cup.
> (222)

Wordsworth's rejection of the nightingale is also echoed some years later by Oscar Wilde in "The Burden of Itys." Hearing in England the song of the "tiny sober-sided advocate . . . for the moon against the day," the poet, cast as a student at Oxford, recalls the stories of gods and men in Greek mythology. The nightingale's song unlocks memories of the heroic past:

> Sing on! sing on! let the dull world grow young,
>   Let elemental things take form again,
> And the old shapes of Beauty walk among
>   The simple garths and open crofts.

But this mood is confronted with the realization that the glorious heritage of the past no longer has a place in the modern world: "Cease, cease, sad bird, thou dost the forest wrong / To vex its sylvan quiet with such impassioned song!" In a gesture like Wordsworth's, Wilde offers the "pastoral thrush," with its simpler song of "jocund carelessness," as a more fitting bird for England, where there is no "cruel Lord with murderous blade" and "no woven web of bloody heraldries."[51] The poem closes with descriptions of the moorhen and the heron and the return of the student to the towers of Oxford. It is not so much the nightingale that Wilde rejects as the conditions of the modern world that make its traditional meanings inappropriate. In this he anticipates the incongruity of the nightingales singing near the brothel visited by Sweeney in Eliot's poem.

In one of his fairy tales, "The Nightingale and the Rose," Wilde carries his disillusionment a step further. The story concerns a student who is required by his lady friend to procure a red rose for her before she will consent to dance with him. A nightingale undertakes to find a rose for him and discovers that her own heart's blood must be used to nurture the rose and tint its petals red. This she does by leaning her breast against a thorn and singing all night "of the Love that is perfected by Death." The bird dies in the process, the student gets his rose, but the lady friend now spurns this token of love in favor of "some real jewels" offered by another admirer. The student, who is unaware of the bird's self-sacrifice on behalf of true love, renounces love as a "silly thing" and returns to his study of logic and metaphysics. In a letter commenting on his story Wilde writes that only the bird retains the old romantic spirit, while "the Student and the girl are, like most of us, unworthy of Romance" (*Letters*, 218).

Wilde was testing Matthew Arnold's conception in "Philomela" of the nightingale as the enduring spirit of classicism, the eternal passion and pain of Greek tragedy, "that wild, unquenched, deep-

sunken, old-world pain." The nightingale also remains the ultimate symbol of art for William Butler Yeats as well as for Arnold,
though it is not the living nightingale but an artificial one representing the poet and his work after death. "Sailing to Byzantium"
begins with the rejection of "birds in the trees," which are for
young people "in one another's arms." Instead of ephemeral passion the poet who is about to die craves the immortality to be
gained from his poetry, an "artifice of eternity." In Plato's legend
of Er, Orpheus chooses to be a swan in his next incarnation; Yeats
chooses to be an artificial bird because it better represents the art
that goes into the making of poetry:

> Once out of nature I shall never take
> My bodily form from any natural thing;
> But such a form as Grecian goldsmiths make
> Of hammered gold and gold enamelling
> To keep a drowsy Emperor awake;
> Or set upon a golden bough to sing
> To lords and ladies of Byzantium
> Of what is past, or passing, or to come.

The emperor Yeats had in mind may have been Theophilus
(A.D. 829–42), in whose garden, the story goes, mechanical birds
sang from a tree of gold and silver. Sir John Mandeville describes
a similar wonder at the feasts of the Great Khan of Cathay: "before the emperoures table men bryngen grete tables of gold. And
thereon ben pecokes of gold and many other maner of dyuerse
foules alle of gold and richely wrought and enameled. And men
maken hem dauncen and syngen clappyng here wenges togydere
and maken gret noyse." Keats in his "Ode to a Nightingale" refers
to an emperor hearing a nightingale, and in one of Hans Christian Andersen's fairy tales, "The Nightingale," a mechanical bird
is fashioned to provide never-failing song for a Chinese emperor.
When the marvelous jeweled contraption breaks down, the real
nightingale has to be called back to restore the emperor's health.
Yeats, however, rejects the implication here and insists on the
superiority of art over nature and, for the aged at least, the need
for quiet contemplation of the past rather than for the passion of
the present moment.[52]

Another traditional bird symbol, the swan-poet, is considered by Yeats in a number of poems. The conventional praise of poetic achievement is omitted, however, since Yeats uses the swan not to honor another poet but to comment on his own career. He renews the beauty of swan imagery, which had grown rather threadbare over the centuries, but in "Nineteen Hundred and Nineteen" he is full of self-doubt about his own adequacy as a poet, especially in a "dragon-ridden" age when "many ingenious lovely things are gone":

> Some moralist or mythological poet
> Compares the solitary soul to a swan;
> I am satisified with that,
> Satisfied if a troubled mirror show it,
> Before that brief gleam of its life be gone,
> An image of its state;
> The wings half spread for flight,
> The breast thrust out in pride
> Whether to play or to ride
> Those winds that clamour of approaching night.
>
> (206)

The poet questions whether his meager accomplishments can bring him the immortality of a place among the stars:

> The swan has leaped into the desolate heaven:
> That image can bring wildness, bring a rage
> To end all things, to end
> What my laborious life imagined, even
> The half-imagined, the half-written page.

In part 3 of "The Tower," after declaring that "it is time that I wrote my will," Yeats leaves us with a beautiful but depressing picture of the dying swan-poet:

> When the swan must fix his eye
> Upon a fading gleam,
> Float out upon a long
> Last reach of glittering stream
> And there sing his last song.
>
> (196)

His last song, though, the last image of the poem, is not the classical swan's triumph but "a bird's sleepy cry / Among the deepening
shades." In "Coole Park and Ballylee, 1931," like Coleridge before
him, Yeats, counting himself one of the "last romantics," worries
about the failure of his poetic imagination, which is represented
by the image of a swan suddenly mounting above a glittering lake:

> Another emblem there! That stormy white
> But seems a concentration of the sky;
> And, like the soul, it sails into the sight
> And in the morning's gone, no man knows why.
>
> (239)

The skylark, as well as the nightingale and swan, has under-
gone a change of symbolical meaning among twentieth-century
writers, who emphasize the pain rather than the joy of being creative. In Ted Hughes's "Skylarks" the bird is still the symbol of the
poet, but its ascent toward the sun is not joyful but terribly painful,
the implication being that poets harm themselves in the pursuit of
their art:

> All the dreary Sunday morning
> Heaven is a madhouse
> With the voices and the frenzies of the larks
> Squealing and gibbering and cursing.
> Heads flung back, as I see them,
> Wings almost torn off backwards—far up
> Like sacrifices set floating
> The cruel earth's offerings
> The mad earth's missionaries.

There are in these lines ironical echoes of Wordsworth's "ethereal
ministers"; a song from Shakespeare's *Cymbeline* ("Hark, hark,
the lark at heaven's gate sings"); and Milton's "high-tow'ring
lark," which he compares to Christ (*Paradise Regained*, 2.279–
83). Although the birds in "Skylarks" safely plummet to earth,
Hughes also may have had in mind the fate of his wife, Sylvia
Plath, a poet who certainly suffered the pains of creativity and
who committed suicide in midcareer a few years before "Skylarks"
was written. The skylark in Theodore Roethke's "The Thing" is

glorious, "flashing between gold levels of the late sun," but it is killed by a flock of larger birds. In "A Presentation of Two Birds to My Son," James Wright compares the chicken, "dull fowl," to the high-flying swift. The chicken's destined end is the chopping block, "a dumb agony," but the flight of the swift is also "stupid and meaningless" agony. Yet it must be undertaken: "The flight is deeper than your father, boy."[53]

The figure of the self-destructing poet-bird is amusingly portrayed in Vladimir Nabokov's *Pale Fire*, a novel presenting the text of John Shade's autobiographical 999-line poem and his editor's lengthy "Commentary," which manages to present the entire life of the ill-fated poet from a different point of view. Shade's poem, titled "Pale Fire: A Poem In Four Cantos" and originally written on eighty index cards, begins with these lines:

> I was the shadow of the waxwing slain
> By the false azure in the windowpane;
> I was the smudge of ashen fluff—and I
> Lived on, flew on, in the reflected sky.

To clinch the analogy of poet and cedar waxwing the editor, who lives in a place called Cedarn, slyly plants a telling detail in a description of Shade just before his death: he sees a "red bandanna handkerchief limply hanging out of one hip pocket"—a reference to the red waxy substance on the outer edges of the bird's secondary feathers.[54]

To register their independence from European literature and their differing views of poetry, some American poets have refused to accept as their mentors the nightingale and skylark, because they do not occur in North America, and instead have adopted native birds. It is not surprising that a regional historian and sometime poet, William Henry Venable, the author of *Literary Culture of the Ohio Valley* (1891), should lavish praise, half-jokingly no doubt, on the North American gray catbird:

> Nightingale I never heard,
> Nor skylark, poet's bird;
> But there is an aether-winger

So surpasses every singer,
(Though unknown to lyric fame,)
That at morning, or at nooning,
When I hear his pipe a-tuning,
Down I fling Keats, Shelley, Wordsworth,—
What are all their songs of birds worth?
All their soaring
Soul's outpouring?
When my Mimus Carolinensis
(That's his Latin name,)
When my warbler wild commences
Song's hilarious rhapsody,
Just to please himself and me!

Henry Van Dyke preferred the veery:

The moonbeams over Arno's vale in silvery flood were pouring,
When first I heard the nightingale a long-lost love deploring,
So passionate, so full of pain, it sounded strange and eerie;
I longed to hear a simpler strain,—the wood-notes of the veery.

In the same vein John Crowe Ransom makes light of the effort to domesticate the nightingale in the American imagination:

Not to these shores she came! this other Thrace,
Environ barbarous to the royal Attic;
How could her delicate dirge run democratic,
Delivered in a cloudless boundless public place
To an inordinate race.[55]

In "The Comedian as the Letter C," an autobiographical poem about his development as a poet from youthful romanticism to various forms of realism, Wallace Stevens rejects the nightingale because of its association with the "evasions" of moonlight rather than with the realities of the sun. To a poet intent on a "vulgar" theme, the nightingale seems "passionately niggling." In "Autumn Refrain" he professes to be moved more by the "skreak and skritter" of grackles at evening than by

The yellow moon of words about the nightingale
In measureless measures, not a bird for me

> But the name of a bird and name of a nameless air
> I have never—shall never hear.

Instead of the nightingale Stevens offers a blackbird as the symbol of the inescapable reality:

> O thin men of Haddam,
> Why do you imagine golden birds?
> Do you not see how the blackbird
> Walks around the feet
> Of the women about you?

Mastery of poetic techniques is fine, but knowing things is also essential:

> I know noble accents
> And lucid, inescapable rhythms;
> But I know, too,
> That the blackbird is involved
> In what I know.
> ("Thirteen Ways of Looking at a Blackbird")

Like Yeats, Stevens has a golden bird, in "Of Mere Being," but it sings in a palm tree and its "fire-fangled feathers dangle down." And like Wordsworth, Stevens realizes that the ascent of the bird, like the high flight of poetry in the realm of the ideal, must end with a return to earth. The pigeons in "Le Monocle de Mon Oncle" illustrate the attempt, perhaps of the young artist, to go beyond the limits of the real world and the necessity, perhaps for the aging artist, to stay within them:

> A blue pigeon it is, that circles the blue sky,
> On sidelong wing, around and round and round.
> A white pigeon it is, that flutters to the ground,
> Grown tired of flight.
> (17)

In "L'Essor Saccadé" ("The Bridled Flight"), as the title suggests, the flight of swallows is bridled or limited to the church steeple, the apple orchard, and a housetop.

As we would expect from a writer whose references to birds are so numerous, Emily Dickinson has many bird mentors. In keeping with her penchant for domestic imagery, all are common back- yard species that she could have seen without stirring from her father's house.

> The Robin's my criterion for Tune—
> Because I grow—where Robins do—
> But, were I Cuckoo born—
> I'd swear by him—
> The ode familiar—rules the Noon.
>   (no. 285)

She is "New Englandy" and sees "provincially," unlike more pre- tentious poets.

> To the Lady
> With the Guinea
> Look—if She should know
> Crumb of Mine
> A Robin's Larder
> Would suffice to stow—
>   (no. 651)

For the same reason she identifies with the phoebe:

> I was a Phoebe—nothing more—
> A Phoebe—nothing less—
> The little note that others dropt
> I fitted into place—
>
> I dwelt too low that any seek—
> Too shy, that any blame—
> A Phoebe makes a little print
> Upon the Floors of Fame.
>   (no. 1009)

A pun may have been intended in the phrase "a little print," since only a few of Dickinson's poems were ever published in her life- time. Her rationalization for remaining an unpublished poet is that she writes for the pleasure of it, just as birds sing for the joy of it:

> The most triumphant Bird I ever knew or met
> Embarked upon a twig today . . .
> And sang for nothing scrutable
> But intimate Delight.
> >   (no. 1265)

She cites the indigo bunting as a fellow of "independent Hues" who "shouts for joy to Nobody / But his seraphic self" (no. 1465). Birds do not sing "for applause"; theirs is an "independent Ecstasy of Deity and Men" (no. 783). Birds can put poets to shame:

> Touch lightly Nature's sweet Guitar
> Unless thou know'st the Tune
> Or every bird will point at thee
> Because a Bard too soon—
> >   (no. 1389)

Consequently she has taken her time in developing her talent:

> I shall keep singing!
> Birds will pass me
> On their way to Yellower Climes—
> Each—with a Robin's expectation—
> I—with my Redbreast—
> And my Rhymes—
>
> Late—when I take my place in summer—
> But—I shall bring a fuller tune—
> Vespers are sweeter than Matins—Signor—
> Morning—only the seed of Noon—
> >   (no. 250)

As well as minimizing her own writing, Dickinson finds poetry in general to be unsubstantial, like bird song:

> A Bird to overhear
> Delight without a Cause—
> Arrestless as invisible—
> A matter of the Skies;
> >   (no. 774)

and like flight:

> As Bird's far Navigation
> Discloses just a Hue—
> A plash of Oars, a Gaiety—
> Then swallowed up, of View.
>
> (no. 243)

"All we secure of Beauty is its Evanescences" is a statement in one of her letters and then developed in a poem describing the almost illusory appearance of a hummingbird.

> A route of Evanescence
> With a revolving Wheel—
> A Resonance of Emerald—
> A Rush of Cochineal . . .
>
> (no. 1463)

Like Dickinson, Robert Frost considered himself to be a late starter in his career as a poet. Like her, he expresses contentment with modest aims in poetry when he notes that the ovenbird, unlike other birds, continues to sing in midsummer when "leaves are old" and flowers few: "The question that he frames in all but words / Is what to make of a diminished thing" (150). The implied answer to the ovenbird's question is that the poet makes what he can of his material, in Frost's case New England, or a world no longer heroic. (Frost addresses the symbolical association of birds and the making of poetry in at least two other poems, "Our Singing Strength" and "On a Bird Singing in Its Sleep.") Thoreau anticipated the point Frost makes in "The Oven Bird" when he chose the red-eyed vireo as his favorite late-summer singer:

> Upon the lofty elm tree sprays
> The vireo rings the changes sweet.
> During the trivial summer days,
> Striving to lift out thoughts above the street.[56]

Always ready to defend American flora and fauna against European detractors, Thomas Jefferson, in a letter to his daughter Martha, claimed that the mockingbird could hold its own with the nightingale because it "has the advantage of singing thro' a great part of the year, whereas the nightingale sings about 5 or 6 weeks in the spring, and a still shorter term, and with a more feeble voice, in the fall." [57] It is also true that the American bird is a night singer in breeding season and has a repertoire as long and varied as the nightingale's. A favorite among American poets, the mockingbird is Walt Whitman's quite accceptable substitute for the nightingale in "Out of the Cradle Endlessly Rocking," a fairly long poem devoted entirely to the influence bird song may have on a budding poet. Originally called "A Child's Reminiscence," the poem tells the story of a boy's encounter with a pair of mockingbirds nesting near the shore of Long Island.

> When the lilac-scent was in the air and the
>   Fifth-month grass was growing,
> Up this seashore in some briers,
> Two feather'd guests from Alabama, two together,
> And their nest, and four light-green eggs spotted with brown,
> And every day the he-bird to and fro and near at hand,
> And every day the she-bird crouch'd on her nest,
>   silent, with bright eyes,
> And every day I, a curious boy, never too close,
>   never disturbing them,
> Cautiously peering, absorbing, translating.
>   (388–89)

The description is ornithologically sound, although sighting a pair of breeding mockingbirds on Long Island would have been a very special event, since that species rarely nested north of Maryland in 1859 when Whitman wrote the poem. Possibly it was on his travels in the South that he found such a nest, for so he reports in an earlier poem, "Starting from Paumanok" (15, sec. 11). Though not a shorebird, the mockingbird may nest in thick cover near the shore, and its eggs are as Whitman describes them. With the last line of this passage, however, the poetic imagination takes over as the boy sets about "translating" bird song into human terms. The rest of the poem consists of Whitman's conversion of the song into language and of the boy's reaction.

The bird at first rejoices that he and his mate can bask in the sun and ride the winds together, presumably on their trip from the South. This happy mood changes quickly when the bird realizes that his mate is missing. Alarmed, he utters loud calls to guide the absent mate homeward, listens for a response, expresses the despair of lost love ("Carols of lonesome love!"), and finally recognizes that the mate will never return ("We two together no more"). At one point the disconsolate male thinks he can see his lost mate in the distance:

> Low-hanging moon!
> What is that dusky spot in your brown yellow?
> O it is the shape, the shape of my mate!
> O moon do not keep her from me any longer.
>
> (390)

Here we have a curious adaptation of an ancient belief: the fact that the silhouette of flying birds may be seen against the background of a full moon led ancient authors to conclude that birds migrate to the moon in winter. As to a bird feeling the loss of a mate, the anthropomorphic weight of Whitman's poetic rendering of the bird's song is eased somewhat by the fact that pair-bonded birds do indeed recognize the absence of a mate and do make persistent calling and searching efforts to restore contact, though hardly over a period of months, as the poet claims. A short time after the disappearance of its mate, even a monogamous male bird, like the mockingbird, will resume singing in order to attract a new mate.

Whitman's mockingbird sings eloquently of love and the loss of a mate that perishes when it is swept out to sea. The boy in the poem interprets the song as having a profound meaning for him:

> Demon or bird! (said the boy's soul,)
> Is it indeed toward your mate you sing? or is it really to me?
> For I, that was a child, my tongue's use sleeping,
>   now I have heard you,
> Now in a moment I know what I am for, I awake,
> And already a thousand singers, a thousand songs, clearer,
>   louder and more sorrowful than yours,
> A thousand warbling echoes have started to
>   life within me, never to die.
>
> (392)

In the bird's grief the boy discovers his own feelings of unsatisfied love:

> The messenger there arous'd, the fire, the sweet hell within,
> The unknown want, the destiny of me.

Paradoxically, the sea cradles both the dead and the living, a mockingbird's lost mate and a boy whose poetic inspiration is born when he begins to understand a bird's song of love and the sound of the sea, personified as "the fierce old mother" whispering the "delicious word death."

"Out of the Cradle Endlessly Rocking" may be like one of those unwritten poems "bridging the way from Life to Death" that Whitman dreams of in "Proud Music of the Storm." Another could be "When Lilacs Last in the Dooryard Bloom'd," one of the "thousand responsive songs" aroused by his boyhood experience of death. Although this poem had for its occasion the death of an actual person, President Lincoln, and incorporates many of the conventions of the traditional elegy, the song of a bird again figures in the process of leading the grieving poet to an understanding of the mysterious conjunction of death and love. In "Lilacs" the bird is a hermit thrush, an even better choice than the mockingbird since its brief song is well known for its consistently transcendent, unearthly quality, while the mockingbird's extensive repertoire may have some rather harsh and clownish sounds. "The Hermit and Wood Thrushes are reflective. They are the deep ones . . . creatures of the spirit," writes Charlton Ogburn; and Louis Untermeyer calls the thrush "our lark, our more than nightingale, / Surpassing interval and scale."[58] Whitman himself had observed earlier in "Song of Myself" that the hermit thrush has none of the mocker's "gurgles, crackles, screams." The bird and its habitat are carefully described in the Lincoln poem:

> In the swamp in secluded recesses,
> A shy and hidden bird is warbling a song.
>
> Solitary the thrush,
> The hermit withdrawn to himself, avoiding the settlements,
> Sings by himself a song.
>
> . . . .

Sing on, sing on you gray-brown bird,
Sing from the swamps, the recesses,
   pour your chant from the bushes,
Limitless out of the dusk, out of the cedars and pines.

(459, 463)

(Eliot's thrush in *The Waste Land* also "sings in the pine trees.")
Poetic convention dictates some of the details here: evergreens
are traditional emblems of immortality, and so it is poetically fitting for a bird with a comforting message about death to be there
even though cedars and pines do not thrive in swamps and hermit thrushes are not particularly drawn to conifers in the eastern
United States. The hermit is certainly in his best voice at dusk, and
it is then that the thrush ventures near enough to human settlements to be heard clearly. Robert Frost hears one from the "edge
of the woods," and his bird sings of death, too:

Far in the pillared dark
Thrush music went—
Almost like a call to come in
To the dark and lament.
      ("Come In")

Some of the details concerning the hermit thrush may have
come from conversations Whitman had with his friend John Burroughs, who had written of the thrush two years before Whitman's
poem, "It is quite a rare bird, of very shy and secluded habits,
being found in the Middle and Eastern States, during the period of
song, only in the deepest and most remote forests, usually in damp
and swampy localities." He describes its song as a "pure, serene,
hymnlike strain." In another essay Burroughs, commenting on a
passage in Virgil's *Georgics* in which a nightingale mourns for the
brood a ploughman destroyed in the nest, observes that a bird's
song cannot be interpreted as an expression of grief: "The poets,
therefore, in depicting the bird on such occasions as bewailing the
lost brood, are wide of the mark; he is invoking and celebrating a
new brood."[59] Having heard this from Burroughs, perhaps Whitman chose not to render in "Lilacs" the song of the bird as he
had done in "Out of the Cradle." Instead, the poet dwells on the

"tallying chant, the echo arous'd in my soul" by a song he interprets as the "carol of death." The poet's responding chant turns out to be a moving celebration of death, beginning with the invocation "Come lovely and soothing death" and closing with an acceptance of death: "I float this carol with joy, with joy to thee O death." Although the burden of the mockingbird's song in "Out of the Cradle" expresses grief over the death of a loved one, the song of the thrush in "Lilacs" inspires the poet, now no longer a boy, to "warble" his own "outlet song" for the man he loved, the poem itself. The love theme in "Lilacs" is represented not by the bird but the "heart-shaped leaves" of the lilac bush, and the lost loved one, Lincoln, is the "drooping star in the west." Together with the bird they form a "trinity sure" ("Lilac and star and bird twined with the chant of my soul") and finally "retrievements out of the night" bringing consolation for the death of Lincoln and, even more important, reconciliation with death. Whitman's joyful acceptance of death invites comparison with Keats's death wish in his "Ode to a Nightingale." There the song of the bird fills the listener with such despair over his own failure as a poet that he longs for the escape that death may afford:

> Now more than ever seems it rich to die,
> To cease upon the midnight with no pain,
>   While thou art pouring forth thy soul abroad
>   In such an ecstasy!
> Still wouldst thou sing, and I have ears in vain—
> To thy high requiem become a sod.
> (lines 55–60)

Whitman's two elegies have shamanistic features in that the poet is able to deal with the mystery of death through his understanding of the language of a bird. The boy in "Out of the Cradle" is "ecstatic" as he learns that he is capable of "translating the notes" of the mockingbird, whose divine origin he recognizes when he addresses it as "demon or bird"—just as Shelley questions whether his skylark is "sprite or bird." In "Lilacs" the song of the thrush interacts with the cosmos (the star) and the earth (the scent of lilacs) to bring the mourner out of despair over the death of a great hero. The poet's account of the whole experience, like the shaman's frenzied message to his less gifted tribesmen, is the poetic production itself. And like the shaman's report, a considerable portion of Whitman's poem is devoted to "visions" of his journeys over vast distances and among the "myriads" of the dead who had fallen in the Civil War, journeys over "the varied and ample land" of America: "While my sight that was bound in my eyes unclosed, / As to long panoramas of visions."

For reporting a purely personal experience in "Out of the Cradle," a hushed, lyrical voice or style was appropriate; for reporting one's reaction to the death of a great national hero, who meant so much to the poet, in "Lilacs," a mixture of intimate and public declamatory voices was required. By comparison a poem celebrating the glory of America, such as "Thou Mother with Thy Equal Brood," is written in a single declamatory style and has for its bird not the secretive thrush or mockingbird but a highly visible soaring bird:

> As a strong bird on pinions free,
> Joyous, the amplest spaces heavenward cleaving,
> Such be the thought I'd think of thee America,
> Such be the recitative I'd bring for thee.
>
> (568)

The poem originally opened with these lines and was later changed to begin with the image of the "brood" of the several states of the American nation. Whitman saw this poem and six others bound with it and titled *As A Strong Bird* (1872) as the expression of a "vast, composite, electric *Democratic Nationality.*" Curiously enough, he thought his best work was inspired more by the flight than by the song of birds:

> I have not so much emulated the birds that musically sing,
> I have abandon'd myself to flights, broad circles,
> The hawk, the seagull, have far more possessed me
>   than the canary or mocking-bird,
> I have not felt to warble and trill, however sweetly,
> I have felt to soar in freedom and in the fullness
>   of power, joy, volition.

But these lines from "To Soar in Freedom and in the Fullness of Power" were written in old age when Whitman perhaps had forgotten the remarkable early successes with the thrush and the mockingbird.[60]

What accounts for those successes are the extensive lyrical passages dealing with the mourning bird and the reflective poet, both as boy and man. Of "Out of the Cradle," Leo Spitzer claims that there is "no other poem in which we find such a heart-rending impersonation of a bird by a poet, such a welding of bird's voice and human word, such an empathy for the joy and pain expressed by nature's singers." [61] In "Lilacs" the lyrical mode is subtly blended with narrative passages recounting the funeral journey of Lincoln's body and the journeys of the poet from city to shore. Part of Whitman's success may be attributed to his actual experience of birds and seashore on Long Island where he spent his childhood. Whitman's love of the shore and shorebirds, continuing into old age when he lived in Camden and took every opportunity to visit the New Jersey coast in spite of his paralytic condition, is celebrated by Stephen Vincent Benét in a fine passage from "Ode to Walt Whitman":

> Always the water about you since you were born,
> The endless lapping of water, the strong motion,
> The gulls by the ferries knew you, and the wild sea-birds,
> The sandpiper, printing the beach with delicate prints.[62]

The theme of the mourning bird was not original with Whitman, of course. The classical nightingale Philomela not only stirred the pain of grief but also allayed grief through the sheer beauty of its song. Because its cooing resembles the tones of human mourning, the dove has long been a favorite symbol of grief over a lost mate. In Edmund Spenser's *Amoretti* a dove

> Sits mourning for the absence of her mate:
>> and in her songs sends many a wishful vow,
>> for his return that seems to linger late.
> So I alone now left disconsolate,
>> mourn to my self the absence of my love:

and wandring here and there all desolate,
seek with my playnts to match that mournful dove.

(Sonnet 89)

Spenser gives the same idea more elaborate treatment in the story
of Timias and Belphebe told in *The Faerie Queene*. Timias, the
character representing Sir Walter Raleigh, falling out of favor with
Belphebe, or Queen Elizabeth, hears the "mournefull notes" of a
dove "that likewise late had lost her dearest love." Like the listener
in Whitman's two poems, Timias feels that the "lamentable lay"
of the bird "much did ease his mourning" because it addressed
his plight as well as the bird's. Later the bird acts as a messenger between the estranged couple and serves to bring about their
reconciliation (4.8). In "Philisides" Sir Philip Sidney writes of the
"wayling till death" of a "widow turtle" whose mate has been
caught on a limed tree branch, and in James Thomson's *The Seasons* a stock dove "coos mournfully hoarse" as it dwells on "the
sad idea of his murdered mate, / Struck from his side by savage
fowler's guile" ("Summer," lines 618–19). A blackbird in an early
Irish poem serves a purpose strikingly like Whitman's:

Sadly talks the blackbird here.
Well I know the woe he found . . .
I myself not long ago
Found the woe now he has found.
Well I read thy song, O bird,
For the ruin of thy love.[63]

Sea and bird song are "two noises too old to end" writes Gerard Manley Hopkins in "The Sea and the Skylark." In antiquity
the image of the sea and the mourning shorebird somehow became attached to the kingfisher, perhaps because the kingfisher is
seldom seen in the company of a mate except in breeding season
and never fails to utter his distinctive call as he flies over water. A
Greek myth tells the story of Alcyone, a grieving wife who walks
along the shore seeking her shipwrecked husband, Ceyx, and leaps
into the sea when she sees his body floating there. Ovid describes
the scene in book 11 of the *Metamorphoses*:

She stripped herself, then ran upon a breaker
That caught the waves, and leaped as if broad wings
Took her to sea; even her cries were birdlike;
And as she neared the floating man beneath her,
She thrust her growing beak between his lips.

At this point Alcyone and Ceyx are turned into kingfishers, and to compensate them for their untimely end as mortals the god Aeolus calms the sea seven days before and seven days after the winter solstice, the period of time when it was believed kingfishers nested on the water. One of the exiled Argive women in Euripides' *Iphigenia in Tauris* compares her condition to that of the forlorn kingfisher:

O sad-voiced ocean-bird, heard in the foam
    Low by the rocky ledge
Singing a note unhappy hearts can hear,
The song of separation from your mate,
    The moan of separation,
I have no wings to seek like you, but I
    Can sing a song like you,
A song of separation from my mate.

In T. S. Eliot's "Marina" there is a particularly fine image combining the sea and a bird, reminiscent of Whitman's, to create a setting for a father's finding a daughter believed lost at sea:

What seas what shores what grey rocks and what islands
What water lapping the bow
And scent of pine and the woodthrush singing through the fog
What images return
O my daughter.
        (72)

The burial at sea of the hero in Melville's *Billy Budd* is attended by seafowl that deliver an ungainly farewell to the sailor whom the world treated so cruelly: "So near the hull did they come, that the stridor or bony creak of their gaunt double-jointed pinions was audible. As the ship under light airs passed on, leaving the burial spot astern, they still kept circling it low down with the moving shadow of their outstretched wings and the cracked requiem of their cries." [64]

Poetic traditions may be modified but never entirely extinguished. The bird as the poet's muse—which we have noted from Stesichorus in the sixth century B.C. to Yeats in the twentieth century—appears even in a piece of prose fiction that has been acclaimed as ushering in the novel of the twentieth century, James Joyce's *Portrait of the Artist as a Young Man.* In one of his more striking "epiphanies," defined in a first draft of the book as "a sudden spiritual manifestation," the young hero, Stephen Dedalus, suddenly comes to the realization that he is destined to be a poet rather than a priest. Walking on the strand like Whitman, he hears friends call out his name and for the first time makes the association between himself and Daedalus, the mythical Greek master craftsman who was noted for making wings that enabled him and his son Icarus to fly away from Crete, where they were being kept prisoner by King Minos.

> Now, as never before, his strange name seemed to him a prophecy.
> . . . Now, at the name of the fabulous artificer, he seemed to hear
> the noise of dim waves, and to see a winged form flying above the
> waves and slowly climbing the air. What did it mean? Was it a
> quaint device opening a page of some medieval book of prophe-
> cies and symbols, a hawklike man flying sunward above the sea, a
> prophecy of the end he had been born to serve and had been fol-
> lowing through the mists of childhood and boyhood, a symbol of
> the artist forging anew in his workshop out of the sluggish matter
> of earth a new soaring impalpable imperishable being?

Stephen feels that he too is a bird soaring in "an ecstasy of flight.
. . . His throat ached with a desire to cry aloud, the cry of a hawk or eagle on high, to cry piercingly of his deliverance to the winds." [65] The bird imagery is Joyce's concrete way of stating his aesthetic principle, put forward elsewhere in the book, that the artist's personality "finally refines itself out of existence."

In this use of the myth of Daedalus and Icarus, Joyce's hero is more concerned with the promise of a career as a writer and his escape from Ireland and the priesthood than with the warning the story offers to the outsetting artist to avoid being overambitious. Icarus, against his father's advice, brings disaster upon himself by soaring so high that the heat of the sun melts the wax binding the feathers to the wings his father fashioned for him, and he falls into the sea and perishes. The artist's risk of failure does not occur to the young Stephen until he makes this entry in his diary, the very last sentence of the book: "Old father, old artificer, stand me now and ever in good stead." These brief references to Daedalus and Icarus anticipate the extensive use Joyce was to make of another Greek myth dealing with a father-son relationship in *Ulysses.*

To bring his "epiphany" closer to reality and to emphasize the importance of love and beauty in the inspiration of the poet, Joyce at this point has his hero encounter a young girl wading in a rivulet of water left by the receding tide:

> A girl stood before him in midstream, alone and still, gazing out to sea. She seemed like one whom magic had changed into the likeness of a strange and beautiful seabird. Her long slender bare legs were delicate as a crane's and pure save where an emerald trail of seaweed had fashioned itself as a sign upon the flesh. Her thighs, fuller and softhued as ivory, were bared almost to the hips where the white fringes of her drawers were like the feathering of soft white down. Her slateblue skirts were kilted boldly about her waist and dovetailed behind her. Her bosom was as a bird's soft and slight, slight and soft as the breast of some darkplumaged dove. But her long fair hair was girlish: and girlish, and touched with the wonder of mortal beauty, her face.
>
> (*Portrait,* 171)

Although the imagery is sensual, the encounter has no sexual overtones for Stephen. Just as the change of Philomela removes her from the taint of lust and murder, so Stephen's identification of the girl with a bird helps to remove her from the world of senses. The bird-girl is his muse: "Her image had passed into his soul for ever and no word had broken the holy silence of his ecstasy." A merely human girl also figures in Stephen's creative life, an acquaintance he fancies as his Beatrice. But he questions whether her life is as "simple and strange as a bird's life . . . her heart simple and wilful as a bird's heart?" She kindles desire in him and is the "temptress" of a villanelle he writes.

Stephen's inspiration to be a writer is as pure as the call to the priesthood that it now replaces. In a second epiphany involving birds he is impelled to wonder whether his giving up the priesthood for the life of a writer may be "folly." Observing from the steps of a library building the flight of a flock of sparrows, he employs the ancient practice of augury to determine whether he has made the right career choice. "A sense of fear of the unknown moved in the heart of his weariness, a fear of symbols and portents, of the hawklike man whose name he bore soaring out of his captivity on osierwoven wings, of Thoth, the god of writers, writing with a reed upon a tablet and bearing on his narrow ibis head the cusped moon" (*Portrait*, 225).[66] Do the migrant swallows foretell his own departure from Ireland to seek out a new life? "Then he was to go away? for they were birds ever going and coming, building ever an unlasting home under the eaves of men's houses and ever leaving the homes they had built to wander." Stephen feels that his own birdlike nature makes him respond to the birds: "that the augury he had sought in the wheeling darting birds and in the pale space of sky above him had come forth from his heart like a bird from a turret quietly and swiftly." Shortly after this he rejects his mother's plea for him to hold on to the church and prepares to leave home. Earlier he had considered Ireland to be like a bird trap: "When the soul of a man is born in this country there are nets flung at it to hold it back from flight. You talk to me of nationality, language, religion. I shall try to fly by those nets" (203). Stephen's leaving Ireland and the church is comparable to the escape of Daedalus from Crete and the tyranny of King Minos.

In both Whitman's "Out of the Cradle Endlessly Rocking" and Joyce's *Portrait of the Artist as a Young Man,* an encounter with birds leads a youth to a writer's career. Also in both, water plays an important part. It is on "Paumanok's gray beach" that Whitman as a young boy witnesses the loss of the mockingbird's mate when it is blown out to sea, when the sea "lisp'd to me the low and delicious word death." It is during a walk along the strand that Stephen has his vision of Daedalus, "a hawklike man flying sunward above the sea," and his view of the wading girl who seems to be like a seabird. The swallows, too, are associated with water even though he sees them in the city: "A soft liquid joy like the noise of many waters flowed over his memory and he felt in his heart the soft peace of silent spaces of fading tenuous sky above the waters, of oceanic silence, of swallows flying through the seadusk over the flowing waters" (*Portrait,* 225–26). A bird singing "carols of lonesome love! death's carols!" and the sea whispering the word "death" inspire the young Whitman to write poetry; visions of a lovely bird-girl, a winged "artificer," and swallows flying over water inspire the young Stephen to give up the "pale service of the altar" and become a writer.

c h a p t e r   t w o

Birds and the Supernatural

*There is the tyranny of Jove in its claws,
and his wrath in the erectile feathers of
the head and neck.*

Henry David Thoreau on the osprey
in "Natural History of Massachusetts"

one. Birds and Gods: The Ancient Legacy

Because they are able to move freely through space, to appear suddenly out of the sky and disappear just as suddenly, birds must have
seemed to primitive humans to be mysterious creatures commanding attention and worship. Their mastery of air space made them
the most apparent link between earthbound creatures and distant
wonders—the sun, moon, stars, wind, thunder—and the powers
that controlled them. "The wing," Socrates says in *Phaedrus,* "is
the corporeal element most akin to the divine" (246e). There is
hardly a pantheon in the history of world religion that does not
include birds serving as the agents and the disguises of gods, if not
the gods themselves. The earliest Hindu, Sumerian, and Egyptian
sky-gods were associated with high-flying birds such as the hawk,
eagle, and vulture, all exceptional animals in that they dared to
approach the source of all life, the sun. As late as the fifth century B.C. it was still possible for Aristophanes to recall—jokingly
at a time when Greece was outgrowing earlier religious beliefs—
that birds not only lived before gods were born but once ruled
over nations: the cock, king of the Persians; the kite, king over the
Greeks; and the cuckoo, king of the Egyptians and Phoenicians.

If the wing served to make the bird miraculously free of earth,
the egg bound the bird to earth, and the brooding hen became a

symbol of the miracle of life. According to the creation stories of many peoples from all over the world, the universe itself was born from a bird's egg.[1] A pre-Hellenic myth has the goddess Eurynome mating with a serpent, then becoming a dove and brooding an egg from which the universe is hatched. In *The Birds* Aristophanes records another early Greek myth that "black-winged Night" lays an egg in the depths of Erebus from which is born the winged Eros, who mates with Chaos and thereby produces the world, the first generation of birds, and the first family of gods. In this recital the fifth-century B.C. playwright was making light of earlier creation stories and yet honoring them in fine verses. As Algernon Swinburne noted at the time he made a translation "Chorus of the Birds," "It is half sacred, half secular, half humorous, half imaginative, and all poetical in the highest degree of its kind." His translation is an attempt to imitate the form of Aristophanes' hexameters:

> It was Chaos and Night at the first, and the blackness of
> darkness, and hell's broad border,
> Earth was not, nor air, neither heaven; when in the depths of
> the womb of the dark without order
> First thing first-born of the black-plumed Night was a wind-egg
> hatched in her bosom,
> Whence timely with seasons revolving again sweet Love burst
> out as a blossom.

In "The Destiny of Nations" Coleridge has a pair of lines describing the part of Eros in the creation story, "when Love rose glittering, and his gorgeous wings / Over the abyss fluttered with such glad noise" (140, lines 283–84). In another group of creation myths the world substance is composed of soil brought up from the bottom of the sea by diving birds—the Loon Who Made the World from an Ojibwa legend and the red-throated loon from a northeastern Siberian myth in the Yenisey-Ostyak language. According to the Finnish *Kalevala* the earth was formed from the broken eggshells of a blue-winged teal nesting on the knees of the Water Mother.[2]

Well into modern times primitive peoples from Australia to North America continued to worship bird-gods. Native Americans took meteors to be fallen gods and wrapped them in feather-cloth for burial; Hawaiians made images of their gods from wicker and feathers and called them "feather-gods." In religions that became more sophisticated as they drew away from childlike identification with animals, the gods assumed either more human or more abstract characteristics and retained only remnant tokens of animals. The Egyptian Horus and Ra, for example, were pictured with falcon heads on human bodies, while Sumerian and Assyrian war gods had human heads on the bodies of winged lions. Eventually, birds were retained merely as the appurtenances of gods. Thus, almost every major deity in the Greek family of gods was linked with a bird that seemed appropriate for that god's origin or function, such as the peacock of Hera, the owl of Athena, and the dove and swan of Aphrodite. Perched on the sceptre of Zeus, the Greek sky-god, was an eagle holding thunderbolts in his talons. The Romans later adopted this image to represent the godhead and power of their Caesars, and from the Romans it passed on to medieval and modern European emperors, as well as to republics such as the United States. In antiquity the soaring hawk and vulture were also symbols of supreme power, and the eagle's alleged ability to look at the sun without blinking gave it an additional claim to represent divinity.[3]

In addition to keeping their favorite birds about them, the gods sometimes took the form of birds to facilitate their transactions with earthlings. The notion of a bird as the lover of a human maiden was common enough to be represented on a series of Cretan coins. Most famous of these impersonators was the Greek god Zeus, who assumed the forms of various animals to conceal his godhead from ladies who were the targets of his amorous designs. To get at his sister Hera he took the form of a cuckoo, according to Pausanias in his explanation of the figure of a cuckoo perched on Polyclitus's statue of Hera in the temple of Argos (*Itinerary of Greece*, 2.17.4). At least twice Zeus appeared as an eagle, once in pursuit of Asterie, who tried to escape by turning herself into a quail and dropping into the sea; and again to abduct the world's most beautiful youth, Ganymede, whom he carried off to Olympus to serve as the cupbearer of the gods, though another account suggests that it was for the purpose of taking the boy for his lover. Ovid uses this version in *Metamorphoses,* possibly to justify pederasty. Ganymede's abduction by an eagle was the subject of a bronze statue by Leochares, a Greek sculptor of the fourth century B.C. In his most celebrated impersonation, Zeus took the form of a swan to force himself upon a recalcitrant maiden named Leda. From this union, according to one version of the story, there were four famous offspring: the sisters Helen of Troy and Clytemnestra and the twin brothers Castor and Pollux.

In spite of their tendency to value spirit over matter, mind over natural phenomena, Judaism and Christianity assimilated a good deal of the animal imagery of earlier religions. Though the Hebrews strictly forbade the worship of animals, they sometimes used the bird imagery of their neighbors to describe the Almighty. His presence is announced by the sound of wings, and he shields Jerusalem "like a bird hovering over its young"; he protects Jacob "as an eagle watches over its nest, hovers above its young, spreads its pinions and takes them up, and carries them upon its wings" (Isa. 31.5, Deut. 32.11, Ps. 91.4). Christians, coming into contact with northern European as well as Mediterranean cultures, went even further. Early churchmen, well-versed admirers of Greek and Roman literature and eager to win converts among the heathen, had no qualms about attaching old imagery to new beliefs. The medieval church and Renaissance art adopted these borrowings, which became important motifs in literature down to modern times.

Christ's resurrection was thus readily associated with the cock's announcement of the sun's return each morning and with the Egyptian phoenix, a mythical bird that renewed itself every five hundred years. The popular fourteenth-century *Travels* of Sir John Mandeville makes the comparison quite specific: "The brid Fenix cometh and brenneth himself to askes. And the first day next after men fynden in the askes a worm; and the seconde day next after men fynden a brid quyk and parfyt; and the thridde day next after he fleeth his wey. . . . And men may wel lykne that bryd vnto God because that there nys no god but on, and also that oure lord aroos from deth to lyue the thrydde day" (34). The eagle, once the bird of the Greek Zeus and the Roman Jupiter, was another symbol of Christ; like the phoenix it renewed itself, in the rays of the sun rather than in fire. As late as the seventeenth century the two-headed eagle, the *Reichsadler* or emblem of the Holy Roman Empire, was explicitly associated with Christ in a popular design on glass tankards (*Humpen*) showing Christ on the cross between trailing feathers. The imagery of the Trinity sometimes incorporated the eagle as the Father, the dove as the Holy Spirit, the cock and the phoenix as Jesus. The eagle, cock, and phoenix all qualified for association with the new Christian god because of their traditional relation with the sun, the natural phenomenon universally worshipped for its life-giving powers. In the Book of Revelation, chapter 12, a pregnant "woman clothed with the sun," presumably Mary, is rescued from a dragon and brings forth "a man child, who was to rule all nations."

A popular analogy between the pelican and Jesus was predicated on the ancient folk belief that the pelican tears open its breast to feed its young, just as Jesus gave his blood to humankind to save the world from sin. A verse by Saint Thomas Aquinas reads:

> Bring the tender tale true of the Pelican;
> Bathe me, Jesu Lord, in what thy bosom ran—
> Blood that but one drop of has the world to win
> All the world forgiveness of its world of sin.

The tale is told in full by the Anglo-Norman trouvère, Philippe de Thaun. First the pelican slays his offspring when they try "to blind their father's eye" and then, after three days, revives them:

> Feeling so strong a woe
>   To see the small birds so
> That he strikes his breast with his beak
>   Until the blood shall leak.
> And when the coursing blood
>   Spatters his lifeless brood,
> Such virtue does it have
>   That once again they live.
>
>   .   .   .   .
>
> Know that this pelican
>   Signifies Mary's Son;
> The little birds are men

> Restored to life again
> From death, by that dear blood
> Shed for us by our God.

In borrowing some of the attributes of Christ for his persona, Walt Whitman touches on the legend of the pelican when he compares his poems to drops of blood offered to his readers:

> O drops of me! trickle, slow drops,
> Candid from me falling, drip, bleeding drops,
> From wounds made to free you whence you were prison'd,
> From my face, from my forehead and lips,
> From my breast, from within where I was conceal'd.

Another curious use of the legend is made by Thornton Wilder in *The Cabala*. At the dinner table of a fashionable house a cardinal asks grace, "a strange affair discovered by our erudite guest among the literary remains of some disappointed Cambridge parson."

> Oh, pelican of eternity,
> That piercest thy heart for our food,
> We are thy fledglings that cannot know thy woe.
> Bless this shadowy and visionary food of substance,
> Whose last eater shall be worm,
> And feed us rather with the vital food of
> Dreams and grace.[4]

Pelicans feed their young with regurgitant, and possibly the violent manner in which young pelicans probe deep into the large pouch of the parent led some observers to think that the breast was torn open. Anyone who has observed a pelican strenuously preening itself might be inclined to agree with Sir Thomas Browne's explanation in his *Vulgar Errors* that "by nibling and biting themselves on the itchy part of their breast . . . their feathers on that part are sometimes observed to be red and tincted with blood" (2:340). Bas-relief sculptures of pelican chicks clustered around the parent bird are still being made and appropriately placed on lecterns in Catholic churches.

Other birds have figured in the life of Jesus in lesser ways. Many etiological folktales about birds have been used to embroider the story of the crucifixion.[5] In Gaelic lore the plumage of the oystercatcher in flight was said to resemble a white cross to honor the bird's attempt to conceal Jesus from his enemies by covering him with seaweed. Sparrows, flying directly, led his enemies to his hiding place at Gethsemane, while swallows tried to lead them away with their irregular, darting flight. The robin got its red breast from a thorn it picked from the crown of thorns, and the crossbill got its crossed mandibles and red breast in attempting to pull out the nails from the hands and feet of Jesus on the cross. In "The Legend of the Crossbill," written by Julius Mosen and translated into English by Henry Wadsworth Longfellow, Jesus takes note of the crossbill:

> Blest be thou of all the good!
> Bear, as token of this moment,
> Marks of blood and holy rood.

Another memeber of the finch family, the European goldfinch (*Carduelis carduelis*) was a common feature of Renaissance paintings of the Madonna and the Child.[6] Held by the infant Jesus or perched nearby, the bird appears in 450 paintings of the time. Its fondness for thorns and its bright red face pattern were explained by the legend that at the crucifixion a goldfinch pulled out a thorn from the crown of Jesus on the cross. The bird in the paintings thus poignantly brings together a grim reminder of the Passion to come and the happy present scene of mother, child, and brightly colored pet. A Spanish folk belief holds that the owl shuns the daylight and no longer sings because it witnessed the crucifixion. A recent addition to this curious collection is a poem in which William Everson asks what birds there were at the crucifixion "to make a graveness in the afternoon / When the nailing was done to the cross hilt." More than a dozen species are named, including the New World roadrunner and the vulture, "that grim gliding keeper of appointments." All these are "quietly there, not come but *sent*, keeping a tryst," and they are

> Better than those who thumbed sharp iron and plaited thorn!
> Better than those who rattled dice for a stranger's shirt
> And sponged galled water!
> > ("What Birds There Were," 170–71)

Perhaps because of its familiarity and ready accommodation to the human environment, the robin has won a reputation for performing acts of Christian piety. In early times it was most commonly known for ritually burying the dead by covering exposed corpses with leaves, a belief prompted perhaps by the robin's method of foraging for food by pulling leaves aside. Shakespeare speaks of the ruddock's "charitable bill" and Izaak Walton commends the "honest robin that loves mankind, both alive and dead." In the ballad called "The Children of the Wood" or "Babes in the Woods," two children who have been betrayed and then killed by their uncle are served by the robin:

> No burial this pretty pair
>   Of any man receives,
> Till Robin-red-breast piously
>   Did cover them with leaves.

John Webster, in a song from his play *White Devil* (1612), has this:

> Call for robin redbreast and the wren,
> Since o'er shady groves they hover,
> And with leaves and flowers do cover
> The friendless bodies of unburied men.
>   (Hebel and Hudson, 393)

In "The Redbreast" Wordsworth commends "the pious bird" for cooling the fever of a sick child "with his passing wing" and bringing comfort to a lonely old man confined to a poorhouse. From his "old Welch mother," John Greenleaf Whittier learned that the "breast-burned" robin brings drops of water to cool sinners in hell:

> He brings cool dew on his little bill,
>   And lets it fall on the souls of sin:
> You can see the mark on his red breast still
>   Of fires that scorch as he drops it in.
>   ("The Robin")

The domestic cock has had a wider range of Christian applications than any other bird, perhaps because its crowing just before daybreak has practical uses that are readily extended to spiritual values. A fourth-century hymn by Saint Ambrose lists the benefits of cockcrow: the "herald of the day" dispels harmful nighttime evils such as prowling highwaymen, serves as a clock that rouses sleepers to their daily tasks, calms the sea for sailors, and calls the faithful to worship each day, thus prompting their renewal of faith in God. To this list a medieval Latin bestiary added the healing power of cockcrow: "It is by this song that hope returns to the sick, trouble is turned to advantage, the pain of wounds is relieved, the burning of fever is lessened, faith is restored to the fallen." Symbolically the cock's welcome of sunlight represents the joyful acceptance of the spiritual light Christ brings to a benighted world. The last stanza of Ambrose's hymn makes this application implicitly:

> Thou Light, illumine with Thy light
> Our sleeping lethargy of soul;
> Thy name the first our lips shall choose,
> Discharging thus our vows to Thee.

The Creator and the cock are brought closer together in Henry Vaughan's magnificent "Cock-Crowing":

> Father of Lights! what Sunnie seed,
> What glance of day hast thou confin'd
> Into this bird? To all the breed
> This busie Ray thou hast assign'd;
> Their magnetisme works all night,
> And dreams of Paradise and light.
>
> . . . .
>
> If joyes, and hopes, and earnest throws [throes],
> And hearts whose Pulse beats still for light
> Are given to birds; who, but thee, knows
> A love-sick soul's exalted flight?
> Can souls be track'd by any eye
> But his who gave them wings to flie?[7]

The cock not only welcomes the sun each day but, according to a belief dating from the fourth century, commemorates the birth of Jesus at the time of the winter solstice when the sun in the northern hemisphere begins to move to a position more directly overhead, bringing more light to the world. The extension of this idea was that every Christmas the cock crows all night to keep the holy time free of evil spirits. This is the background for the observation that Marcellus makes in *Hamlet:*

> Some say that ever 'gainst that season comes
> Wherein our Savior's birth is celebrated,
> This bird of dawning singeth all night long,
> And then, they say, no spirit dare stir abroad,
> The nights are wholesome, then no planets strike,
> No fairy takes, nor witch hath power to charm:
> So hallowed and so gracious is that time.
>
>   (1.1.157–64)

John Milton, in his ode "On the Morning of Christ's Nativity," uses the legend of Alcyon and Ceyx to make the same point, that a period of calm at the time of the winter solstice was granted by the gods to give kingfishers a chance to nest safely on the water.

> But peaceful was the night,
> Wherein the Prince of light
>   His reign of peace upon the earth began:
> The Winds, with wonder whist,
> Smoothly the waters kiss't,
>   Whispering new joys to the mild Ocean,
> Who now hath quite forgot to rave,
> While Birds of Calm sit brooding on the charmed wave.
>
>   (lines 61–68)

In *The Tempest* Ariel's song soothes Ferdinand's grief over the presumed loss of his father in a shipwreck:

> Hark, hark! I hear
> The strain of strutting chanticleer
>   Cry cock-a-diddle-dow.
>
>   . . . .
>
> This music crept by me upon the waters,
> Allaying both their fury and my passion.
>
>   (1.2.386–95)

In the well-known New Testament story told in Matthew, chapter 26, and Mark, chapter 14, a cock's crowing serves as the omniscient Christ's surrogate presence that rebukes Peter for the denial
of his Master on the occasion of his arrest at Gethsemane. As
Christ had predicted, Peter thrice denies his discipleship "before
the cock crow," but he repents and weeps bitterly before the cock
stops crowing—"washes his guilt in the last crow," as Ambrose has
it. The story has had immense circulation in literature as a symbol of betrayal or weak faith, though it is clear in Ambrose and
Prudentius, another fourth-century Christian writer, that Peter's
denial is an example of the power of evil night spirits to lead a good
man into sin, which he immediately forswears at dawn. Forgiveness is the emphasis in Elizabeth Bishop's "Roosters," a fine poem
touching many of the cock's traditional meanings. With "horrible
insistence" at four o'clock in the morning, the first cock wakes us
to grim realities, "unwanted love, conceit, and war." At that hour
of "gun-metal blue dark," the cock appears brutal:

> The crown of red
> set on your little head
> is charged with all your fighting-blood.
>
> Yes, that excrescence
> makes a most virile presence
> plus all that vulgar beauty of iridescence.

The poet here draws on the tradition of the fighting cock as a symbol of military might—it was once a favorite emblem in French
armed forces. She then sets this image of the cock over against
the Christian tradition as it is represented in "old holy sculpture"
depicting the Biblical scene in which Peter's tears "run down our
chanticleer's / sides and gem his spurs." Bishop sees in Peter's
weeping that the cock may "come to mean forgiveness." The
weather vane on the basilica of Saint John Lateran assures us that

> there would always be
> a bronze cock on a porphyry
> pillar so the people and the Pope might see

> that even the Prince
> of the Apostles long since
> had been forgiven, and to convince
>
> all the assembly
> that "Deny deny deny,"
> is not all the roosters cry.[8]

Even though the popular religious significance of the cock has diminished with the secularization of the Western world since the eighteenth century, some writers have continued to adapt the cock's light- and life-giving power. A well-versed but not particularly observant Christian, Herman Melville adheres to some of the traditional conceptions in his extended treatment of the bird in "Cock-A-Doodle-Doo!" This curious short story begins with the narrator in a state of depression over the terrible calamities that befall people in this "miserable world." He is "full of hypos" (hypochondria)—the same expression used by Ishmael at the beginning of *Moby-Dick* only two years before—but instead of going down to the sea for relief, this melancholy man goes for a walk in the countryside, where he hears a most wonderful cockcrow. "What a triumphant thanksgiving of a cockcrow! '*Glory be to God in the highest!*' It says those very words as plain as ever cock did in this world." His spirit is restored: "Shanghai sent up such a perfect paean and *laudamus*—such a trumpet blast of triumph that my soul fairly snorted in me" (39, 42). Melville aggrandizes the cock as he did the great white whale, calling it a "cock, more like a golden eagle than a cock. A cock, more like a Field-Marshal than a cock." After a long search, the narrator discovers that the cock belongs to a poor woodchopper, Merrymusk, who refuses to sell it to him because the bird means so much to his family, all of whom are bedridden with disease. It gives them "stuff against despair," he explains. The presence of the resplendent cock in the woodchopper's humble house is striking: "There was a strange supernatural look of contrast about him. He irradiated the shanty; he glorified its meanness" (53–54). Ironically, however, everyone in the family dies to the accompaniment of cockcrow: "He seemed bent upon crowing the souls of the children out of their wasted bodies. He seemed bent upon rejoining instanter this whole family in the upper air. The children seemed to second his endeavors. Far, deep, intense longings for release transfigured them into spirits before my eyes. I saw angels where they lay" (57). The narrator has a family gravestone made, "with a lusty cock in act of crowing, chiseled on it" and an inscription from Saint Paul:

> *O death, where is thy sting?*
> *O grave, where is thy victory?*

And never again does he feel "the doleful dumps."

"Cock-A-Doodle-Doo!" has a number of the traditional Christian beliefs about cockcrow—the glorification of God and his creation, the stirring of the listener's soul and revival of his spirit, the apotheosis of the woodchopper's family after death. But the reader can hardly avoid suspecting that the tale is quite ambiguous if not bitterly ironical.[9] The cock is overly aggrandized in the manner of the Western tall tale, the usual sign of a mock-heroic mood. It does seem strange that the cock, whom Melville knew to possess curative powers, should preside over the untimely demise of an entire family and that all should accept death so readily. Can Melville be implying that they are fools for rejoicing in the cock? Still, Socrates went to his death without complaint; his last words, "I owe a cock to Asclepius," presumably refer to a cock that is to be sacrificed in payment of a cure the god of medicine had effected for him in the past. But it could also be in payment of the cure of Socrates' present situation, in which he is being falsely accused by his enemies, the cure being the death he is about to receive on the order of the Athenian court. "Oh, brave cock!" exclaims Melville's narrator, "oh, bird rightly offered up by the invincible Socrates, in testimony of his final victory over life." The Socrates of the *Apology* is scorned by his countrymen, yet he is cheerful and dies "unappalled." In similar fashion perhaps death is the cure the cock brings to the woodchopper and his family. At least they die quietly in their beds, not violently like those unfortunates at the beginning of the story who have been "knocked on the head" or "sloped into eternity" in train and steamboat wrecks. Admiration for those who face hardship and death bravely is a common enough theme in Melville—Ahab and Bartleby immediately precede Merrymusk. But Ahab and Bartleby are psychopaths, one driven by a maniacal will to vanquish life and the other by a catatonic withdrawal from life. The narrator of "Cock-A-Doodle-Doo!" is fortunate to witness an ordinary man's reaction to the inevitable "knockings on the head" in this life. If there is a victory over death here, it is not the Christian victory of resurrection that the cock tradition-ally represents. Rather the cock in Melville's story inspires in both Merrymusk and the narrator a purely human stoicism in the face of the cruel circumstances of the human condition.

There is no question about the tone of two paragraphs on cock-crow in Thoreau's essay "Walking." Here the traditional Christian attributes of the cock are clearly adapted to suit Thoreau's tran-scendental philosophy of living in the present and living in nature.

> Unless our philosophy hears the cock crow in every barn-yard within our horizon, it is belated. That sound commonly reminds us that we are growing rusty and antique in our employments and habits of thought. His philosophy comes down to a more re-cent time than ours. There is something suggested by it that is a newer testament,—the gospel according to this moment. He has not fallen astern; he has got up early and kept up early, and to be where he is to be in season, in the foremost rank of time. It is an expression of the health and soundness of Nature, a brag for all the world,—healthiness as of a spring burst forth, a new fountain of the Muses, to celebrate this last instant of time. Where he lives no fugitive slave laws are passed. Who has not betrayed his master many times since last he heard that note?

The new day announced by the cock holds a good many of Tho-reau's ideals: the need for new ways of thought, a new literature, and a new spirit of individual freedom and self-determination. In-stead of Peter's repentance for denying his master, the cock calls for the slave to turn against his master. The second paragraph further underscores Thoreau's departure from the traditional in-terpretation of cockcrow as a call to worship:

> The merit of this bird's strain is in its freedom from all plain-tiveness. The singer can easily move us to tears or to laughter, but where is he who can excite in us a pure morning joy? When,

in doleful dumps, breaking the awful stillness of our wooden
sidewalk on a Sunday, or, perchance, a watcher in the house of
mourning, I hear a cockerel crow far or near, I think to myself,
"There is one of us well, at any rate,"—and with a sudden gush
return to my senses.[10]

The absence of "plaintiveness," the morning walk, the "watcher
in the house of mourning," and the recovery from the "doleful
dumps"—all these are elements in Melville's story. But there can
be no question of influence here, unless Melville heard Thoreau
deliver "Walking" as a lecture in 1851 or 1852, since the essay was
not published until 1862, nine years after Melville's story appeared
in *Harper's New Monthly Magazine.*

So well did Thoreau like what cockcrow represented for him
that he printed this statement on the title page of the first edition
of *Walden:* "I do not propose to write an ode to dejection, but to
brag as lustily as chanticleer in the morning, standing on his roost,
if only to wake my neighbors up." And we have this from his journal: "I would crow like Chanticleer in the morning, with all the
lustiness that the new day imparts, without thinking of the evening, when I and all of us shall go to roost—with all the humility
of the cock that takes his perch upon the highest rail and wakes the
country with his clarion" (June 2, 1853). Certainly, the long-term
impact of Thoreau's writings has been to arouse his countrymen
to the new possibilities of life that he had tested.

There is a hint of the anticlerical in Thoreau's cockerel that
breaks "the awful stillness" of a Sunday morning. In *Cock-a-
Doodle Dandy* (1949) Sean O'Casey also uses the figure of the cock
to mount an attack against the repressiveness of the Irish church
and propertied class. What the playwright calls "the joyful, active
spirit of life" is portrayed by a character dressed like a cock: "He
is of deep black plumage, fitted to his agile and slender body like
a glove on a lady's hand; yellow feet and ankles, bright green flaps
like wings, and a stiff cloak falling like a tail behind him. A big
crimson crest flowers over his head, and crimson flaps hang from
his jaws." Like one of Aristophanes' bird characters, O'Casey's
cock romps around the stage, flapping, dancing, and crowing. His

wild and sometimes supernatural antics inspire the women in the play to join him; the stodgy menfolk and the parish priest are put to rout. When Loreleen, the most outspoken of the women, appears as a cock, a frightened man exclaims, "Jasus, she's changin' into th' look of a fancy-bred fowl! It's turnin' to face us; it's openin' its bake as big as a bayonet!"[11]

In *The Man Who Died* D. H. Lawrence brings to the traditional association of Christ and the cock new materials from the classical anthropologists of his time who had called attention to the similarity of the Christian deity to pagan vegetation gods, particularly the Egyptian god Osiris. The fable demonstrates Lawrence's belief that a grave weakness of Christianity is its failure to do justice to the physical aspects of Christ's resurrection. Lawrence's unnamed hero is roused from a long sleep "inside a carved hole in the rock" by the "shrill wild crowing of a cock just near him, a sound which made him shiver as if electricity had touched him." Inspired by the cock's vitality, the twice-born man sets out to lead a life quite different from that of his first incarnation. The "health and soundness of Nature" that Thoreau saw in cockcrow is narrowed by Lawrence to the sexual experience that his hero had denied himself in his first incarnation and actively seeks in his second. But more of this in a later discussion.

Another unconventional treatment of Jesus that makes even more extensive use of birds is Yeats's *Calvary*. Looking back on his life on earth, Jesus comes to realize that some people do not regard him as a savior. Lazarus resents having been raised from the dead because he prefers death to facing Christ's love; Judas feels that his freedom to develop his own individuality was impaired by his being under the Master's control; Martha and the three Marys flee in terror on the way to the crucifixion; and the three dice-playing Roman soldiers have no use for a god that is not a god of chance. Three of these denials are accompanied by bird imagery that emphasizes the isolation of people who cannot surrender to something greater than themselves. Lazarus must search for death "among the desert places where there is nothing / But howling wind and solitary birds." When Judas planned his treachery, "there was no live thing near me but a heron / So full of itself that it seemed terrified" (292). The devotion of Martha and the three Marys cannot survive without the actual presence of Christ:

> Take but his Love away,
> Their love becomes a feather
> Of eagle, swan or gull,
> Or a drowned heron's feather
> Tossed hither and thither
> Upon the bitter spray
> And the moon at the full.

The effect of these denials is to isolate Jesus by showing him the failures of his mission, and this result is reinforced by the deployment of forlorn birds: a lone heron at the beginning of the drama—

> Motionless under the moon-beam,
> Up to his feathers in the stream;
> Although fish leap, the white heron
> Shivers in a dumbfounded dream;

and at the end a lonely seabird, a gull—

> Blown like a dawn-bleached parcel of spray
> Upon the wind, or follows her prey
> Under a great wave's hollowing crest—

a ger-eagle, or gyrfalcon, "content with his savage heart," and yearling cygnets that have not returned to their lake—"What can a swan need but a swan?" After each verse in this series there is the refrain "God has not appeared to the birds," presumably no more than Jesus has rescued people from their isolation. As in the Philomela legend birds serve as a means of approaching the human condition without wholly entering it. Yeats is aware of the difference in a comment he made on his play: "I have used my bird-symbolism in these songs to increase the objective loneliness of Christ, by contrasting it with a loneliness, opposite in kind, that unlike His can be, whether joyous or sorrowful, sufficient to itself." Some birds, he felt, "such lonely birds as the heron, the hawk, eagle, and swan, are the natural symbols of subjectivity, especially when floating upon the wind alone or alighting on some pool or river." [12]

Of all the animals used in Christian symbology, the dove has been the most popular. It could not fail to appeal to early Christians since it was honored in the Old Testament for having brought to Noah proof of the world's renewal after the Flood, and it was one of the few birds the Hebrews found to be ritually clean for sacrifices. Even more important than these considerations is the implication in the creation story that when "the spirit of God moved upon the face of the waters" it had the form of a bird (Genesis 1.2). The Hebrew word that is translated as "moving" in the King James Bible could mean hovering, as in Isaiah 31.5: "Thus the Lord of Hosts, like a bird hovering over its young, will be a shield over Jerusalem." In Psalms 91:4 the Almighty is even more explicitly compared to a brooding bird: "He shall cover thee with his feathers, and under his wings shalt thou trust." Moreover, the primitive association of wind and wing with life-giving power appears to be retained in Genesis with the use of the Hebrew word *ruach* or *ruh* (wind or breath) for the spirit of God.

This background prepared the way for Christian clerics, starting with Basil the Great in the fourth century, to accept pagan notions of the cosmogonic egg in their comments on the biblical story of creation.[13] Thus, it was not unusual for a learned poet like John Milton to open his *Paradise Lost* with the figure of the Holy Spirit taking the form of a dove for this singular act of creation:

> Thou from the first
> Wast present, and with mighty wings outspread
> Dove-like sat'st brooding on the vast abyss
> And mad'st it pregnant.
> (1.19–22)

Later in the poem Milton backs away a little:

> on the wat'ry calm
> His brooding wings the Spirit of God outspread,
> And vital virtue infus'd, and vital warmth.
> (7.234–36)

In a similar figure from "God's Grandeur," Gerard Manley Hopkins sees that despite humanity's abuse of the earth its grandeur is renewed each morning "because the Holy Ghost over the bent / World broods with warm breast and with ah! bright wings" (66).

There was strong pagan precedent for the deification of the dove in the widespread worship of two goddesses of reproduction, the Sumerian Ishtar (the Semitic Astarte or Esther) and the Greek Aphrodite, to whom the dove was sacred because of its prolificness. Early Christian sects transferred the reproductive powers of these goddesses to the Holy Spirit, along with the imagery of dove, wings, and wind. The identification of the dove with the Holy Spirit was firmly established in the New Testament with all four Gospels agreeing that at Christ's baptism "the heavens were opened unto him, and he saw the Spirit of God descending like a dove, and lighting upon him." [14] In like manner the Egyptian sun-god Ra sent a falcon to perch on a pharoah at his coronation. In "The Three Languages" the Grimm brothers preserve a legend in which the election of a pope is determined by the descent of doves on an unlikely candidate, a young man whose only merit is that he understands the languages of dogs, frogs, and birds. The frogs direct him to a church where the college of cardinals is meeting to elect a new pope, and just as they decide that a divine miracle should guide them, he enters the building:

> Suddenly two snow-white doves lighted on his shoulders and remained there. In this the clergy recognized a sign from God and at once asked him if he would become pope. He was undecided, for he didn't know whether he was worthy of this, but the doves persuaded him to accept. . . . Then he had to sing a mass and didn't know a word of it, but the two doves stayed right on his shoulders and whispered it in his ear.

In his *History of the World* Sir Walter Raleigh tells the story of Mahomet's dove to illustrate the "petty witchery, (if it be not altogeyther deceit), which they call charming of beasts and birds." The prophet, he writes, had a pet dove, "which he had used to feed with wheat out of his ear; which dove, when it was hungry, lighted on Mahomet's shoulder, and thrust his bill therein to find his breakfast; Mahomet persuading the rude and simple Arabians, that it was the Holy Ghost that gave him advice." [15]

The dove is to be found in innumerable Renaissance paintings of the feast of the Pentecost and the ascension of Christ as well as many saints. The dove's presence in paintings of the Annunciation is accounted for by the legend that the Holy Spirit in the form of a dove descended upon Mary to impregnate her through the ear. Although this bizarre notion derived from primitive beliefs that pregnancy is caused by spirits penetrating various body orifices and that birds deliver messages from the gods, it served to reinforce the important theological principle of the Word becoming flesh in the person of the infant Jesus.

The impregnation of Mary by a god in the form of a bird is of the same order of imagery as the story of Leda and the swan. Yeats treated both subjects, but the violent sexual assault described in "Leda and the Swan" is missing in "The Mother of God." The part played by the Holy Spirit is known only by the fluttering of wings, and light from a flare is the means of insemination. The account is from Mary's viewpoint and begins,

> The threefold terror of love; a fallen flare
> Through the hollow of an ear;
> Wings beating about the room;
> The terror of all terrors that I bore
> The Heavens in my womb.
>   (244)

The key elements in these few lines appear in W. S. Merwin's long and complex poem "The Annunciation." From the scene in Luke 1.35—"The Holy Ghost shall come upon thee, and the power of the Highest shall overshadow thee"—Merwin picks up two details that figure prominently in his own version: the word *come* and the darkness accompanying the descent of the dove. The double meaning of *come*, a word repeated at least a dozen times in Merwin's poem, serves to emphasize the sexual nature of the incident; sudden darkness and the sound of wings are used to suggest the presence of some mysterious force:

> . . . and the black coming down
> In its greatness, between my eyes and the light,
> Was like wings growing, and the blackness
> Of their shadow growing as they came down
> Whirring and beating.
> (lines 59–71)

To Mary the sound of the wings is

> Like a whisper in the feathers there, in the wings'
> Great wind, like a whirring of words, but I could not
> Say the shape of them, and it came to me
> They were like a man, but none has yet come to me,
> And I could not say how.
> (lines 84–88)

After the dove departs Mary becomes aware of the change within her even though nothing has changed around her:

> But I did not doubt
> For the wonder that was in me, quickening,
> Like in your ear the shape of a sound
> When the sound is gone.
> (lines 150–53)

These few lines can only suggest the skill with which Merwin succeeds in adapting ancient images to modern sensibilities in describing the process whereby the Word is made flesh.

A recent interesting attempt to treat the participation of a dove in the virgin birth is John Pielmeier's play *Agnes of God*, produced on the stage in 1980 and on film in 1985. The impetus for this work was a series of questions the author had been asking himself: "Are there saints today? miracles? Did these phenomena ever exist and, if so, have they or our perception of them changed?" Perhaps "the asking of the questions was answer enough: that our determined search for *any* solution today has eliminated from our lives the mystery and wonder of the universe around us."[16] Neither work makes a firm commitment to either a miraculous or natural explanation of the fact that Agnes, a novice at a convent, has borne

a child without an ostensible father. Agnes is too modest to consider herself a saint, yet her vivid imagination and strong, simple
faith lead her to believe that she has been visited by the winged
spirit of God. "I stood in the window of my room every night for
a week. And one night I heard the most beautiful voice imaginable. It came from the middle of the wheat field beyond my room,
and when I looked I saw the moon shining down on Him. For six
nights He sang to me. Songs I'd never heard. And on the seventh
night He came to my room and opened His wings and lay on top
of me. And all the while He sang" (109). The film has some elements of mystery—religious mystery—that the play lacks, because
the camera is able to display flying doves at strategic moments. In
order to lend a medieval "feeling of stopped time," as the author
puts it, the scene is now a convent in Quebec, and we are given a
strong clue supporting a natural explanation. We learn that Agnes
has been stealing out of the convent by way of a secret passage-
way that an aged nun has shown her. It comes out in a barn used
by the men who work the convent farm, a barn, too, where doves
roost. Though it is never stated, there is a possibility that she may
have met one of the laborers there—perhaps a man with "the voice
from the middle of the wheat field." Or the aged nun may have
led a man from the barn to Agnes's room, like the procuress of
medieval tradition or the "old beldame" in Keats's "The Eve of St.
Agnes" who leads a young man to the chamber of Madeline on the
night of January 21 when, according to folk belief, maidens hope
to discover who will be their husbands. In the last scene Agnes lies
prone on the floor of the barn and gazes on a glorious display of
doves fluttering in bright light. The scene is reminiscent of Saint
Teresa's vision of a dove flying over her head with wings "made
of little shells which emitted a great brilliance." [17]

The famous line from Gertrude Stein's *Four Saints in Three Acts*
("Pigeons on the grass alas") is a reference to the doves seen by the
saint as she is seated in a garden. Saint Ignatius questions whether
they are pigeons: "If they were not pigeons on the grass alas what
were they. He had heard of a third and he asked about it it was
a magpie in the sky. . . . He asked for a distant magpie." Commenting on her play in *Lectures in America*, Stein observes that the
magpies at Avila, the birthplace of Saint Teresa, are "exactly like

the birds in the Annunciation pictures the bird which is the Holy Ghost and rests flat against the wide sky very high." [18]

Long after the peaking of Christian iconography in medieval and Renaissance times, the Christian dove continues to attract even writers who work in the realistic mode of prose fiction. In Flaubert's "A Simple Heart," Félicité, an old woman who has been a servant all her life and is now without anyone to serve, finds companionship and beauty in her pet parrot Loulou. "His body was green and the tips of his wings rose-pink; his forehead was blue and his throat golden." Though deaf she can hear the few phrases the bird speaks. "Loulou was almost a son and a lover to her in her isolated state." A devout Catholic but unable to understand Christian doctrine, she is bound to her faith largely by visual images, in particular the likeness she sees between her parrot and the symbolical figure of the Holy Ghost pictured on the stained glass of the church she attends. "They were linked in her thoughts, and the parrot was consecrated by his association with the Holy Ghost." After its death she has the bird stuffed and places it in her room beside "a crude colour-print representing the baptism of Our Lord" in which the Holy Ghost is pictured as a dove with "purple wings and emerald body." There she kneels to say her prayers. On her deathbed, while a religious procession passes in the street below her window, "she thought she saw an opening in the heavens, and a gigantic parrot hovering over her head." Félicité experiences the miracle of the dove as it appears in the Ascension of Christ and the saints.[19]

Taking Félicité's parrot as his starting point, Julian Barnes has written a fascinating book on Flaubert. Called by some readers a novel because we get a good deal of narrative concerning the author's research of his subject, *Flaubert's Parrot* is actually a brilliant and discerning piece of literary criticism that attempts to discover the truth about Flaubert the man and the writer. Barnes's quest began when he was shown what was reputed to be the stuffed parrot that Flaubert borrowed from the Museum of Rouen and kept before him on his desk while he was writing "A Simple Heart." When another museum claimed to have the authentic stuffed parrot that Flaubert had on his desk, Barnes had the problem of determining which was the legitimate bird and who was the real Flaubert. The parrot had come to symbolize the author: "to Félicité, it was a grotesque but logical version of the Holy Ghost; to me, a fluttering, elusive emblem of the writer's voice."[20]

It is in keeping with the unrelenting realism of Flaubert that the glowing idealisms of the past are sympathetically reduced to childlike fancies. A great admirer of Flaubert, whose story he had read, Henry James uses the religious symbolism of the dove, but without ironical undertones, in *The Wings of the Dove*. Because of his psychological realism and avoidance of ideologies, James does not often strike a religious note in his fiction. The exception is his characterization of Milly Theale, an American heiress who is the target of a conspiracy conceived by Kate Croy and Merton Densher, a betrothed couple whose marriage has been put off for lack of sufficient funds to support a genteel life-style. The plot is for Densher to engage the affection of Milly, get her to marry him, and inherit her immense fortune upon her death, which they know is imminent because she is suffering from a fatal disease. Then Kate and Densher would have the means to make a marriage that meets the materialistic standards of Mrs. Lowder, Kate's wealthy and domineering aunt. The plot backfires when Densher's feeling for Milly develops into something far beyond mere pose and when Milly, even when she learns of the conspiracy, bears no grudge against the scheming couple but returns duplicity with love and forgiveness, leaving Densher a handsome bequest in her will. Her saintly act has such a powerful effect on Densher that he finds it impossible to accept the money. James leaves us to surmise what the effect is on Kate, who is left with the choice of taking Densher without riches or riches without Densher.

In the characterization of Milly, James uses no more than a half dozen references comparing her to a dove, and these are of the order of brief suggestions to be savored by readers familiar with the two aspects of the dove as it is treated in the Bible. First, there is the gentle dove of Psalm 124, fearful of "the snare of the fowlers" from whom it would fly; second, there is the dove as symbol of the protective power of the Almighty under whose wings the faithful find comfort, as in Psalm 91. The two doves correspond to the two sides of James's character, the heroine as victim and the heroine as savior. On the one hand, Milly is so shy and gentle that she is afraid to venture outside her Venetian palace, "the ark of her deluge," and she asks "nothing more than to sit tight in it and float on and on." [21] Unlike Noah's dove, Milly at this time does not seek out news of the outside world but has it brought in to her by others. Her passive attitude toward her fatal disease is reflected in the title of the novel, an echo from a line in Psalm 55: "O that I had wings like a dove! for then would I flee away, and be at rest."

Yet Milly, like all of James's young heroines, does venture out into the world to experience one passionate moment—what James calls "life"—when she responds to the attentions of Densher. Seeing her dressed in resplendent garments and pearls, Kate comments, "She's a dove, and one somehow doesn't think of doves as bejewelled. Yet they suit her down to the ground" (2:218). At this time Kate is so intent upon her mercenary aims that she fails to see in Milly the sign of the savior dove, which in Christian iconography is always richly ornamented, like the dove with "purple wings and emerald body" in Flaubert's story and the dove in Psalm 68, the prototype of the Holy Spirit in Christian symbolism: "Though ye have lain among the sheepfolds, yet shall ye be as the wings of a dove covered with silver, and her feathers with yellow gold." Later, however, when Milly's act of forgiveness and generosity is known, both Kate and Densher are struck with a sense of awe. "Something incalculable wrought for them—for him and for Kate—something outside, beyond, above themselves" (2:239). It turns out that the woman who wanted wings to carry her away from her enemies also has wings that "spread themselves for protection" over the erring couple in both the spiritual and material sense. They "cover us," Kate says, and at the very end of the book she comes to a realization of the effect Milly has had: "We shall never be again as we were." This is as far as James dares to go toward the redemption of sinners. The imagery of the savior dove enables him to avoid making a too explicit statement that Milly is a divine presence exerting an appreciable influence on people. In this manner James manages to devise what is for his writing a rare "irruption of the divine order into the natural," as one reader puts it; another finds evidence that Milly herself is aware of the special role she is playing: when she receives Kate's denomination of her as a dove, "she met it on the instant," in James's words, "as she would have met the revealed truth. . . . She should have to be clear as to how a dove *would* act" (1:283–84).[22]

Milly Theale was modeled after Mary (Minny) Temple, James's cousin, who died of tuberculosis at age twenty-four. Another saintly figure James must have had in mind was a heroine from Hawthorne's *The Marble Faun,* Hilda, a New England girl "unacquainted with evil and untouched by impurity," as James himself observes in his book on Hawthorne. An art student in Rome, Hilda lives in an old tower that is a shrine of the Virgin, where Hilda always keeps a lamp burning. (The tower sheltering doves was often used, as in Hieronymous Bosch's fifteenth-century *Madonna and Child,* to call attention to Mary's being the benefactress of church buildings.) Hilda shares her tower with a flock of white doves, "high above the evil scents of Rome." Her worldly friend Miriam notes "how like a dove" Hilda is herself, "the fair, pure creature!" (chap. 6). Like Milly Theale, Hilda encounters evil in the behavior of Miriam and her Italian friend Donatello, but, unlike Milly, she does not have the power of divine mediation. Distraught with having witnessed a crime committed by her friends, she leaves her tower, and the birds abandon their roost, returning only when she does. Hawthorne probably got his cue for Hilda from Sir Walter Scott's *Marmion,* in which Saint Hilda, abbess of Whitby in the seventh century, is described as a "feeble girl" who yet has a "constant mind and hate of wrong" (6.4); snakes turn to stone under her spell and

> sea-fowls' pinions fail,
> As over Whitby's towers they sail,
> And, sinking down, with flutterings faint,
> They do their homage to the saint.
> (2.13)

Scott repeats the tradition, recorded in Bede, that the ghost of Saint Hilda still appears in the highest church window at Whitby. In Hawthorne's novel Miriam speculates that Catholics will make a saint of her friend just as of her "namesake of old."

Both James and Hawthorne make use of the familiar opposition of the white dove and the evil black bird. The innocent Milly must contend with those who are counting on her demise for their benefit: the worldly Mrs. Lowder, who is compared to a vulture and an eagle "with a gilded beak," and Kate Croy, whose name may well be a play on *crow*—a device not beneath James, who had a weakness for allegorical naming. The name of Madame Merle, who plots against the virginal Isabel Archer in *The Portrait of a Lady*, is derived from the French word for blackbird; Theale, a thin disguise for teal, a small elegant duck, is an appropriate surname for Milly. Hawthorne, in his even more elaborate allegorical manner, sets up a labored contrast between Hilda's tower frequented by doves and the tower occupied by Donatello after he flees Rome following his crime. It is called the Owl Tower after the two birds that share it with him, birds of ill omen that tolerate his presence now that he is a murderer. "They do not desert me, like my other feathered acquaintances," he observes. "When I was a wild, playful boy, the owls did not love me half so well." Instead of keeping vigil at the Virgin's shrine as Hilda does, Donatello broods over his sin in a room decorated with "ugly little prints, representing the sufferings of the Saviour, and the martyrdom of saints." In Hawthorne's *House of the Seven Gables*, Phoebe is another bird-like girl who, like the bird for which she is named, makes the best of a forbidding human dwelling and brings some joy into the lives of Hepzibah and Clifford, "two owls" living under the shadow of a crime.

Like other traditional symbols the dove has been impaired a little in the twentieth century because of the familiar association of the airplane with the bird and the wide use of the airplane as an indiscriminate war weapon. World War I produced many reactions such as Isaac Rosenberg's: "Death could drop from the dark / As easily as song." The tremendous increase in the use of bombers in World War II led to further disillusionment, which was often expressed in a bitterly ironical inversion of the traditional reverence for the dove as Holy Spirit and symbol of peace. Postwar poetry abounds with references to "the duraluminium dove . . . bringing peace to many," "dove of death," "charnel birds / That drop their excrement of death," "lumbering death-laden birds."[23] Best known are Picasso's dove in *Guernica*, standing among ruins and pointing its beak heavenward, and Eliot's dove in the description of the bombing of London in "Little Gidding":

> The dove descending breaks the air
> With flame of incandescent terror
> Of which the tongues declare
> The one discharge from sin and error.
> The only hope, or else despair
>   Lies in the choice of pyre or pyre—
>   To be redeemed from fire by fire.
>
>   (143)

The irony of Eliot's wartime "dark dove with the flickering tongue" is all the more effective when we recall how the Holy Spirit descended upon the assembled apostles in the form of a dove at the Feast of the Pentecost: "And suddenly there came a sound from heaven as of a rushing mighty wind, and it filled all the house where they were sitting. And there appeared unto them cloven tongues like as of fire. And they were all filled with the Holy Ghost" (Acts 2.2–3).

"Who will not change a raven for a dove?" asks Lysander in *A Midsummer's Night Dream* (2.2.114). While the dove enjoys a good reputation despite its often quarrelsome behavior, the raven and other large birds with which it was often confused, such as the crow and the vulture, have been considered evil, undoubtedly because of their jet-black plumage and carrion-eating proclivities. From paleolithic times there was a belief in twin goddesses who opposed each other, one a life-giving water bird and the other a death-dealing vulture or owl. This kind of pairing gets into the Judeo-Christian tradition by way of the Bible story of the Flood: the raven's failure to return to the ark signifies the continued reign of death on the earth; the dove's return with an olive leaf in its beak announces the revival of life on earth. In an earlier Flood story from the Babylonian *Gilgamesh* a dove and a swallow return to the boat and a raven does not. At the beginning of *Paradise Lost* the Holy Spirit is portrayed as a dove creating the world; in contrast, Satan in book 9 is seen perched like a cormorant on the Tree of Life, "devising death" to those who live, or, in effect, plotting the destruction of God's creation, and in book 3 he is compared to a vulture gorging the "flesh of Lambs or yeanling [new-born]

Kids." To Christians the affiliation of ravens with pagan deities of northern Europe made them particularly abhorred as the messengers of death and evil, creatures employed by the devil to bear bad tidings and carry off the souls of the dead.

Many folktales have explained how the raven got its disagreeable traits. In some elaborations of the Bible story, the raven becomes so engrossed with feeding on flood victims that it forgets the important mission Noah had given it and consequently is doomed to feed thereafter on carrion exclusively. So it is in the Old English poem "Noah's Flood": "The foul one perched on the floating corpses; / The dusky-feathered would not return." Ovid, in book 2 of *Metamorphoses*, tells the story of Apollo's crow, a white bird that was turned black by the angry god because it informed him of his mistress's infidelity. Retelling the story in the Manciple's Tale, Chaucer reduces the characters to an ordinary married couple and a caged crow that sings "Cokkow! Cokkow!" to warn the husband "how that his wyf had doon hire lecherye." The husband kills the wife, immediately regrets the rash deed, then turns on the bearer of bad news, pulling out all of the crow's white feathers and depriving him of song and speech. There is a similar French version, contemporary with Chaucer, in which a pet magpie reports that the wife has eaten an eel that the husband was saving for his friends. After being scolded by her husband, she plucks all the feathers on the bird's head, and "ever after, whanne the pie sawe a balled or a pilled man, or a woman with an high forhede, the pie saide to hem: 'Ye spake of the ele.'" A modern version of the story, written by John Collier, involves an American couple and their pet parrot, which is mysteriously bred by a giant night bird, resulting in an all-black offspring. This bird informs the husband of the wife's infidelity by repeating the intimate conversation of the lovers. After killing his wife, Jack turns the gun on himself: "The parrot, or whatever it was, sailing down, seized what came out of his ruined mouth, and wheeled back through the window, and was soon far away, visible for a moment only as it swept on broader wings past the new-risen moon." Collier's "Bird of Prey" manages to combine the motif of the erring woman and the tell-tale bird with association of the black bird and the devil.[24]

The idea of ravens feeding on carrion was made more horrible by the popular belief, supported by Aristotle (9.609b5), that the raven pecks out the eyes of corpses, a practice actually employed by scavengers to get at the choice contents of the brain cavity. In Proverbs 30.17 the eagle, also a carrion feeder, joins the raven: "The eye that mocketh at his father, and despiseth to obey his mother, the ravens of the valley shall pick it out, and the young eagles shall eat it." One medieval English ballad, "The Twa Corbies," is particularly graphic in its description of the work of ravens on a "new slain knight" whose body has been abandoned by his hounds, his hawk, and his lady. One crow says to the other,

> Ye'll sit on his white hause-bone [neck-bone]
> And I'll pike out his bonny blue een;
> Wi ae lock of his gowden hair
> We'll theek our nest when it grows bare.

The honor of birds and ladies is redeemed, however, in a related ballad, "The Three Ravens," in which the knight's body is protected from scavengers:

> His hounds they lie downe at his feete,
> So well they can their master keepe.
> His haukes they flie so eagerly,
> There's no fowle dare him come nie.

The lady carries him off the field and gives him proper burial.

> God send every gentleman,
> Such haukes, such hounds, and such a leman.

Alexander Pushkin favors the first version of the tale in his "Raven Doth to Raven Fly," in which the hawk flies off and the bride takes "a new love, warm and breathing." Two crows are the subject of a lugubrious image in a song from Thomas Lovell Beddoes's *Death's Jest-Book;* a carrion crow whose beak is "heavy with marrow" addresses his mate:

> Our nest it is queen Cleopatra's skull,
>   'Tis cloven and cracked,
>   And battered and hacked,

But with tears of blue eyes it is full.
Let us drink then, my raven of Cairo.

In "Birdwatchers of America" Anthony Hecht brings the eye-gouging image home to "our part of the country" where the corpse of a man is found:

> He seemed in ultimate peace
> Except that he had no eyes. Rigid and bright
>   Upon the forehead, furred
> With a light frost, crouched an outrageous bird.[25]

Another mark against large black scavengers was their congregating at battlefields to feast on the corpses of fallen soldiers, the worst imaginable desecration of the dead. "Where the slain are, there the vulture is," declares the writer of Job 39.30, this being the translation from the New English Bible, whereas the bird is called an eagle in the King James Version. An Egyptian battle palette dating from 4000 B.C. pictures vultures and crows pecking at fallen men.[26] The scene of feasting ravens was a common one in Old English battle epics. The herald announcing the hero's death in *Beowulf* has this report of the battle in which he died:

> No harp shall sound
> The warriors to wake, but the wan-hued raven
> Shall croak o'er the carcass and call to the eagle,
> To tell how he fare'd at the feast after battle
> When he and the gray wolf gorged on the slain.[27]

A similar fate awaited the fallen at the Battle of Brunanburh, in Tennyson's translation of the Old English poem dating from the tenth century:

> Many a carcase they left to be carrion,
> Many a livid one, many a sallow-skin—
> Left for the white-tailed eagle to tear it, and
> Left for the horny-ribbed raven to rend it, and
> Gave to the garbaging war-hawk to gorge it, and
> That gray beast, the wolf of the weald.
>   ("Battle of Brunanburh," st. 14)

In *Paradise Lost* Milton compares the allegorical figure of Death to the "ravenous Fowl" that come from

> many a League remote,
> Against the day of Battle, to a Field,
> Where Armies lie encampt, come flying, lur'd
> With scent of living Carcasses design'd
> For death, the following day, in bloody fight.
> (10.274–78)

Having once fed well on the battlefield, the birds anticipate opportunities wherever they spy marching armies. In "Advice to a Raven in Russia" Joel Barlow tells of the "feather'd cannibals" who follow their good friend the Emperor Napoleon "to the world's bleak end," devouring the dead on battlefields from the deserts of Egypt to Moscow. Shelley adapts the image of battlefield ravens in "Adonais" to express his horror at what he considered to be the mistreatment of Keats by literary critics:

> The obscene ravens, clamorous o'er the dead;
> The vultures to the conqueror's banner true
> Who feed where Desolation first has fed,
> And whose wings rain contagion.
> (st. 28)

The raven is not always a villain. In folklore from all over the world one finds many helpful ravens, among them the god Odin's two ravens named Hugin and Munin, who, according to *The Prose Edda of Snorri Sturluson*, were sent out each morning to spy on the world and faithfully returned each night with a report for their master, unlike Noah's derelict bird. Pliny devotes an entire section of his *Natural History* to "repay due gratitude to the ravens" for their usefulness and accomplishments, particularly the talking raven who was given an elaborate public funeral in the reign of Tiberius, "the draped bier being carried on the shoulders of two Ethiopians and in front of it going in procession a flute-player and all kinds of wreaths right to the pyre" (10.60). There are at least two complimentary references to the raven in the Bible: in Psalms 147.9 the Lord provides food for "the young ravens which cry," and in turn ravens obey the Lord's command to bring "bread and flesh" to Elijah in 1 Kings 17. A recent descendant of Elijah's raven appears in Peter S. Beagle's novel *A Fine and Private Place.* His mission is to bring food to a certain Mr. Rebeck, who lives in a cemetery and has the ability to converse with the dead. At great risk he steals food in the city, a baloney from a delicatessen on one occasion, but he affects to be indifferent: "Ravens bring things to people. We're like that. It's our nature. We don't like it. . . . You think we brought Elijah food because we liked him? He was an old man with a dirty beard." The gentle Mr. Rebeck has a more charitable explanation: "We both had delusions of kindness."[28]

Even the vulture has its champions, principally for the beauty of its flight, remarked by Robinson Jeffers—

> But how beautiful he looked, gliding down
> On those great sails; how beautiful he looked,
>   veering away in the sea-light over the precipice—[29]

as well as for the valuable function it performs in nature, noted by Richard Wilbur in "Still, Citizen Sparrow":

> Then you'll see
> That no more beautiful bird is in heaven's height,
> No wider more placid wings, no watchfuller flight;
> He shoulders nature there, the frightfully free,
>
> The naked-headed one. Pardon him, you
> Who dart in the orchard aisles, for it is he
> Devours death, mocks mutability,
> Has heart to make an end, keeps nature new.
>   (318)

For the same reason William Everson's "What Birds There Were" includes the vulture among the birds at Christ's crucifixion:

> That grim gliding keeper of appointments, that dark
> Ceremonial purist the vulture, a frown on the sky,
> Methodical as an undertaker, adaptive
> And deferential as the old woman of griefs
> Who wraps up the dead.
>   (170–71)

The large black bird is not the only supernatural agent of evil. Something in the modern imagination is still attracted to the idea that even seemingly innocent small birds may have demonic power to bring evil upon people. In James Thurber's "Whip-Poor-Will" a bird's annoying early-morning singing drives a man insane. What appears to be a comic irritation is described in garbled echoes from classic sources. We have the distraught Mr. Kinstrey recalling the "brazen-breasted bird murdering sleep" and "the fatal bellman cried the livelong night," a line conflating two figures of speech from *Macbeth;* from the myth of Prometheus and from Edgar Allan Poe we have this:

> Its dawn call pecked away at his dreams like a vulture at a heart.
> It slowly carved out a recurring nightmare in which Kinstrey was
> attacked by an umbrella whose handle, when you clutched it,
> clutched right back, for the umbrella was not an umbrella at all
> but a raven. Through the gloomy hallways of his mind ran the
> thing's dolorous cry: nevermore, nevermore, nevermore, whip-
> poor-will, whip-poor-will.

Driven mad by their failure to credit his complaints, Kinstrey kills his wife and butler. The story ends with an exchange between the policemen assigned to the case. "You ever hear the old people say a whip-poor-will singing near the house means death?" asks one. "Take more'n a whip-poor-will to cause a mess like that." There is nothing humorously mock-heroic in the case of the hero in Patrick Süskind's *Pigeon.* Jonathan Noel lives a reclusive, well-organized life until one morning upon opening his apartment hall door he finds a pigeon sitting

> not eight inches from the threshold, in the pale reflection of dawn
> that came through the window. It was crouched there, with red,
> taloned feet on the oxblood tiles of the hall and in sleek, gray-blue
> plumage: the pigeon.
>   It had laid its head to one side and was glaring at Jonathan with
> its left eye. This eye, a small, circular disc, brown with a black
> center, was dreadful to behold. It was like a button sewn onto the
> feathers of the head, lashless, browless, quite naked, turned quite
> shamelessly to the world and monstrously open; at the same time,

however, there was something guarded and devious in that eye; and yet likewise it seemed to be neither open nor guarded, but rather quite simply lifeless, like the lens of a camera that swallows all external light and allows nothing to shine back out of its interior. No luster, no shimmer lay in that eye, not a spark of anything alive. It was an eye without sight. And it glared at Jonathan.

Only one other detail is reported of the pigeon: "On the tile where it had sat there was now an emerald green splotch about the size of a five-franc piece and a tiny white downy feather that trembled softly in the draft from the door crack." The encounter with the pigeon causes a radical disorientation in Jonathan's life, a breakdown of all the rigid arrangements of his daily existence. Unable to bring himself to return to his apartment, he takes a room in a cheap hotel, eats his lunch among derelicts in a park, and begins to falter in the performance of his duties as a bank guard. Finally he succeeds in getting the concierge to close the hall window outside his apartment and clean up the green splotches on the floor. He is reprieved, but not until he has looked with horror at the suspension of the regimen supporting his life.[30]

In both of these stories the ordinary routines of civilized existence are threatened by the irruption of nature in the form of a bird that somehow gets a demonic hold on a person. The result for Thurber's character is tragicomic; Süskind's bank guard narrowly avoids disaster. The result is tragic for Clyde Griffiths in Theodore Dreiser's *American Tragedy*. While the great bulk of the novel is devoted to the accumulation of the social forces acting upon Clyde, particularly the materialistic standards of success in America, there is another force that comes into play when Clyde decides to remove the one obstacle in his way, his involvement with Roberta. That force is what Clyde perceives, given his childhood background in Christian fundamentalism, as the demonism in nature in the form of a wilderness setting and a bird dominating that setting. Nothing in his rather ordinary existence ever moves Clyde as deeply as Big Bittern Lake and the strange bird; they seem to offer him the place and occasion for a plan to do away with Roberta. The bird is never precisely identified, though it appears to be a bittern. Dreiser calls it a "weir-weir," perhaps to imitate the sound it makes—"the weird, haunting cry of that unearthly bird"—or more likely to suggest the fate or *wyrd* toward which the bird is leading the hapless youth. It is "one of the solitary water-birds of this region . . . flying from somewhere near into some darker recess within the woods." It is present at the time when Clyde conceives of his "miserable plan" to drown Roberta in the lake, again when they set out in the boat, and finally after she sinks for the last time when he hears "once more the voice of that weird, contemptuous, mocking, lonely bird."[31]

two. Bird Signs and Bird Souls

> *Comme si je planais dans l'air qui me réclame,*
> *Et comme si j'avais une âme*
> *Faite avec des plumes d'oiseau.*
>
> Victor Hugo, "Le Cantique de Bathphagé"

It seemed plausible to early man that the close association of birds with deities gave them privileged knowledge of what actions would be pleasing to the gods. If only a way could be found to tap that knowledge, birds would be of immense benefit to man. In Chaldea and Greece there developed elaborate systems of observing the behavior of birds—especially the details of their flight, feeding, and song—and determining not precisely what the gods had willed for man, but what courses of action the gods might have a disposition to approve. As early as the eighth century B.C., Hesiod had written a treatise called *Divination by Birds*, no longer extant, which probably explained how bird signs could be used by farmers, sailors, and rulers to avoid disasters in the conduct of their affairs. A pair of eagles rending a pregnant hare is interpreted by the seer Calchas, in Aeschylus's *Agamemnon*, to mean that the sons of Atreus would be successful in their war against Troy (lines 113–27). Reading bird signs grew to be so important in ancient Rome that the official College of Augurs for many years practically ran the affairs of state. A course of action could not be undertaken until it was declared that "the birds allow it" (*aves admittant*). Obviously the whole process was open to corruption, since the augurs could shape their interpretations for personal gain and political influence. But even before the flagrant abuses of the practice were widely known, there was a good deal of skepticism about augury as early as Homer, who reports Hector's scorn of the practice:

> you tell me to put my trust in birds, who spread
> wide their wings. I care nothing for these, I think nothing of them,
> nor whether they go by on our right against dawn and sunrise
> or go by to the left against the glooming mist and the darkness.

The historian Eusebius tells the story of another great warrior, Alexander, shooting a bird whose signs were to be used for determining military strategy and saying to his horrified seers, "What folly is this? In what way could this bird, which could not foresee its death by this arrow, predict the fortunes of our journey?" In Euripides' *Bacchae* the King of Thebes accuses the respected seer Tiresias of practicing augury as "another trick of yours to squeeze some profit out of bird-watching and burnt offerings." [32]

Some of the details of augury have been preserved in folklore and by that route have found their way into recent literature. For example, the children's rhyme that tells what the future holds in store for a maiden according to the number of perching birds one may see—

> One for sorrow,
> Two for mirth,
> Three for a wedding,
> Four for a birth—

appears in D. H. Lawrence's *The White Peacock* in this form:

> One for sorrow, two for joy,
> Three for a letter, four for a boy,
> Five for silver, six for gold,
> And seven for a secret never told. [33]

A scene near the end of James Joyce's *Portrait of the Artist as a Young Man* dramatizes for the modern reader some of the obscure details of Roman augury. Stephen Dedalus stands on the porch of his school library and studies a flight of swallows to determine whether it is an "augury of good or evil" for the choice he has just made to leave Ireland and become a writer instead of a priest. He is careful to count the number of birds in the flight, whether odd or even, the cries they utter, and the direction of their flight. The results are not auspicious: there are thirteen swallows, "ever flying from left to right, circling about a temple of air." The learned Stephen knows that the Roman *auspex* (observer of birds), in order to facilitate his observations, made a pattern on the ground to correspond with the four sections of sky within which the flight of birds was to be watched and used a stick (*lituus*) to scratch the pattern (*templum*) on the ground. Stephen is well aware that "for ages men had gazed upward as he was gazing at birds in flight. The colonnade above him made him think of an ancient temple and the ashplant on which he leaned wearily of the curved stick of an augur" (224–25).

In addition to their use in the formal practice of augury, birds were assumed to utter warnings and prophecies, a power derived not only from their access to omniscient gods but from their association with the dead, who were supposed to have the privilege of foreseeing the future. Night birds and large, black-plumaged birds were the favorite prophets of doom. In *Macbeth* the murder of Duncan is foretold in act 2.2 by a shrieking owl, "the fatal bellman, / Which gives the stern'st good-night" (2.2.3–4)—the line Thurber had fun with—and it is an owl that "rehearses the hollow note of death" before the murder of Becket in Eliot's *Murder in the Cathedral*. In *The Jew of Malta* Christopher Marlowe rolls out some of his darkest lines to describe the prophetic powers of the

> sad presaging raven that tolls
> The sick man's passport in her hollow beak,
> And, in the shadow of the silent night,
> Does shake contagion from her sable wing.
> (2.1.1–4)

It could be either a raven or an owl that Shakespeare describes in the opening of "The Phoenix and the Turtle" as the

> shrieking harbinger,
> Foul precurrer [precursor] of the fiend,
> Augur of the fever's end.

It is a seemingly harmless robin that carries a grim prophecy in

Sir Walter Scott's song "Proud Maisie," used in *The Heart of Mid-lothian:*

> "Tell me, thou bonny bird,
> When shall I marry me?"
> "When six braw gentlemen
> Kirkward shall carry ye."
> (chap. 40)

The most common visualization of the soul is a winged creature. To the primitive mind human and animal were not so far apart that they could not easily trade places, and the aerial agility and lightsomeness of a bird must have prompted the belief that upon death the incorporeal and therefore immortal part of us could pass from an earthbound creature to a flying bird. This idea explains in part the frequency of metamorphosis in Greek myth, including the change of Philomela from maiden to nightingale. Some degree of philosophical respectability was given to the primitive notion by the Pythagoreans, who believed in the transmigration of souls, but it has always been the target of ridicule, as in this amusing exchange from Shakespeare's *Twelfth Night* when the Clown "makes a trial" of Malvolio's sanity:

> *Clown.* What is the opinion of Pythagoras concerning wild fowl?
> *Malvolio.* That the soul of our grandam might happily inhabit
>   a bird.
> *Clown.* What think'st thou of his opinion?
> *Malvolio.* I think nobly of the soul and no way approve his opinion.
> *Clown.* Fare thee well. Remain thou still in darkness. Thou shalt
>   hold th' opinion of Pythagoras ere I will allow of thy wits, and
>   fear to kill a woodcock, lest thou dispossess the soul of thy gran-
>   dam. Fare thee well.
>
> (4.2.50–61)

Poised at the point of contact between man and immortal gods, birds were thought to have access to the underworld or upperworld places where the dead dwelt for all eternity. Upon death the soul either became a bird or was carried by a bird to the realm of the afterlife. The earliest record of the soul's bird flight is to be found

in one of the Lascaux Cave paintings, dating from the end of the
Ice Age, about 18,000 years ago. Beside a man who has been killed
by a bison a bird is pictured standing on a pole and ready to take
flight. Ancient Egyptian burial pictures often show a bird flying
up from the body of the deceased, and in the Book of the Dead
the phoenix represents the soul. The phoenix was adopted for this
purpose by Lactantius, a Christian author of the fourth century,
whose Latin poem inspired a much superior ninth-century Old
English work, "The Phoenix." In this manner the miraculous rebirth of a mythical Egyptian bird from the ashes of its previous
existence became a symbol of the shriven soul's assurance of a
place in the Christian heaven:

> So each blessed soul through somber death
> After his life-days of sore distress
> Gains life everlasting, knowing God's grace
> In bliss never-ending; and ever thereafter
> Resides in glory as reward for his works.[34]

The flight of the bird-soul to an upper world has always been
an attractive image. A common motif in early Christian paintings
was a bird flying out of the mouth of dying saints, and even to this
day the dove carved on gravestones signifies hope in the escape of
the soul to an existence in heaven. Saint John's ascent to heaven,
according to legend, was made on the back of an eagle, an image
that Christians borrowed from the Roman practice of releasing
an eagle at the funeral of a Caesar to carry his soul to Olympus.
On the other side of the world and at a much later date, it was
the custom of the Iroquois to set a bird free on the death of a
chief. The sonnet John Keats wrote upon the death of his grandmother combines the ascent of the soul with the role of birds as
the messengers of the gods:

> As from the darkening gloom a silver dove
> Upsoars, and darts into the eastern light,
> On pinions that naught moves but pure delight,
> So fled thy soul into the realms above.
>
> . . . .

There thou or joinest the immortal quire
In melodies that even Heaven fair
Fill with superior bliss, or, at desire
Of the omnipotent Father, cleav'st the air
On holy message sent.
                    ("As from the Darkening Gloom")

A fine passage from Robert Penn Warren's "Picnic Remembered" compares the departing soul to the flight of a hawk:

Or is the soul a hawk that, fled
On glimmering wings past vision's path,
Reflects the last gleam to us here
Though sun is sunk and darkness near
—Uncharted Truth's high heliograph?
                    (308–9)

The descent into a dark underworld has been an alternate, and not necessarily pejorative, image of the journey of the soul after death. In one of the earliest known writings, a seventh-century B.C. Assyrian version of *Gilgamesh,* souls of the dead are described as wearing feathers in a dream of Enkidu, Gilgamesh's dear companion. He tells how his arms were transformed into wings and how he was led by a great black bird to the place of the dead: "There is the house where people sit in darkness; dust is their food and clay their meat. They are clothed like birds with wings for covering."[35] One of the functions of the winged god Hermes was to conduct the souls of the dead to the underworld. In Virgil's *Aeneid* a pair of the doves sacred to Venus leads her son Aeneas to the entrance of the Roman underworld at Lake Avernus. Both Virgil and Dante are carried down to the deepest part of hell on the back of Geryon, a monstrous flying reptile in the *Divine Comedy.* A recent striking adaptation of the bird's trip to the underworld is this description by W. S. DiPiero of the ground-feeding brown thrasher:

curved beak cutting trenches,
he hammers, he feeds, down
where earth's muscled rind wraps
around its molten core.

sea of blue mud flames,
combed fine, swell, cooling foam,
where our dead are waiting,
where we await ourselves,
he works, hungry, fearless,
our only messenger.[36]

It is not uncommon for the souls of departed lovers to appear as birds. The souls of lovers in the Circle of the Lustful in Dante's *Divine Comedy* are buffeted about by a strong wind like cranes and starlings. Thoreau comes close to the Gothic mood when in *Walden* he imagines the "dismal scream" of screech owls to be the cries of doomed lovers:

It is no honest and blunt tu-whit tu-who of the poets, but, without jesting, a most solemn graveyard ditty, the mutual consolations of suicide lovers remembering the pangs and the delights of supernal love in the infernal groves. . . . They are the spirits, the low spirits and melancholy forebodings, of fallen souls that once in human shape night-walked the earth and did the deeds of darkness, now expiating their sins with their wailing hymns or threnodies in the scenery of their transgressions.

("Sounds," 327)

The same mood is found in C. Day Lewis's "Buzzards over Castle Hill" when three hawks, "three celestial bodies," are seen "balancing on the wind" and heard uttering "a wraith-like rumour" of sound:

you might well surmise
They are earth-souls doomed in their gyres to unwind
Some tragic love-tangle wherein they had mortally pined,
When you hear those phantom, famishing cries.[37]

The bird as prophet and the bird as the soul of a deceased lover form the substance of the harrowing experience recounted by Edgar Allan Poe in "The Raven." The midnight visitor of a student who is desperately trying to find "surcease of sorrow" for the death of his lady, the "rare and radiant" Lenore, the raven perches on a bust of Pallas Athena above the chamber door. (The owl is commonly Athena's token, but the raven is also permissible if we accept the testimony of Pausanias that he saw a statue of the goddess with a raven.) To the mystified student's questions the intruder replies with the single word "Nevermore," which the narrator first accepts as a word the bird has learned to repeat by rote from a master who had suffered some "unmerciful Disaster" that has left him without hope. This realistic explanation, reflecting the narrator's own situation, is soon rejected for a more symbolical one: perhaps the bird is God's messenger bringing "respite and nepenthe from the memories of Lenore." The answer is the same: there is to be no "balm in Gilead." The bird is then asked to prophesy whether the sorrowing lover will ever embrace Lenore in the "distant Aidenn" [Eden]. The negative answers to the last two questions drive the distraught lover to determine whether his mysterious visitor is a "bird or devil"—the traditional reaction to a spectral appearance. We are given no definitive answer, though the climactic last two stanzas strongly suggest that the raven is a "thing of evil," a messenger from "Night's Plutonian shore," or the land of the dead, that has come to taunt the narrator with the prophecy that he will never be able to stop grieving for his deceased Lenore. "Take thy beak from out my heart!" he shouts.

There is some evidence in the poem to support another identity for the raven, one suggested by Beryl Rowland in his discussion of the lore of the raven. It is consistent with the traditional use of birds in literature and with Poe's fondness for revenants that the bird may be seen as the soul of Lenore herself, a ghost returned from death to haunt her lover as so many of Poe's women are wont to do. When the narrator opens the door of his chamber in response to the raven's tapping, he actually believes, "dreaming dreams no mortal ever dared to dream before," that his visitor may be Lenore herself. He whispers her name "and an echo murmured back the word, 'Lenore.'" When he sees it is a bird that enters the room, he notes that it has the "mien of lord or lady." The last stanza of the poem depicts the shadow of the raven crushing the soul of the narrator to the floor in a manner very much like that at the close of "The Fall of the House of Usher" when the buried-alive sister of Roderick Usher returns from the tomb and falls on him—"bore him to the floor a corpse."

And the Raven, never flitting, still is sitting, *still* is sitting
On the pallid bust of Pallas just above my chamber door;
And his eyes have all the seeming of a demon's
   that is dreaming,
And the lamp-light o'er him streaming throws his shadow
   on the floor;
And my soul from out that shadow that lies floating on the floor
     Shall be lifted—nevermore!

Death is not the fate of the raven's victim but rather the burden of a sorrowful memory, the "shadow" under which he must live. The same motif is to be found in Poe's "Ligeia," a short story in which the deceased wife, with hair "blacker than the raven wings of the midnight," returns from the tomb to inhabit the body of the narrator's second wife. In "The Philosophy of Composition," an essay sometimes more appropriately titled "How I Wrote the Raven," Poe declares the raven to be "emblematical of Mournful and Never-ending Remembrance."[38]

There is not a little similarity between Poe's poem and the two encounters Goethe's Faust has with a demonic animal. In the first encounter a small dog keeps circling Faust while he is walking outside the town gate. Like Poe's narrator, Faust at first accepts the rational explanation of this behavior offered by his student Wagner, that it is but an ordinary black poodle trying to find his master's tracks. But upon returning to his study, he soon learns that it is not a real dog he has brought home but a specter taking on a variety of forms and finally appearing in the guise of a traveling scholar. Faust's first question is to ask the stranger's name. "I am the spirit which always denies" is the reply. Mephistopheles, among his other temptations, offers Faust the chance to find relief from despair: "Stop playing with your grief which battens / Like a vulture on your life, your mind" (*Faust*, 48, 57).

In his role as a book reviewer Poe may have gleaned the lore of the raven from a number of sources, including an essay by Christopher North on Selby's *Ornithology*. It was widely thought that he got his idea for the talking raven from Charles Dickens's *Barnaby Rudge*, a novel he reviewed three years before "The Raven" first appeared. One of his objections to the novel was that Dickens did not make enough of Barnaby's pet raven: "Its croakings might have been *prophetically* heard in the course of the drama" (*Essays*, 243). Poe's raven, of course, is all dire prophecy, while Dickens's is a comical bird patterned after his own pet raven, Grip. It is fond of saying "I'm a devil" but has no effect on the course of action or tone of the novel even though the book is replete with scenes of death. Upon being imprisoned with his master in Newgate, Grip returns to his natural state, and "for a whole year he never indulged in any other sound than a grave, decorous croak." The association of Poe with Dickens in this matter gave James Russell Lowell an opportunity to write a famous couplet in "A Fable for Critics":

> There comes Poe, with his raven, like Barnaby Rudge,
> Three fifths of him genius and two fifths mere fudge.[39]

Immensely popular in Poe's lifetime, "The Raven" was the sort of poem that easily inspired parodies, like this by a supporter of temperance:

> I invited him to drink of, saying there was plenty more—
> But the owl he shook his head, he threw the whiskey
>   on the floor,
>   Plainly saying, "nevermore!"[40]

It is likely that Walt Whitman recalled "The Raven" when he composed "Out of the Cradle Endlessly Rocking" fourteen years later. Among the striking similarities are the midnight tone, the late-risen moon, the appearance of a spectral "demon or bird" speaking of a departed lover, and the shore dividing the living from the dead. The experience of losing a loved one has opposite results for the two poets, however. For Poe, as he states in "The Philosophy of Composition," the death of a beautiful woman is the "most poetical topic in the world," and sorrow over such a loss the very essence of beauty. The bereaved lover, Poe goes on to say, "experiences a phrenzied pleasure in so modeling his questions as to receive from the *expected* 'Nevermore' the most delicious because the most intolerable of sorrow" (*Essays*, 19). At the close of the poem a soul lying crushed by unending sorrow is a sort of consummation. The mockingbird grieving for his mate in Whitman's poem teaches quite a different lesson. It serves a kindly, creative purpose. The listening boy accepts mortality—the "delicious word death"—and makes it the origin of his awakening as a poet. Thereafter he will "fuse" the song of his "dusky demon and brother" with his own "thousand responsive songs." Death for Whitman is a natural process associated with love and the release of his poetic voice.

In "The Raven" Poe draws on the tradition of birds bringing bad news to the living and even snatching souls to death before their time. Primitive Greeks were terribly afraid of a large assortment of legendary winged creatures—keres, Harpies, Erinyes, Sirens (originally winged rather than fish tailed)—that seized the souls of the unwary and the guilty. Christian symbolism makes use of these primitive fears but reverses the figure by having the trapped bird represent the soul in danger of damnation. Thus the wicked man is "cast into a net by his own feet, and he walketh upon a snare. The gin shall take him by the heel" (Job 8.9). Scriptural commentaries on passages of this sort explain that the wicked fowler is Satan and the birds are Christian souls susceptible of temptation. Odo of Cluny, a tenth-century abbot, admonishes readers of his *Occupatio*

> just as bait draws flying birds to the snare
> Wicked appetite draws those moved by its sweetness.
> Fixed in the lime, they cannot stretch their wings;
> They lack devotion to virtue and the wings to fly.

God rescues the faithful from the trap: "Surely he shall deliver thee from the snare of the fowler" (Ps. 91.3). In Chaucer's *Legend of Good Women* small birds themselves give thanks that they have escaped the fowler over the winter when everyone is subject to spiritual tribulations:

> The foule cherl that, for his coveytise,
> Had hem betrayed with his sophistrye.
> This was hire song, "The foweler we deffye,
> And al his craft." [41]

Herman Melville reverts to the more primitive—and more playful—image of a bird snatching a sailor's soul as represented by his cap. Near the end of *Moby-Dick*, when bad omens multiply, Ahab's hat is seized by "one of those red-billed savage sea-hawks," probably an Egyptian vulture: the bird "came wheeling and screaming round his head in a maze of untrackably swift circlings." (One recalls the spiraling circles the black poodle runs around Faust in Goethe's drama). The bird drops the hat far out at sea, and it is never recovered. In the poem *Clarel*, written many years after *Moby-Dick*, much is made of the story of a sailor whose "old wool cap" is seized by a "big bird, red-billed and black." Bird and man fall into the sea, and when the sailor is rescued and revived, he swears that the "shrill gird," or sneer, the bird uttered while he was sinking was "bitterer than the brine he drank." He was not the sinner that Ahab was, however:

> Bird? but he deemed it was the devil,
> And that he carried off his soul
> In the old cap, nor was made whole
> 'Till some good vicar did unravel
> The snarled illusion in the skein,
> And he got his soul again.

An older Melville does not press the incident as hard as he did earlier: the narrator calls it "a bit of Nature's allegory." [42]

As well as carrying souls into the realm of death, birds also represent the souls of the living. Andrew Marvell in "The Garden" creates this happy picture of the bird-soul of Adam before Eve appears on the scene:

> Here at the fountain's sliding foot,
> Or at some fruit tree's mossy root,
> Casting the body's vest aside,
> My soul into the boughs does glide;
> There like a bird it sits and sings,
> Then whets, then combs its silver wings;
> And till prepared for longer flight,
> Waves its plumes in the various light.
>   (Hebel and Hudson, 854)

In a charming passage from the Venerable Bede's eighth-century *Ecclesiastical History of the English People* the soul in its journey through this life is compared to a sparrow passing through the great hall of an Anglo-Saxon king. Wordsworth adapts the image in one of his "Ecclesiastical Sonnets":

> Man's life is like a sparrow, mighty King!
> That—while at banquet with your Chiefs you sit
> Housed near a blazing fire—is seen to flit
> Safe from the wintry tempest. Fluttering,
> Here did it enter; there, on hasty wing,
> Flies out, and passes on from cold to cold.
>
> (1.16)

Thoreau tried his hand at this in the poem "Speech of a Saxon Ealderman," and with the typical New England thriftiness of the time his sparrow "flutters through the hall" briefly and "barely picks the scattered crumbs" at the feast (213). Reflecting on his life as a watcher of men and birds, the narrator of Wallace Stegner's *The Spectator Bird* acclaims the story of Bede's sparrow as "the truest vision of life that I kow." At the end of the novel he and his wife return to their house after a walk in the cold misty night and then go out again to see if there is a lunar rainbow—"Of course there wasn't one." The house is Bede's hall, the place from which they can observe the world, where they may "sit among the rafters while the drinking and boasting and reciting and fighting go on below." A literary agent, the narrator feels that he has always been a spectator of life, not a true participant.[43]

The restrictiveness of life on earth is also expressed in the common image of the soul imprisoned in the body like a bird held captive in a cage. Thus in the words of the Persian poet Hafiz, "My soul is as a sacred bird, the Highest Heaven its nest: / Fretting within the body's bars, it finds on earth no rest." The bird in the cage became a cliché as this from John Webster's *The Duchess of Malfi*—"Didst thou ever see a lark in a cage? / Such is the soul in the body"—although Gerard Manley Hopkins was able to give it force in a striking image from "The Caged Skylark":

> As a dare-gale skylark scanted in a dull cage
>   Man's mounting spirit in this bone-house,
>   mean house, dwells.
>
> (70)

three. The Modern Revival of Bird-Gods

> *Let not a god disappear. We need all of them time and again;*
> *let every image once formed count with us even today.*
> *Treat nothing deigning to speak deep in the heart with*
> *disdain.*
>
> Rainer Maria Rilke

One of the more curious features of twentieth-century literature is the renewal of interest in the ancient association of birds with gods. It is but one aspect of the primitivistic movement that grew out of turn-of-the-century studies in anthropology and depth psychology, followed by the analysis of myth and archetypes undertaken by literary criticism. In the first half of the twentieth century the primitivistic style of writing filled a need to counter the excessive mechanization that the industrial revolution had fostered in society. In a sense it was an extension of the romantic movement, concentrating on the revival of ancient forms of feeling and belief that rationalism and science had discredited and attempting to restore some residue of influence for long-neglected forms of religious worship. One of these was the belief in animal-gods. We have noted that pagan elements crept into Judeo-Christian symbology, but primitivist writers have gone well beyond the dove for their animal-gods. As though to register their dissatisfaction with the gentler aspects of Christianity, often they have chosen to revive animal-gods representing the fiercer and more destructive forces of nature, the kind of "evil" gods, indeed, that Christianity had incorporated in the figure of Satan. The revival of the supernatural power of birds has been especially effective. For example, the twentieth-century reader of Yeats's "Leda and the Swan"—agnostic, skeptical, without compelling religious convictions—believes for a moment in the power of a god whose worship came to an end over two thousand years ago. The poem gives him the feeling of, if not the belief in, a divine presence. The animal disguise makes the impression more vivid and perhaps more acceptable to the reader who may find it more congenial to entertain a reminiscent belief in the primitive face of divinity than in the full panoply of official religious doctrine.

Impetus to this aspect of twentieth-century literature came in part from the belated recognition of Herman Melville's impressive deification of the white whale in *Moby-Dick*. The voluminous material Melville presents concerning whales in general all goes to aggrandize the great white whale and prepare for his overwhelming appearance near the end of the book when the "grand god revealed himself." It is noteworthy that birds are closely associated with this god. In his wake, like a horde of attending angels, are "hundreds of gay fowl softly feathering the sea," and on a harpoon stuck in the whale's back "one of the cloud of soft-toed fowls hovering, and to and fro skimming like a canopy over the fish, silently perched and rocked on this pole, the long tail feathers streaming like pennons" (chap. 133: 689). Long before this, however, the crew had seen what they believed to be the spout of Moby Dick at midnight: "Lit by the moon it looked celestial; seemed some plumed and glittering god uprising from the sea." Typically, Melville avoids accountability by assigning the attribution of divinity to the supposedly superstitious crew and not the learned narrator.

A "screaming gull" ominously ushers the *Pequod* out of Nantucket harbor on Christmas day. At the very end of the book a bird goes down with the sinking ship: a "sky-hawk," or frigate bird, that had come down from "its natural home among the stars" to peck at a new flag being installed by a sailor, is accidentally nailed to the mast: "and so the bird of heaven, with archangelic shrieks, and his imperial beak thrust upwards, and his whole captive form folded in the flag of Ahab, went down with his ship, which, like Satan, would not sink to hell till she had dragged a living part of heaven along with her, and helmeted herself with it. Now small fowls flew screaming over the yet yawning gulf." It is as though man, in his desperate contest with the gods, succeeds in pulling one down, the sky-god represented by the bird, while another, the earth-god represented by the whale, escapes unharmed and unconcerned.

What could have been another impressive deification of a bird is relegated by Melville to a footnote in his famous chapter on the whiteness of the whale, perhaps because he knew that it had been already so used by another writer, Coleridge, in his "wild Rhyme." It has to do with a white albatross seen in a storm:

I saw a regal, feathery thing of unspotted whiteness, and with a hooked, Roman bill sublime. At intervals, it arched forth its vast archangel wings, as if to embrace some holy ark. Wondrous flutterings and throbbings shook it. Though bodily unharmed, it uttered cries, as some king's ghost in supernatural distress. Through its inexpressible, strange eyes, methought I peeped to secrets which took hold of God. As Abraham before the angels, I bowed myself.

(chap. 42: 256)

Melville's white whale is unique in Western literature in that it is purely an animal-god, not an agent of a god nor a disguise of one. A more common primitivistic method among modern writers is to adapt gods with more or less well-known histories of worship and celebration in art and literature. Such is the ancient Greek god Zeus, and the most popular choice among all of his animal disguises has been the swan, the form he took in his seduction of Leda. The bizarre affair was a common subject of Renaissance art. A painting of the school of Leonardo da Vinci shows the nude Leda standing demurely beside the swan, one wing clapped around her thigh, while at their feet are the newborn babes and the broken eggshells from which they have just emerged. In copies of Michelangelo's Leda and the Swan the principals are at least in a semireclining position and embracing, but there is no sign of sexual assault. Other Italian paintings include several by Tintoretto, one fairly sensual work by Veronese, and a Correggio in which the swan and a gently yielding Leda are surrounded by smiling maidens who serve as Leda's attendants. Rubens portrays the incident as well as a painting can, though an ancient Roman limestone bas-relief copy of a Greek original is even more effective in representing the massive proportions of the swan-god fronting the woman.

Among the many literary treatments of the rape of Leda, Edmund Spenser's in *The Faerie Queene* deserves notice. To distance himself a little from a subject that many moralists deplored, Spenser is careful to describe not the actual event but a portrayal of it in a tapestry hanging in the House of Busyrane:

> Then was he turned into a snowy Swan,
>   To win faire Leda to his lovely trade:
>   O wondrous skill, and sweet wit of the man,
>   That her in daffodillies sleeping made,
>   From scorching heat her daintie limbes to shade:
>   Whiles the proud Bird ruffing his feathers wyde,
>   And brushing his faire brest, did her invade;
>   She slept, yet twixt her eyelids closely spyde,
> How towards her he rusht, and smiled at his pryde.
>
>   (3.11.32)

Spenser's prettiness is almost exceeded by Goethe in *Faust*, in which the influence of Correggio's painting dominates a long passage about swans and bathing girls in the scene "On the Lower Peneios" in part 2. Leda remains unnamed, and there is no clearly defined contact with the swan. A dream Faust has in "Wagner's Laboratory" is more explicit. Clashing wings suddenly strike the stream where Leda is bathing; while her attendants flee, she remains undisturbed and looks at the princely swan with proud womanly delight ("*stolzem weibliche Vergnügen*") as the swan embraces her knees. It is importunate yet tame ("*zudringlich-zahm*").

Hilda Doolittle's version of the exchange between Leda and the swan, though quite beautiful in its way, is even more tenuous, drawing as it does on the flower language of love that was so popular in the nineteenth century:

> Ah kingly kiss—
> no more regret
> nor old deep memories
> to mar the bliss;
> where the low sedge is thick,
> the gold day-lily
> outspreads and rests
> beneath the soft fluttering
> of red swan wings
> and the warm quivering
> of the red swan's breast.[44]

The affair was not successfully rendered in literature until it became the subject of a sonnet by a writer for whom swans and the
story of Leda were of crucial importance, William Butler Yeats.
Rainer Maria Rilke had touched on the Leda story briefly in some
lines about Zeus, which Yeats may have read:

> Blindly submerging
> himself in the plumes of a wing-beating swan, he released
> streams of existence, showering untold constellations
> into that timorous domain, and far-off generations.[45]

This sets the general significance of divine intervention in human
affairs, but it is through precise details of the swan's sexual assault
and the girl's shock in being so strangely confronted that Yeats
achieves, as those before had not, a convincing sense of a god
manifesting himself as a terrifying presence in the natural world.

> Leda and the Swan
> A sudden blow: the great wings beating still
> Above the staggering girl, her thighs caressed
> By the dark webs, her nape caught in his bill,
> He holds her helpless breast upon his breast.
> How can those terrified vague fingers push
> The feathered glory from her loosening thighs?
> And how can body, laid in that white rush,
> But feel the strange heart beating where it lies?
>
> A shudder in the loins engenders there
> The broken wall, the burning roof and tower
> And Agamemnon dead.
>   Being so caught up,
> So mastered by the brute blood of the air,
> Did she put on his knowledge with his power
> Before the indifferent beak could let her drop?
>   (211)

The poem's dynamism, as Leo Spitzer points out, depends on two
sharply drawn contrasts: the girl's helplessness in the grip of a
mysterious force, and the far-reaching historical consequences of

a brief, isolated act.[46] For the god knows, as we do, that one child resulting from this union, Helen, would one day be the cause of the Trojan War with its heavy toll of death and destruction. We might take these as the tragic results of sexual passion involving a god and a human, but from Yeats's rather idiosyncratic point of view the poem symbolizes the idea that the great turning points in history are the result of the intervention of gods in human affairs. Greco-Roman civilization was thus brought about by what he called the "annunciation" of Leda, Christianity by Mary's conceiving Jesus through the agency of the Holy Spirit in the form of a dove. "The Mother of God" presents Mary and the dove but in terms almost abstract compared to those used with Leda and the swan.

Yeats's scenario of the history of the Western world calls for a third annunciation in the year 2000, when the fall of our present civilization will make way for the birth of a new one. "The Second Coming" is not about Christ's return to earth, however, but the appearance of a new divinity to supplant him. The world's present confusion is suggested in the poem's opening lines with the image of a falconer (humankind) who can no longer communicate with his falcon (symbol of Christ): "Turning and turning in the widening gyre / The falcon cannot hear the falconer" (184). A contrasting image occurs in the closing lines that describe the new god as a "rough beast" that "slouches towards Bethlehem to be born." Ponderous, it is hardly birdlike and is resented by real birds:

> A shape with lion body and the head of a man,
> A gaze blank and pitiless as the sun,
> Is moving its slow thighs, while all about it
> Reel shadows of the indignant desert birds.
>
> (185)

Yeats's falcon is like one in Dante's *Inferno* that

> wheels away
> In a hundred circlings, and sets her far aloof
> From her master, sullen and scornful.[47]

What is remarkable about Yeats's three annunciations is his assumption that animals play an important part in the history of humankind. The point is made by Giorgio Melchiori in a study of the development of the poet's images: "Yeats saw the crucial events, the most important moments in universal and personal history, as produced by the conjunction and the conflict of human and animal forms. The animal symbolizes not only the lowest physical impulses uncontrolled by reason (the 'beastly,' 'rough,' 'brute' side of life), but also the superhuman, transcendental powers, the miraculous and the prodigious which cannot be accounted for in rational terms."[48] If we can assume that the bird represents a combination of the animal and the divine, then each annunciation reflects the creation of a new type of personality at various points in history: in the first, the ancient world, the divine and the animal, the swan, are beautifully balanced; in the medieval and Renaissance world the divine, the Christian dove, predominates; and the monstrous apocalyptic animal completely takes over in the last, the modern world.

The retrospective view of ancient beliefs allows a humorous as well as serious treatment of divinity. Of his beautiful friend, Maud Gonne, Yeats could write in "His Phoenix" that she "might be that sprightly girl trodden by a bird." His seriocomic verse play *The Herne's Egg* in some ways is a parody of the legend of Leda and the swan. In this version Attracta claims to be the bride of the Great Herne (an archaic dialect form of *heron*), enduring like Leda the terror of "beak and claw," but there is some doubt of her honesty. She is called "a crazed loony / Waiting to be trodden by a bird" and inventing the story "to feed [her] sensuality." She admits to the inadequacy of the Great Herne's embrace; he begets in her only an image of his own spirit, and something more tangible is required:

> there's a work
> That should be done, and that work needs
> No bird's beak nor claw, but a man,
> The imperfection of a man.
>   (*Collected Plays*, 427)

Attracta is later accused of having seven men in one night.
Oliver St. John Gogarty wrote his own "Leda and the Swan,"

and it turned out to be a long comic parody of his good friend's
poem:

> Of the tales that daughters
>   Tell their poor old mothers,
> Which by all accounts are
>   Often very odd;
> Leda's was a story
>   Stranger than all others.
> What was there to say but:
>   Glory be to God?

The last stanza is almost a paraphrase of Yeats's sestet:

> When the hyacinthine
>   Eggs were in the basket,—
> Blue as at the whiteness
>   Where a cloud begins;
> Who would dream there lay there
>   All that Trojan brightness:
> Agamemnon murdered;
>   And the mighty Twins? [49]

   Taking a humorous view of the extramarital affairs of gods was
not unknown even in antiquity, as we know from reading Homer.
The story of Leda and the swan offered pornographic opportunities, from this seventh-century squib by Bassus in *The Greek
Anthology*—

> I'll never turn to gold; let someone else become
> A bull, or a shore-haunting swan that tuneful sings;
> Such tricks I leave to Zeus: two obols is the sum
> Corinna I will give, instead of sprouting wings—

to the reenactment of the event by the courtesan Thais in Anatole
France's novel of that name and, in Pamela Hansford Johnson's
Unspeakable Skipton, by a "boot repairer's" assistant, who reclines
on a "mossy bank contrived by means of a greengrocer's baize
spread over pillows" while "Le Cygne" is being played on an old
gramophone. In Guy de Maupassant's "Madame Tellier's Estab-
lishment" the choicest room in the brothel of a small French town

is "embellished with a large drawing representing Leda stretched out under a swan." [50]

An interesting revision of the traditional version of Leda and the swan is Mona Van Duyn's "Leda Reconsidered." As might be expected of a poem written in the era of new feminism, her Leda is hardly the terrified maiden being overwhelmed by a god, but rather the experienced woman who is only a little startled by "the strangeness of the thing." In fact she feels the "joy of being used," and in that she is the god's equal:

> Deep, in her inmost, grubby
> female center
> (how could he know that,
> in his airiness?)
> lay the joy of being used,
> and its heavy peace, perhaps,
> would keep her down.
> To give: women and gods
> are alike in that ceremony,
> find its smoke filling and sweet.
> But to give up was an offering
> only she could savor,
> simply by covering
> her eyes.

Her womanly self-possession leads the god to treat her with care:

> She waited for him so quietly that
> he came on her quietly,
> almost with tenderness,
> not treading her.
> Her hand moved into the dense plumes
> on his breast to touch
> the utter stranger.[51]

D. H. Lawrence took an interest in swan imagery about the same time as Yeats. In a 1915 essay, "The Crown," he writes that Leonardo da Vinci's and Michelangelo's paintings of Leda and the swan represent "mankind in the clasp of the divine flux of corruption, the singing death." He sees the swan as "one of the symbols of divine corruption with its reptile feet buried in the ooze and mud, and its voluptuous form yielding and embracing the ooze of water, its beauty white and cold and terrifying, like the dead beauty of the moon, . . . its neck and head like the snake, it is for us the cold white fire of flux . . . the salt cold burning of the sea which corrodes all it touches, coldly reduces every sun-built form to ash, to the original elements." After destruction, however, "something new must arise."[52] This view of the swan comports with the implication in Yeats's "Leda and the Swan" that the violent assault upon Leda is both destructive and creative, but whereas the inspiration of Yeats had been Greek myth, Lawrence seems to draw on the Hindu god Siva the force in the universe that both destroys and regenerates. In his role as destroyer, Siva reduces human beings to the basic world substance ("the nectar of deathlessness," Amrita, ambrosia), and in his phallic role he produces new creatures from the eternal substance, for which Lawrence, in subsequent developments of the swan symbol, gives twentieth-century scientific equivalents—atoms, neutrons, fusion—as in this passage from "Spiral Flame":

> There is a swan-like flame that curls round the centre of space
> and flutters at the core of the atom,
> there is a spiral flame-tip that can lick our little atoms
>   into fusion
> so we roar up like bonfires of vitality
> and fuse in a broad hard flame of many men in a oneness.
>
> (440)

In "Give Us Gods" the basic components of matter are merged with the natural watery habitat of the swan, "the father of all things" swimming "in a mist of atoms." What we have in Lawrence's swan is the attempt to combine twentieth-century atomic theory with the traditional imagery of an animal deity. The first attribute of his swan is its identification with formless matter as it exists in space, what he called "the divine flux" in his 1915 essay. The second is its more familiar role as the progenitor of new life from that eternal supply of matter. The two functions of the swan are brought together in "Swan," a poem in which the "vast white bird" is seen as not merely "nesting passive upon the atoms" but "treading our women . . . with unknown shocks" (436). With this Lawrence comes close to the creative act of a god that Yeats described in "Leda and the Swan."

The ending of *Moby-Dick* especially pleased Lawrence because he could see the bird there as "the eagle of the spirit," or the "white mental consciousness," and the whale as "our deepest blood-consciousness." For the union of earth and heaven, of body and spirit, that Melville symbolized with the whale and his attendant birds, Lawrence, in *The Plumed Serpent,* uses the figure of Quetzalcoatl, an ancient Aztec god having the combined form of a bird and a serpent, and reflecting the importance Aztecs placed on the pairing of opposed forces to maintain balance in the universe. The quetzal (*Pharomarchus mocinno*), a member of the trogon family and the national emblem of Guatemala, is described accurately by Lawrence as "a bird that lives high up in the mists of tropical mountains, and has very beautiful tail feathers, precious to the Aztecs."[53] It was considered sinful to kill the quetzal, and Montezuma's headdress was made of feathers plucked from live birds. Coatl is a snake and together with quetzal constitutes the plumed serpent. On his visit to Mexico in 1923 Lawrence was impressed with the statue of Quetzalcoatl in Mexico's National Museum—"so hideous in the fanged, feathered writhing stone." What also appealed to him was the origin of the symbol in the prehistoric past of Mexico, "when the mind and the power of man was in his blood and his backbone, and there was the strange, dark intercommunication between man and man, and man and beast" (415). The complex of varied and confused traditions about Quetzalcoatl gave Lawrence an opportunity to give the figure some substance of his own invention.

Lawrence makes the avian component of Quetzalcoatl a sky-god, wind-god, and sun-god somewhat resembling the eagle of Greek and Roman myth: a "roaming Bird of the Beyond, with thunder in your pinions and the snake of lightning in your beak. . . . You sit in the middle of the sun, and preen your feathers" (*Serpent,* 198). The serpent is the earth principle, the source of life. The human race dwells between the two forces, "exposed naked betwixt sky and land, belonging to neither," as Lawrence expresses it in the opening of his "Study of Thomas Hardy" (*Phoenix,* 398). It is essential, though, that men and women must establish a relation with the elemental forces represented by the bird-serpent figure, the power and wisdom of the bird and the life force of the snake.

Lawrence's symbol cannot be accounted successful, however. The novel deals exclusively with the attempt of two fanatical Mexican revolutionaries, Don Ramon and General Cipriano, to return to the worship of ancient Aztec gods for the purpose of revitalizing the religious and political life of Mexico as well as the lives of all who espouse this cause. Counting on the lingering paganism of the Mexican masses, they hope that the revived Quetzalcoatl will replace Christ as savior and that Mexico will be his "bride between the seas." The background for their idea of revival is the ancient Aztec legend in which Quetzalcoatl, after being banished by the dark god Tezcatlipoca, throws himself on a pyre and, like the phoenix, is reborn from the ashes. For Lawrence the legendary phoenix had immense importance as a symbol of the possibility of individuals to create a new life for themselves. At the height of the cult of Quetzalcoatl there were always two high priests serving as the god's representatives on earth, now incarnated as Ramon and Cipriano. The idea of a political revival may have been derived from an Aztec belief that an ancient Toltec ruler, Topiltzin, who identified himself with Quetzalcoatl and became the Morning Star after his death, will someday return to life and resume his kingship. Thus Don Ramon is "the living Quetzalcoatl" as well as a political leader; he has the bird of heaven on his brow and the serpent in his loins, which is to say he unites heaven and earth, or all the opposites of reality. In one of his hymns he declares,

> I am Quetzalcoatl of the eagle and the snake.
> Of earth and air.
> Of the Morning Star.
> I am the Lord of the Two Ways.
> (*Serpent,* 341)

But in spite of an elaborate ritual devised for its worship, complete with sacred hymns and dances, the bird-serpent is never a real enough presence in the novel, never the point where act and meaning intersect, as they do in *Moby-Dick*, in which the detailed description of the whale's entire existence is made to correspond in some way to the fate of the *Pequod*'s crew members. Since Quetzalcoatl was a purely mythical creature, it was not possible for Lawrence to give it the kind of experiential reality that so informs Melville's whale. Lawrence never achieves a convincing union of the fantasy "world of Quetzalcoatl" and the real world. Lawrence's surrogate in the novel, the Englishwoman Kate Leslie, whom Ramon and Cipriano attempt to proselytize, remains skeptical even though she becomes the wife of Cipriano. He is the living incarnation of Huitzilopochtli, the god who confers immortality on fallen warriors by transforming them into hummingbirds. (The *uitzil* in his name means hummingbird.) Kate must passively bear his fiery passion, like the brown hen being trod by the great bird. One cannot escape the final impression that the bird-serpent turns out to be but a metaphor of the male's sexual domination of the female, a subject to be treated fully in a later chapter.

Others besides Lawrence have been interested in the revival of the god Quetzalcoatl. At Dartmouth College there is a painting by José Clemente Orozco, "The Departure of Quetzalcoatl," in which the bird-god bears a resemblance to the figure of God in Michelangelo's "Creation of Man." The reappearance of Quetzalcoatl is the subject of a 1982 film, *Q, The Winged Serpent,* a melodrama in which the great bird terrorizes New York after it has been "prayed back into existence" by cultists.

The eagle episode in Saul Bellow's *Adventures of Augie March* may be seen as a corrective, if not a parody, of Lawrence's plumed serpent. Like Lawrence and his revolutionaries, Augie feels the spell of the old myths in the Valley of Mexico, where "worshipers disguised as gods and as gods in the disguise of birds, jumped from platforms fixed on long poles, and glided as they spun by the ropes—feathered serpents, and eagles too, the *voladores,* or fliers. There still are such plummeters, in the market places, as there seem to be remnants or conversions or equivalents of all the old things."[54] The pre-Columbian myth that Bellow adopts, however, is not the same as Lawrence's winged serpent, but rather the Toltec image featured on the Mexican flag since 1821, an eagle seizing a snake in its beak. Whereas Lawrence's Aztec symbol represents the harmony of two opposite forces, Bellow's represents the more familiar Western conception of the unavoidable conflict of heavenly good with earthly evil, symbolized by the early Christian image of battle between Christ the eagle and the serpent, followed by the better-known image of Saint George and the dragon.[55]

Augie's eagle exploit is set in motion by his girlfriend, who has a plan to train an eagle to catch giant iguanas. She enlists the help of Augie, who is skeptical but must admit "the nobility of the project, how ancient it was." A city boy whose knowledge of eagles is limited to "the eagle of money . . . and the NRA eagle with its gear and lightnings," he is willing to "catch up with legends, more or less." He admires the bird's flight "in the deep air of the mountainside, once again up toward the high vibrations of blue," and the assault on the iguana: "Feathered and armored he looked in his black colors, and such menace falling swift from heaven." But their bird proves to be no fighter and releases his grip on the reptiles as soon as they show the least resistance. Thea abandons the eagle and turns her attention to collecting snakes—like the man in Edmund Wilson's *Memoirs of Hecate County* who gives up raising ducks in favor of their predators, turtles. Augie has a "cold eye" for Thea's snakes "less from horror than from antagonism," and the couple breaks up. But all is not lost for Augie: like a later Bellow hero, Henderson, Augie has learned "to bear the gaze" of a fierce animal and in taming an eagle "could claim a certain amount of courage." In the spirit of comedy his encounter with mythic experiences results in a modest personal gain, not the soul-shaking cataclysms Lawrence wanted.

Both Lawrence, seriously, and Bellow, half-seriously, are responding to the Nietzschean idea that people must revert to the instincts of their animal heritage in order to free themselves from the restraints that civilization has put in the way of their proper self-realization. Both use a combination of bird and serpent like the central image of *Thus Spake Zarathustra*. Nietzsche's symbol represents the same union of sky and earth as Quetzalcoatl, only now the figure is given an application that accords with a philosopher's intellectual adventures: the eagle, proudest of birds, ascends to the exhilarating heights of philosophical speculation, and the serpent, wisest of animals, delves into the dangerous depths of tragic knowledge. The two animals function almost as Zarathustra's divine muse, both attending the prophet at the start of his

career in the prologue and the eagle calling him to a triumphant renewal of his mission at the end. Because of Nietzsche's fascination
with heights and his belief that the depths may be surveyed only
from the heights, more is made of the eagle than of the serpent.
"Man is a rope stretched between the animal and the Superman—
a rope over an abyss," and to explore the abyss man must look
into it from the height of a soaring bird. "He who seeth the abyss,
but with eagle's eyes—he who seizes the abyss with eagle's talons
graspeth the abyss, he hath courage." The courage is that of the
thinker who pursues the truth wherever it may be found, even in
the darkest corners of reality, and declaims it fearlessly. As well
as courage, Zarathustra's bird is described as a fierce predator in
order to represent the harsher side of nature that the Superman
must recover. At one point the eagle is compared to a panther in
the way it viciously attacks lambs:

> On *lambkins* pouncing,
> Headlong down, sore-hungry,
> Fierce 'gainst all lamb-spirits,
> Furious-fierce 'gainst all that look
> Sheeplike, or lambeyed, or crisp-woolly,
> —Grey, with lambsheep kindliness![56]

This seems to be a complete rejection of the Christian spirit, yet
at the close of the book when Zarathustra fearlessly confronts the
ultimate animal, the "blond beast" or lion, a flock of doves hovers
lovingly over his head. It is a lion that the hero must confront in
Bellow's second adaptation of Nietzsche in *Henderson, the Rain
King.* Augie and Henderson succeed in winning the same balance
of savage courage and human love that Zarathustra displayed.

Zarathustra's fierce and probing eagle joins the company of
other eagles with a bent for philosophy—the eagle that carried
Saint John to heaven in honor of the sublimity of his gospel and the
eagle Emanuel Swedenborg refers to in a paragraph comparing
different kinds of thinkers to birds:

There are some who the moment they hear a truth perceive that it
is true: and these in the spiritual world are represented by eagles.
There are others who have no perception of truth, but reach con-

clusions by means of confirmation from appearances; and these are represented by singing birds. Others believe a thing to be true because it has been asserted by a man of authority; these are represented by magpies. Finally, there are some who have no desire and no ability to perceive what is true, but only what is false, for the reason that they are in a delusive light, in which falsity appears to be true, and what is true seems either like something overhead concealed in a dense cloud, or like a meteor, or like something false. The thoughts of these are represented by birds of night, and their speech by screech owls.[57]

While Lawrence in *The Plumed Serpent* attempted without much success to revive an old Central American Indian religious symbol, another British author has found in Native American legends of bird-gods inspiration for a remarkable body of poems. In *Crow* and other collections of poetry Ted Hughes develops a significant animal character based in part on the trickster crow of the Tlingit of the Pacific Northwest. It appears that Crow is both the unruly agent of a creator god and himself a perverse Satanic deity who is opposed to his creator and his works. He presides over the dissolution of the world today. Other birds may have dwelt in a beautiful natural environment, but Crow thrives on the refuse of human beings:

> When the eagle soared clear through a dawn distilling emerald
> When the curlew trawled in seadusk through
>   a chime of wineglasses
> When the swallow swooped through a woman's song
>   in a cavern
> And the swift flicked through the breath of a violet.
>
> . . . .
>
> Crow spraddled head-down in the beach-garbage, guzzling
>   a dropped ice-cream.[58]

His origin is the subject of diverse explanations, including one, "Lineage," that places Crow in a biblical line of descent:

> In the beginning was Scream
> Who begat Blood

Who begat Eye
Who begat Wing.

Until we get to Crow, who is begotten of "Nothing" and "Never." The Christian elements in the characterization of Crow are always inverted in their emphasis on negativism, blackness, and death. "Examination at the Womb-Door" is a parody of the catechism, in this instance the questioning of Crow at his birth:

Who owns these scrawny little feet? *Death.*
Who owns this bristly scorched-looking face? *Death.*

. . . .

Who is stronger than hope? *Death.*
Who is stronger than the will? *Death.*
Stronger than love? *Death.*
Stronger than life? *Death.*
But who is stronger than death?
　　　Me, evidently.
Pass, Crow.

"King of Carrion" employs a familiar repetitive form—this one reminiscent of the Psalms—to describe the ultimate desolation of Crow's kingdom:

His palace is of skulls.

His crown is the last splinters
Of the vessel of life.
His throne is the scaffold of bones, the hanged thing's
Rack and final stretcher.

His robe is the black of the last blood.

His kingdom is empty.
　　　(*Crow*, 81)

The ugliness and nihilism of Hughe's *Crow,* accented by Leonard Baskin's macabre drawings that accompany the text, are uncompromising. Another of his poems about an avian deity, however, stands quite apart from his characterization of Crow. "Hawk

Roosting" again presents a cruel and remorseless bird, except that this bird makes a sympathetic impression, perhaps because it is a hawk and speaks in a series of strongly affirmative statements.

> I sit in the top of the wood, my eyes closed.
> Inaction, no falsifying dream
> Between my hooked head and hooked feet:
> Or in sleep rehearse perfect kills and eat.
>
> The convenience of the high trees!
> The air's buoyancy and the sun's ray
> Are of advantage to me;
> And the earth's face upward for my inspection.
>
> My feet are locked upon the rough bark.
> It took the whole of Creation
> To produce my foot, my each feather:
> Now I hold Creation in my foot
>
> Or fly up, and revolve it all slowly—
> I kill where I please because it is all mine.
> There is no sophistry in my body:
> My manners are tearing off heads—
>
> The allotment of death.
> For the one path of my flight is direct
> Through the bones of the living.
> No arguments assert my right:
>
> The sun is behind me.
> Nothing has changed since I began.
> My eye has permitted no change.
> I am going to keep things like this.[59]

Hughes's hawk-god is but one of many in modern literature, all owing a little to Nietzsche's eagle that looks into the abyss of a cruel and remorseless nature. Certainly another is Robinson Jeffers's collection of godlike raptors, "all fierce, all flesh-eaters." His falcon in "Rock and Hawk" is frankly offered as a replacement for Christ and his Church:

I think, here is your emblem
To hang in the future sky;
Not the cross, not the hive,

But this bright power, dark peace;
Fierce consciousness joined with final
Disinterestedness.
                    (*Rock and Hawk*, 167)

The "unsocial birds," he asserts in "The Caged Eagle's Death Dream," are a "greater race" than humans, who are "sieves leaking desire." In "Hurt Hawks" he declares, "I'd sooner . . . kill a man than a hawk." "Give your heart to the hawks," he advises in the long narrative poem of that name, because the state is "only a herd of people." In "People and a Heron," he writes that "a lone bird was dearer to me than many people." Immortality is to be won by being eaten by a vulture,

     To be eaten by that beak and
       become a part of him, to share those wings and those eyes—
     What a sublime end of one's body, what an enskyment,
       what a life after death.
                    ("Vulture," 288)

In "Shiva" Jeffers reflects the same principle of destruction and regeneration that so intrigued Lawrence and Yeats in their imagery of the swan. A hawk representing the Hindu god Siva destroys the world—"picks out the stars' eyes," kills "the white swan of the beauty of things"—and then begins to hatch a new world. Only in one of his latest poems, "The Beginning and the End," does Jeffers retreat a little from the barbaric extreme to which his primitivism carried him when he admits that one day we may surpass the hawk by reason of our minds.

Robert Penn Warren also tries his hand with the image of the hawk-god. In "Red-Tail Hawk and the Pyre of Youth," a young boy sights the distant approach of a hawk:

Except for the center of
That convex perfection, not yet
A dot even, nameless, no color, merely

> A shadowy vortex of silver. Then,
> In widening circles—oh, nearer!
> And suddenly I knew the name, and saw,
> As though seeing, it come toward me,
> Unforgiving, the hot blood of the air:
> Gold eyes, unforgiving, for they, like God, see all.

On his deathbed he prays that

> I'll again see the first small silvery swirl
> Spin outward and downward from sky-height
> To bring me the truth in blood-marriage of earth and air—
> And all will be as it was
> In that paradox of unjoyful joyousness.
>   (146–50)

The flight of the bird brings him that all-important awareness of the union of heaven and earth that we have seen in Yeats's "Leda and the Swan" and Lawrence's *Plumed Serpent.*

Warren mitigates somewhat the terror of the modern hawk-god. Wallace Stevens uses the image for satirical purposes in "The Bird with the Coppery, Keen Claws," a poem made difficult by a number of obscure puns, starting with the very first stanza:

> Above the forest of the parakeets,
> A parakeet of parakeets prevails,
> A pip of life amid a mort of tails.
>   (82)

The parakeet is the Holy Spirit (Paraclete) but without the powerful creative force of the dove in Christian symbology. This bird emits but a chirp ("pip") among mortals ("mort of tails"), or, to render another meaning for the same line, the parakeet is impotent in the midst of impotence. He is blind and "broods," but not in the sense of Milton's dove incubating the world; rather he "munches a dry shell" as he sits still "in the sun-pallor of his rock."[60]

Serious and even bitter attacks on Christian dogma are made by Ted Hughes, whose Crow presides over the destruction of God's creation, and Stevens, whose powerless parakeet replaces the miracle-working dove. Quite a different view of the Judeo-

Christian tradition is presented in *Solomon Gursky Was Here*, a novel by Mordecai Richler, who produces a delightfully comic effect with materials like those used by Hughes, Native American myths of a trickster raven. True, this bird-god "has an unquenchable itch to meddle and provoke things, to play tricks on the world and its creatures," and some of his exploits may seem rather bloodthirsty, such as misleading some Eskimos to build their igloos under a cliff and then causing an avalanche of snow to bury them: "The trusting inhabitants were buried, never to waken again. The raven waited for spring. Then, when the snows melted, revealing the bodies of the unfortunate people, he amused himself emptying their eye sockets. According to legend, the raven did not lack for tasty provisions well into summer." But the pranks of Tulugaq are hilarious, not heinous, and quite in accord with the audacious opportunism of the Gursky family. Its first member in North America is Ephraim, who is deported from England as a criminal and yet is clever enough to become a member of Sir John Franklin's 1845–46 Arctic voyage to discover the Northwest Passage. The sole survivor of the ill-fated expedition, Ephraim manages to win the confidence of Eskimos from King William Island, whom he organizes into the Church of the Millenarians, a religious cult mixing native Haida myths with Jewish ritual. Ephraim is their shaman, wearing both a tallith and a clerical collar, and enjoying supernatural powers, as well as the favors of the women of his sect, by virtue of his identificaiton with the raven-god. Eventually his powers are passed on to his grandson, Solomon, who evinces for his suffering fellows more sympathy than his conniving grandfather ever did. On one occasion he calls upon the raven to lead a group of starving Chinese to safety during the famous Long March of 1935: "Just before the appearance of the big black bird Solomon had tramped up and down, searching the skies, some sort of sad clacking noise, an inhuman call, coming from the back of his throat." After Solomon is presumed dead in the crash of his private aircraft, the plane buzzes the home of his biographer, Moses Berger, who "believed that he saw it turn into a big menacing black bird." Moses suspects that Solomon is still alive and could be found "in the Gulag or a stadium in Latin America," wherever, echoing Job 39.30 "ravens would have gathered."[61] From Solomon the power of the raven will devolve on his grandson, Isaac, who like his great-great-grandfather, Ephraim, is suspected of having practiced cannibalism on a journey to the far north.

In an age divided by skepticism at one extreme and religious fundamentalism at the other, the revival of bird-gods in literature has given some writers an opportunity to occupy a kind of middle ground on which to display a variety of basically religious images and feelings that are certainly worth preserving. The bird is well suited to this sort of imaginative endeavor because it lends itself so readily to both the distance and the nearness divinity requires.

Birds Caged, Hunted, and Killed

o n e . Pet Birds

The great affection people have for birds makes them favored as pets. Their value as food and ornamentation subjects them to severe economic exploitation, and their elusiveness in flight makes them exceptionally challenging targets for sport hunters. Little is ever said about the practical uses birds have, but literature has had much to say about the treatment of birds as pets and objects of sport.

The problem with making pets of birds is that most species, especially those valued for their singing, cannot be wholly tamed either by training or breeding and consequently must be kept under restraint of some sort. The practice of keeping caged birds is worldwide and goes far back into antiquity as evidenced in the art of ancient Egypt and Greece. By the first century A.D. it was fashionable for wealthy Romans to maintain an aviary in their homes. The most famous *ornithon* measured forty-eight by seventy-two feet and was constructed at the villa of the writer Varro in Casinum.[1] According to Pliny "our practice of imprisoning within bars living creatures to which Nature had assigned the open sky" was begun by the historian Marcus Laenius Strabo. With mounting disgust Pliny reports that a nightingale famous for its singing and priced at 600,000 serteces was given as a gift to Agrippina, the consort of the emperor Claudius, and that the actor Clodius Aesop liked to dine on pet birds that "sang some particular song or talked with human speech" (10.141).

Pliny's concern for animals was rather unusual for his time and anticipates by almost two thousand years the widespread sentiment against keeping caged birds. From ancient times through the Renaissance there was no particular outcry, though there were exceptions, of course. Saint Francis released doves in the market square of Sienna, and Leonardo da Vinci is reported by Vasari to have made a frequent practice of buying birds at the market and immediately releasing them. Chaucer, who took such delight in birds, paints this affecting picture of the caged bird in *The Canterbury Tales:*

> Taak any bryd, and put it in a cage,
> And do al thyn entente and thy corage
> To fostre it tendrely with mete and drynke
> Of alle deyntees that thou kanst bithynke,
> And keep it al so clenly as thou may,
> Although his cage of gold be never so gay,
> Yet hath this brid, by twenty thousand foold,
> Levere in a forest, that is rude and coold,
> Goon ete wormes and swich wrecchednesse.
> For evere this brid wol doon his bisynesse
> To escape out of his cage, yif he may.
> His libertee this brid desireth ay.
>   (The Manciple's Tale, lines 163–74)

The passage is substantially repeated in The Squire's Tale and ultimately derives from *The Consolation of Philosophy*, a work by Boethius that Chaucer himself had translated. Like Pliny, Boethius disapproved of keeping birds in a "streyt cage" on the philosophical principle that "alle thynges seken ayen to hir propre cours, and alle thynges rejoysen hem of hit retournynge ayen to his nature" (book 3).

The great turning point in attitudes about keeping wild pets occurred in the late eighteenth and early nineteenth centuries when the romantic movement in art and literature began to reemphasize the close relation of man to nature, not nature in the abstract but nature as it is experienced through the senses. To this end nothing would serve but the emotional identification of the sensitive poet with all natural phenomena, both animate and inanimate, with earth, sky, water, and with all forms of plant and animal life. Inevitably, in this process human desires and aspirations, such as the right of individuals to fulfill themselves freely, were read into animal behavior. To romantic sensibilities the caging of birds was particularly offensive because the power of flight had grown to be such a powerful symbol of freedom that to deny a bird flight seemed the grossest violation of both nature and philosophical principle. Among romantic poets the plight of a captive bird became a common metaphor for any restraint imposed upon a person's freedom. Living in a city was considered comparable to being caged since it denied one the benefit of close contact with nature.

Romantic writers objected to tampering with nature or removing a wild creature from its habitat on grounds we would now call ecological. In "Each and All" Emerson proves that he had the feeling if not the scientific knowledge of environmental integrity:

> I thought the sparrow's note from heaven,
> Singing at dawn from the alder bough;
> I brought him home, in his nest, at even;
> He sings the song, but it cheers not now,
> For I did not bring home the river and the sky;—
> He sang to my ear,—they sang to my eye.
>
> (14)

In similar fashion Elizabeth Barrett Browning writes of the sea mew dying when it is taken from the sea to its prison in a "grassy place." To satisfy ecological requirements the collector would have to go to the same trouble as Sir John Mandeville's Mongolian conqueror, who, in Saint-John Perse's words, "brought back with bird and nest and song the whole natal tree itself, torn from its place with its multitude of roots, its ball of earth and its border of soil, a remnant of home territory evoking a field, a province, a country, and an empire" ("Oiseaux," no. 3).

One of the earliest and most famous outcries against the practice of keeping caged birds was William Blake's in "Auguries of Innocence":

> A Robin Red breast in a Cage
> Puts all Heaven in a Rage.
> A dove house fill'd with doves & Pigeons
> Shudders Hell thro' all its regions.
>
> .   .   .   .
>
> A Skylark wounded in the wing,
> A Cherubim does cease to sing.
>
> .   .   .   .
>
> He who shall hurt the little Wren
> Shall never be belov'd by Men.

Ever since he wrote this in 1803, Blake's sentiment and even his wording have echoed in English poetry, as for example in this from Emily Dickinson:

> to be
> Assassin of a Bird
> Resembles to my outraged mind
> The firing in Heaven,
> On Angels—squandering for you
> Their Miracles of Tune—
> (no. 1102)

Among those violently opposed to keeping caged birds was Thomas Hardy, who took the trouble to register his protest in a letter to the *Times* of December 19, 1913: "The assertion that a caged skylark experiences none of the misery of caged man makes demands upon our credulity. . . . It seems marvellous that the 20th century, with all its rhetoric on morality, should tolerate such useless inflictions as making animals do what is unnatural to them or drag out an unnatural life in a wired cell."[2] In "The Bird-Catcher's Boy" a man who makes his living trapping larks and nightingales suffers terrible retribution when his son runs away from home to avoid following his father's trade and dies at sea. In "The Blinded Bird" Hardy was able to bring himself to write about the incredibly cruel practice of blinding caged birds with a red-hot needle in order to make them sing more. The poem closes with the suggestion that an abused bird may meet the high standard of charity set by Saint Paul in 1 Corinthians 13:

> Who hath charity? This bird.
> Who suffereth long and is kind,
> Is not provoked, though blind
> And alive ensepulchred?
> Who hopeth, endureth all things?
> Who thinketh no evil, but sings?
> Who is divine? This bird.
>
> (446)

Some writers have been able to find extenuating circumstances for keeping caged birds: imprisonment may strengthen the spirit of the captive bird and by example the human spirit. Mrs. Browning's doves adjust to their "city prison," the bird in Hardy's "Blinded Bird" sings "zestfully" without resenting the wrong done to him, and Coleridge's lark in "La Fayette" rejoices that other birds are free in spite of his own pitiable state:

> He bathes no pinion in the dewy light,
>   No father's joy, no lover's bliss he shares
>   Yet still the rising radiance cheers his sight—
> His fellows' freedom soothes the captive's cares!
>
> (82)

And so the imprisoned Marquis de La Fayette shall "mock with raptures high the dungeon's might" when the cause of freedom for which he fought shall one day triumph in his own country. The title of Maya Angelou's first novel, *I Know Why the Caged Bird Sings*—derived from the last line of Paul Laurence Dunbar's "Sympathy"—is explained in the dedication as a reference to black poets, "all the strong black birds of promise who defy the odds and gods and sing their songs," the songs that helped to sustain African Americans in their struggle for equality.[3] Perhaps the last best word on this theme is Marianne Moore's in "What Are Years?" that one can only make the best use of the inevitable restrictions faced by both humans and birds.

He
sees deep and is glad, who
   accedes to mortality
and in his imprisonment rises
upon himself as
the sea in a chasm, struggling to be
free and unable to be,
    in its surrendering
    finds its continuing.

So he who strongly feels,
behaves. The very bird,
   grown taller as he sings, steels
his form straight up. Though he is captive,
his mighty singing
says, satisfaction is a lowly
thing, how pure a thing is joy.
    This is mortality,
    this is eternity.
      (105–6)

The sentimental romantic objection to keeping caged birds still persists and even finds scientific corroboration among ornithologists who warn that taking wild animals for pets will hasten the extinction of some species. The nightingale and goldfinch were almost exterminated in England because they were so popular as cage birds, the nightingale as far back as Elizabethan times. Francis Willughby's *Ornithology,* in 1678 one of the earliest European scientific writings on birds, devotes considerably more space to the care of the captive nightingale than to the bird in the wild. In America the indigo bunting and painted bunting were decimated. Nevertheless, while sympathy for caged birds has inspired some impassioned poetry, it does not necessarily change people's tastes. In spite of the entreaties of poets, the general public has never seen anything reprehensible in keeping wild animals captive. Even during the height of the romantic era, the practice of keeping cage birds was so popular in Europe that it supported many editions, in several languages, of G. M. Bechstein's *Natürgeschichte der Hof-und-Stubenvögel* (1795). Between 1812 and 1895 there were at least twenty-seven English translations of this work, the most popular being one by H. G. Adams, *Cage and Chamber-Birds: Their Natural History, Habits, Food, Diseases, Management, and Modes of Capture.*

There remains to this day a clear difference of opinion between well-meaning people on the subject of keeping cage birds, and, for that matter, between different moods of the same person. In "The Caged Bird" May Sarton expresses the embarrassment of people whose friends have a pet bird:

> He was there in my room,
> A wild bird in a cage,
> But I was a guest and not for me
> To open the gate and set him free
> However great my gloom
> And unrepenting rage.

In "A Parrot," however, Sarton admits to having a cage bird herself and claims he is content with his life except when he sees wild birds outside the house.[4]

People who see nothing wrong in keeping pet birds may defend themselves from the charge of insensitivity with the argument that it is hardly reasonable to assume that a bird feels the way humans do about restrictions upon its freedom of movement. They may also question the assumption that birds are altogether free and "happy" in a natural environment where the law of the survival of the fittest must appear from a human perspective to be quite cruel. Thoreau observes in the "Tuesday" section of *A Week on the Concord and Merrimack Rivers* that "Nature herself has not provided the most graceful end for her creatures. What becomes of all these birds that people the air and forest for our solacement? . . . We do not see their bodies lie about. Yet there is a tragedy at the end of each one of their lives. They must perish miserably" (165). Only recently have field studies documented the heavy toll exacted on birds by natural conditions of weather, disease, predation, and fluctuating food supply. In her summary of these studies Sally Carrighar states that "most birds live to only a tenth of their possible lifetimes."[5] One activity that appears to be so charming, the care of the young, is so terribly onerous that many parent birds die

from exhaustion in their efforts to bring in enough food (475 feed-
ings a day for a pair of titmice, 1,000 caterpillars a day for a pair of
English robins), and as a result the undernourished nestlings die
of starvation and predation. There is some kind of inconsistency in
assuming that it is permissible to use all the means at our disposal
to rescue humans but not animals from the operation of the law
of the survival of the fittest. In countries where vast numbers of
birds are slaughtered for much-needed food, as in China, it is no
wonder that keeping a pet bird is considered an act of the greatest
kindness.

Konrad Lorenz, the distinguished zoologist and pioneer in the
science of ethology, condones keeping wild animals under restraint, if not in cages, for two worthy purposes: it provides an
opportunity to make close scientific observations of animal behavior, as he himself did so well in his study of the greylag goose,
and it may awaken in the lay person a deeper understanding of
nature. He feels that William Blake's objection "need not be taken
too seriously," pointing out that many males in the wild do not
find mates and are not distressed but continue to sing, just as
"the singly kept male songbird does not suffer, nor is his song
the expression of sorrow and desire, as sentimental people like to
believe."[6]

Lastly, there is something to be said for the desire that some
people have to enjoy a closer contact with a wild creature than a
state of nature can afford. Richard Wilbur takes account of their
motivation in "Marché aux Oiseaux": on the one hand there is the
ancient and profitable business of marketing pet birds—

> Here are the silver-bill, the orange-cheek,
> The perroquet, the dainty coral-beak
> Stacked in their cages—

but on the other hand there are the buyers, who are driven by
"their termless hunt for love":

> Here are the old, the ill, the imperial child;
> The lonely people, desperate and mild;
> The ugly; past these faces one can read
> The tyranny of one outrageous need.

(296)

Their need to love some creature small and defenseless enough to be kept nearby is "outrageous" but understandable, especially in an age of such extensive urbanization that normal contact with wild animals is quite rare for a great number of people. Unfortunately, few can live like Thoreau in the woods where he built his simple abode: "I found myself suddenly neighbor to the birds; not by having imprisoned one, but having caged myself near them." Even those living in the countryside may not have access to wildlife. Early photographs of many sod houses in which the first American settlers lived on the bleak and treeless Great Plains reveal canary cages "hanging under the eaves and porches."[7]

Since the pet bird must someday die, escape, or fall victim to an accident, it follows that mourning for a deceased bird is a frequent theme in poetry dealing with caged birds. The earliest examples are from Catullus, the first of whose two famous bird poems, "*Passer, deliciae meae puellae,*" celebrates his sweetheart's pet sparrow; the second, "*Lugete, o Veneres Cupidinesque,*" mourns its passing. It was inevitable, given the subject, that the slight suggestion of a mock-heroic tone in Catullus should be greatly elaborated by Ovid in a poem mourning the death of a pet parrot. As Peter Green points out in the notes of his translation of *Amores*, Ovid's poem is "a detailed parody of the *epicedion*, or commemorative dirge," in classical literature. It begins with a call to mourners:

> Parrot, that feathered mimic from India's dawnlands,
>   Is dead. Come flocking, birds,
> To his funeral: come, all you godfearing airborne
>   Creatures, beat breasts with wings,
> Mourn, claw your polls, tear out soft feathers (your hair) and
>   Pipe high your sad lament.

There follows praise of the dead:

> So green his feathers, they dimmed the cut emerald; scarlet
>   His beak, with saffron spots.
> No bird on earth could copy a voice more closely
>   Or sound so articulate.

Some consolation is found in the assurance that Polly is now in a place where all good birds go:

> Beneath a hill in Elysium, where dark ilex clusters
>   And the moist earth is for ever green,
> There exists—or so I have heard—the pious fowls' heaven
>   (All ill-omened predators barred).
> Harmless swans roam after food, there dwells the phoenix,
>   That long-lived, ever-solitary bird;
> There Juno's peacock spreads out his splendid fantail
>   Amid the billing and cooing of amorous doves;
> And there, in this woodland haven, the feathered faithful
>   Welcome Parrot, flock round to hear him talk.

In the spirit of Ovid, Dorothy Parker imagines what the real girl-friend of Catullus may have felt about her poet-friend's reflections on a dead bird:

> That thing he wrote, the time the sparrow died—
>   (Oh, most unpleasant—gloomy, tedious words!)
> I called it sweet, and made believe I cried;
> The stupid fool! I've always hated birds.[8]

A Christian form of mourning is used by John Skelton in "Philip Sparrow," an early sixteenth-century poem, which E. M. Forster is certainly right in calling the "pleasantest Skelton ever wrote." A young girl at a convent school consoles herself over the death of her pet sparrow by expressing her grief in a form modeled after the vesper service for the dead. Skelton's parody, though, is a gentle one, for Jane Scrope is quite innocent in assuming that her pet bird has a soul that may be mourned, just as the simple Félicité of Flaubert confuses her parrot with the dove of the Holy Spirit. The poem begins with the customary "Pla-ce-bo" and then goes on to a prayer for the deceased:

> For the soul of Philip Sparrow,
> That was late slain at Carrow
> Among the Nunes Black.
> For that sweet soules sake
> And for all sparrows' souls
> Set in our beadrolls,
> *Pater noster qui*
> With an *Ave Mari,*

> And with the corner of a Creed,
> The more shall be your meed.

Jane's lament goes on for more than eight hundred lines. It seems that Gib the cat did the foul deed:

> Caught Philip by the head,
> And slew him there stark dead.
>> *Kyrie, eleison,*
>> *Christe, eleison,*
>> *Kyrie, eleison!*

Following the classical form of the elegy, Jane calls for mourners from the bird world to participate in a kind of requiem mass:

> To wepe with me look that ye come,
> All maner of birdes in your kind.

About seventy-five species are named:

> The woodcock with the longe nose;
> The throstle with her warbling;
> The starling with her brabling;
> The rook, with the osprey
> That putteth fishes to a fray;
> And the dainty curlew,
> With the turtle most true.[9]

Throughout the Renaissance and well into the nineteenth century, the elegy for the deceased pet bird supported a minor subgenre of poetry, bearing such titles as "On the Death of Mrs. Throckmorton's Bulfinch" by William Cowper and "Epitaph on a Robin Redbreast" by Samuel Rogers. The sentimentality of the theme is satirized in *The Adventures of Huckleberry Finn* in Mark Twain's account of the Grangerfords, a family whose womenfolk shed copious tears as a kind of compensation for the blood shed by their feuding menfolk. On the walls of their home are displayed the black crayon drawings of one of the daughters: "Another one was a young lady with her hair all combed up straight to the top of her head, and knotted there in front of a comb like a chair-back, and she was crying into a handkerchief and had a dead bird laying on its back in her other hand with its heels up, and underneath the picture it said 'I Shall Never Hear Thy Sweet Chirrup More Alas!' " (chap. 17).

two. Birds Trapped and Hunted

Before successful methods of breeding wild birds were developed, trapping and nest robbing supplied markets with pet birds and fowl for food. While Plato rejected trapping as a "lazy contrivance" for the true hunter (*Laws* 7.824a), many writers have been fascinated with the various ways to trap animals, perhaps because the devices could be readily used in metaphors comparing the plight of trapped animals to human beings caught in some sort of desperate situation. Aristophanes mentions four bird traps—nets, nooses, limed twigs, decoy-baited cages—in *The Birds*; Shakespeare also names four—net, lime, pitfall, and gin [trap]—in *Macbeth* (4.2.34–35). In the Bible there are seven kinds of bird traps in over a hundred animal-trap images, many of these, as we have noted before, being used to compare sinners to birds that run the risk of being trapped. It is not surprising that half of the avian imagery in Milton, a writer fairly saturated with the Bible, has to do with snaring birds.[10]

The noose, or snare, consists of a length of animal hair or thread looped at one end and secured to a fixed object at the other end; it is then set in a place where grain has been spread in the hope that a bird will get its foot or head caught in it. Ancient wall paintings picture nets of various designs that were used by the Egyptians as early as 2000 B.C. to catch vast numbers of waterfowl for food and pets. Both the net and the noose are used in one of the earliest and most moving images of bird traps, Homer's epic simile at the close of the *Odyssey* comparing the mass hanging of the false maiden servants to the capture and killing of birds:

> As when either thrushes with their long wings or doves
> Rush into a net that has been set in a thicket,
> As they come to roost, and a dreadful bed takes them in;
> So they held their heads in a row, and about the necks

Of all there were nooses, that they might die most piteously
They struggled a little with their feet, but not very long.[11]

Liming—spreading a sticky substance on tree branches—is
another method of trapping birds often used in poetic imagery, the
most famous instance being from the soliloquy of Claudius when
he tries to repent for the murder of his brother in *Hamlet:* "O limèd
soul, that struggling to be free / Art more engaged!"

Trapping wild animals has always been the farmer's solution to
the problem of protecting crops from depredation. We learn of a
Roman technique by way of a comic passage in the play *Asinaria*
by Plautus in which a character compares his method of attracting
lovers to the fowler's use of nets to capture birds:

> They choose a place and scatter first the grain,
> For you must spend ere you can hope to gain.
> The birds become familiar with the spot,
> And eat, and eat—until he gets the lot.
> And so with me. My lodgings will be found
> To take the place of fowlers' trapping ground.
> Girls are my bait, and beds are my decoys;
> The birds I angle for are you bright boys.[12]

In Longfellow's *Song of Hiawatha* we find an interesting description of the methods employed by Native Americans to protect their
cornfields from foraging birds. Minnehaha draws a magic circle
around the field to keep out creatures that approach on the ground,
and the wily Hiawatha finds an answer to the ravens, crows, and
blackbirds that have been laughing at him from the treetops. Before dawn he sets snares throughout the field, and when the "black
marauders" are caught in them as they begin to feed on the corn,
he comes out of hiding and easily despatches them.

> Without mercy he destroyed them,
> Right and left, by tens and twenties,
> And their wretched, lifeless bodies
> Hung aloft on poles for scarecrows
> Round the consecrated cornfields,

As a signal of his vengeance,
As a warning to marauders.

(pt. 13)

There is quite a different outcome, however, when the farmers of Killingworth, in Longfellow's *Tales of a Wayside Inn*, kill all the birds in their fields and orchards: their crops that summer are devoured by insects, who find "no foe to check their march." Next spring the chastened farmers collect as many birds as they can "from all the country round" and turn them loose in their township.

It is curious that falconry, which combines both the caging and the hunting of birds, has escaped censure in literature. This is perhaps because the proud demeanor of raptors used in falconry, their position at the top of the food chain, and their adaptability to the formal hunt have endeared them to privileged classes. Hunting with a trained bird enjoys the special status of a noble sport, but hunting with firearms has received mixed reactions. Of the several passages describing bird hunting in Alexander Pope's "Windsor-Forest," at least one seems to express disapproval:

With slaught'ring Guns th'unweary'd Fowler roves,
When Frosts have whiten'd all the naked Groves;
Where Doves in Flocks the leafless Trees o'ershade,
And lonely Woodcocks haunt the wat'ry Glade.
He lifts the Tube, and levels with his Eye;
Strait a short Thunder breaks the frozen Sky.
Oft, as in Airy Rings they skim the Heath,
The clam'rous Lapwings feel the Leaden Death:
Oft as the mounting Larks their Notes prepare,
They fall, and leave their little Lives in Air.

Sympathy is expressed for the spectacularly plumaged pheasant brought down by a hunter:

See! from the Brake the whirring Pheasant springs,
And mounts exulting on triumphant Wings;
Short is his Joy! he feels the fiery Wound,
Flutters in Blood, and panting beats the Ground.
Ah! what avail his glossie, varying Dyes,

His Purple Crest, and Scarlet-circled Eyes,
The vivid Green his shining Plumes unfold;
His painted Wings, and Breast that flames with Gold?

On the same page, however, Pope compares ("if small Things we may with great compare") the trapping of partridges to British soldiers taking a prized enemy town. The implication is that hunting animals is like war, a "Sylvan War," which in the enlightened time to come will be a fitting substitute for the kind of war that kills people.

The shady Empire shall retain no Trace
Of War or Blood, but in the Sylvan Chace,
The Trumpets sleep, while chearful Horns are blown,
And Arms employ'd on Birds and Beasts alone.[13]

Seventeen years later, in 1730, James Thomson, an early precursor of romanticism, takes an entirely different view in *The Seasons: "Autumn"*:

Oh, let not, aimed from some inhuman eye,
The gun the music of the coming year
Destroy, and harmless, unsuspecting harm,
Lay the weak tribes, a miserable prey,
In mingled murder fluttering on the ground!
(lines 983–87)

By the middle of the nineteenth century feeling against hunting was strong enough to support organizations devoted to its abolition. Yet we cannot attribute this change of heart to romanticism alone; true hunters have great respect for their prey, and there has always been sympathy for birds whose young are destroyed or who themselves are killed while tending their young. Here is Matthew Arnold's affecting description of a family of eagles in *Sohrab and Rustum:*

As when some hunter in the spring hath found
A breeding eagle sitting on her nest,
Upon the craggy isle of a hill-lake,
And pierced her with an arrow as she rose,
And follow'd her to find her where she fell

Far off;—anon her mate comes winging back
From hunting, and a great way off descries
His huddling young left sole; at that, he checks
His pinion, and with short uneasy sweeps
Circles above his eyry, with loud screams
Chiding his mate back to her nest; but she
Lies dying, with the arrow in her side,
In some far stony gorge out of his ken,
A heap of fluttering feathers—never more
Shall the lake glass her, flying over it;
Never the black and dripping precipices
Echo her stormy scream as she sails by—
As that poor bird flies home, nor knows his loss,
So Rustum knew not his own loss, but stood
Over his dying son, and knew him not.

(lines 556–75)

This work was written in 1853 at about the same time Arnold was recalling the ancient story of the nightingale in his poem "Philomela," and it must have given him a good deal of pleasure to honor another legendary bird, the eagle, when he adapted in *Sohrab and Rustum* the material and form of a speech from the fifth-century B.C. drama *Agamemnon* by Aeschylus. The passage in question tells of the departure of the Greek warriors on their exploit to rescue Helen from her Trojan abductors:

and they shouted a great shout, War!
So eagles scream as they circle aloft
on their feathered oars,
high over their nest on a lonely crag,
when the eaglets are stolen away.
And they grieve for their young
and the nest never more to be tended.
But in heaven there is one who hears,
or Pan or Zeus or Apollo,
hears the shrill, screaming cry of the dwellers in air,
and slow-footed vengeance
he sends to those who transgress.[14]

Ancient writers could be just as sensitive about wildlife as those moved by the romantic feelings of the modern era. Ambivalent attitudes about hunting birds have persisted, however, even among those who devote themselves to cultivating in the public a better appreciation of wildlife. John James Audubon loved shooting as much as he did drawing birds. The need to have models for his art justified him, of course, though procuring a "basketful" of Carolina parakeets "with a few shots" does appear excessive, especially since we know that the species became extinct early in this century.[15] We cannot question the need that ornithologists have to gather specimens for scientific examination. In "Higher Laws," a section of *Walden*, Thoreau admits having used a gun to collect specimens, but he gave it up before he went into the woods to live: "I confess that I am now inclined to think that there is a finer way of studying ornithology than this. It requires so much closer attention to the habits of the birds, that, if for that reason only, I have been willing to omit the gun" (385–86). In discovering the "finer way" Thoreau anticipated the present-day emphasis on ethology rather than taxonomy, which requires numbers of animal corpses for study. Emerson probably had the reformed Thoreau in mind when, in "Forbearance," he asks, "Hast thou named all the birds without a gun?" (78); if so, you are his friend, and it must have been after Thoreau had surrendered his gun that Emerson commended his friend's love and knowledge of birds:

> He saw the partridge drum in the woods;
> He heard the woodcock's evening hymn;
> He found the tawny thrush's broods;
> And the shy hawk did wait for him;
> What others did at distance hear,
> And guessed within the thicket's gloom,
> Was showed to this philosopher,
> And at his bidding seemed to come.
> ("Woodnotes," 45)

Before his sojourn at Walden Pond, on a trip with his brother on the Concord and Merrimack rivers, Thoreau describes how he "obtained" a passenger pigeon (also now extinct) that "had lingered too long on its perch and broiled it. . . . It is true it did not seem to be putting this bird to its right use to pluck its feathers, and extract its entrails, and broil its carcass on the coals; but we heroically persevered, nevertheless, waiting for further information" (164). The humor is worthy of Mark Twain. Sometime after Walden Pond, Thoreau found that red-headed woodpeckers were "good to eat," and as late as 1856 he still indulged in the once-popular hobby of collecting birds' eggs. He could admire the construction of a nest—"How well suited the lining of a bird's nest, not only for the comfort of the young, but to keep the eggs from breaking!"—and a few days later throw sticks at a brooding pewee to scare it off its nest.[16]

William Wordsworth in his youth was also a bird hunter and egger, admitting in *The Prelude* that

> 'twas my joy
> With store of springes o'er my shoulder hung
> To range the open heights where woodcocks run
> Along the smooth green.
> (1.309–12)

He made his rounds at night and his "scudding away from snare to snare" seemed to him to disturb the peace of the stars above, though not the birds. He admits to a feeling of guilt only when he steals a bird from another trapper's snare. The final 1850 edition of the poem, however, omits a line from the original 1799 text: "I was a fell destroyer." (In Wordsworth's youth a pair of woodcocks brought sixteen to twenty pence.) As for stealing eggs from a raven's nest high on a rocky ridge,

> though mean
> Our object and inglorious, yet the end
> Was not ignoble.
> (1.328–30)

The noble end Wordsworth had in mind was that each of his boyhood experiences contributed to the "fair seed-time" of his soul, in this case overcoming the fear of falling from the slippery rock he had to climb. The practical end, however, was probably to supply people with a delicacy or to complete some hobbyist's egg collection.

W. H. Hudson, whose books in the early years of the twentieth century were so influential in turning people toward an interest in nature, admits to killing a heron in order to complete his collection of local birds. His rationalization: because the heron had an oversize fish stuck in his bill he concluded that "the bird would never have been able to free himself, and that by shooting him I had only saved him from the torture of a lingering death from starvation." [17] This is of a piece with Huck Finn's tongue-in-cheek confession that he sometimes "lifted a chicken that warn't roosting comfortable."

In defense of what seems to be the calloused attitudes of earlier times, it must be said that when game was plentiful there was little concern about killing wild animals because it was difficult to imagine a time when they would be threatened with extinction. In exculpation of Thoreau we must note that as late as 1868 John Burroughs was still able to report, in "Spring at the Capitol," that red-headed woodpeckers were "more common than the robin." That might also excuse Franklin Delano Roosevelt, whose "Bird Diary" for May 8, 1896, records that he "shot a red-headed woodpecker." Roosevelt was also an avid collector of birds' eggs, a hobby pursued so relentlessly by so many enthusiasts that by 1895 some bird species faced extinction, causing Burroughs to revile collectors as "these human weasels." [18] We must give Thoreau the last word on mankind's ambivalent love and misuse of nature. After dining on the passenger pigeon he had shot on the trip with his brother, he reflected: "We are double-edged blades, and every time we whet our virtue the return stroke straps our vice" (165).

By far the most destructive and least defensible assault upon birds was the industry that supplied attractive feathers for use in ladies' millinery. Before the practice was outlawed in the first decade of the twentieth century, the population of egrets and herons in America was almost exterminated. A native Floridian in Peter Matthiessen's *Killing Mister Watson* describes the slaughter in which he participated but lived to regret, as is the case with so many people who have become sensitive toward wildlife in recent times.

Plume hunters never shot cept in the breeding season when egret plumes are coming out real good. When them nestlings get pretty well pinfeathered, and squawking loud cause they are always hungry, them parent birds lose the little sense God give 'em, they are going to come in to tend their young no matter what, and a man using one of them Flobert rifles that don't snap louder than a twig can stand there under the trees in a big rookery and pick them birds as fast as he can reload.

A broke-up rookery, that ain't a picture you want to think about too much. The pile of carcasses left behind when you strip the plumes and move on to the next place is just pitiful, and it's a piss-poor way to harvest, cause there ain't no adults left to feed them starving young 'uns and protect 'em from the sun and rain, let alone the crows and buzzards that come sailing and flopping in to tear 'em to pieces.[19]

As distinguished from the commercial, playful, or merely thoughtless killing of animals, the hunting of birds for sport has often been regarded as an abuse of class privilege. John Ruskin was among those who never missed an opportunity to scold the English aristocracy for its devotion to the ceremonial hunt. "It is fast becoming the only definition of aristocracy that the principal business of its life is the killing of sparrows," he declared in a lecture at Oxford; "no English gentleman in recent times has ever thought of birds except as flying targets, or flavourous dishes" (25:18–19).[20] Thomas Hardy, who was as much opposed to the hunting as to the caging of birds, was also thinking of the gentry when in "The Puzzled Game-Birds" he imagines the dismay of carefully raised game birds as they are being shot down:

> They are not those who used to feed us
> When we were young—they cannot be—
> These shapes that now bereave and bleed us?
> They are not those who used to feed us.
>
> (148)

The poem was occasioned by a battue (beating bushes to flush game in the direction of the shooters) in which 700 pheasants were killed in a single day and 150 left to die in the bush. The

horror of it remained with Hardy, for nine years later the heroine of *Tess of the D'Urbervilles* comes upon a number of wounded
pheasants the hunters had left behind: "Some were dead, some
feebly twitching a wing, some staring up at the sky, some pulsating
quickly, some contorted, some stretched out—all of them writhing in agony, except the fortunate ones whose tortures had ended
during the night by the inability of nature to bear more" (354).
The hunters were "quite civil persons save during certain weeks
of autumn and winter" when they go about "looking over hedges,
or peering through bushes, and pointing their guns, strangely ac-
coutred, a bloodthirsty light in their eyes." Though Tess does not
make the connection, the reader realizes that she has been abused
and abandoned by men in the same way as the birds.

The politics of the Bolshevik Revolution are underscored by a
battue-style bird hunt in Rebecca West's *Birds Fall Down*. Much
to the horror of his granddaughter, Count Nikolai, an emigré who
was once in charge of the Russian security police, tells how Russian
aristocrats hunted woodcocks at the very time when the birds were
so intent on their elaborate mating ritual that they were unaware
of their danger. For the count the image of the hunt represents the
murderous struggle between the Tsarist government and the revolutionaries. One system, the mating ritual of woodcocks, "perfect
in itself, and exquisitely ingenious, is destroyed at the very moment when it is implementing its perfection, by another system,
just as perfect and ingenious," the methods and technology man
has devised for hunting wildfowl.[21] From the count's philosophical point of view the conflict is like the cosmic clash of galaxies
that are "simply being what they are, by their mass, their momen-
tum. . . . The galaxies may be only birds, whom we think fixed in
the sky but which are falling through it at the slow pace of a larger
time, while hunters to whom the universe is not knee-high level at
them with guns that were loaded outside infinity." From a political
point of view the woodcock hunt represents the murderous battle
between government agents and terrorists that forms the subject
of the novel.

An elaborate battue is the subject of a fine novel by Isabel Colegate, *The Shooting Party*, in which an upper-class hunt serves as
the symbol of an era that is passing. The title is used advisedly,

for in this kind of affair the participants do not track or stalk the prey but simply shoot at game that a small army of beaters has been busy flushing into the range of fire. On the last day of the weekend party held by Sir Randolph Nettleby on his Oxfordshire estate, the count of pheasants shot by his guests reaches over five hundred even before the last drive. The sport is deemed excellent, though it has a fatal flaw that goes uncorrected: one of the shooters wants to show off his prowess before the married woman he is attempting to seduce, and, against all shooting etiquette, he initiates a competition with the party's acknowledged champion shooter. The contest in killing the greatest number of birds has the desired effect: "Lionel, his sense of glory endowing him with an extraordinary alertness, shot with complete carelessness and complete accuracy, Olivia beside him in what seemed to her a column of divine flame, hardly noticing the noise or the smell of cordite or the shouts and cries of the beaters or the continual thumps of birds falling dead on the grass round her. She was absorbed in the wonder and amazement of her discovery, deaf to everything except the soundless shout of triumphant love."[22] Spurred on by the ungentlemanly competition and his hatred of the younger man for his looks and his good fortune in love, the expert shooter, to increase his count, fires at a low-flying woodcock and accidentally kills one of the beaters.

The tragic outcome has it ironies: the champion shooter gets a reputation as a "dangerous shot" and moves to Kenya; the unfortunate beater was a known poacher, not a shooter but a true hunter taking game for his pot; the young lover is killed two years later in World War I, and Sir Randolph's estate is turned into a wartime convalescent home for wounded soldiers. Another victim of the ill-fated hunt is Cornelius Cardew, a perpetual supporter of lost causes, who walks all the way from Oxford so that he might appear in the middle of the proceedings and display a sign reading THOU SHALT NOT KILL. The death of the beater is such a shock to this idealist that he begins to despair of making people recognize the absurdity of some of their traditional activities, and two months later he joins a monastic order—"became more cheerful and even grew fat."

Only Sir Randolph's ten-year-old grandson Osbert remains unscathed. During the hunt his pet mallard escapes, and the boy spends all day frantically searching for it, fearing that it may be shot by the hunters when at the end of the day, according to custom, they are invited to "take the duck" on the river running through the estate. Because of the accident the shooters do not go for the ducks, and Osbert retrieves his pet, tired but unharmed. The boy's concern for his duck draws this comment from one of the guests: "He will have to be educated and taught the ways of the world and made to be on the side of the guns, and against the ducks." Only Osbert and Cardew are truly opposed to the killing of birds, the only ones who have an interest in nongame birds. As he approaches the scene of the battue, Cardew observes the birds with an appreciative eye:

> As he strode along he noticed with pleasure the small flurries
> of finches among the hawthorn berries in the hedge, and the flash
> of a yellowhammer darting ahead of him; he had time to notice a
> tiny wren making her way along the inside of the hedge towards
> a pleasant tangle of bramble, hawthorn and dogrose in which
> several blue tits were already finding nourishment; a pair of mag-
> pies were churring at each other (or at him) in the field just over
> the hedge, and the rooks in the tall elms by the gates of the park
> were settling back into the branches from which the shooting had
> earlier disturbed them. (89)

Just after this pleasant spectacle, however, he comes upon one of the gamekeeper's "gibbets," a contraption made of rails on which are suspended the corpses of mammals and birds that had been slaughtered to protect the precious pheasants' eggs and chicks from would-be predators.

> The topmost rail held a row of small mammals, some of them
> hardly more than a leaf-like shape of dried skin or a bedraggled
> tail. . . . Below these were the black feathers and evil beaks of
> crows, magpies with their tail feathers gone and a couple of
> brightly colored jays which could not have been there for more
> than a day or two. Below again came the multifariously speckled
> feathers of kestrels and sparrow hawks, miniscule and soft on their
> breasts, long and curved for swiftness of flight on their wings, their

fine-boned heads mostly skeletal, eye sockets void; and beneath them hung the owls, three tawny owls and a barn owl, wings hanging open, swaying from time to time as the breeze touched them.   (90)

Anton Chekhov's similarly titled *The Shooting Party*, written in 1894, also ends tragically when a young woman, who has been debauched by the local count and the local magistrate, his drinking companion, is killed by the latter in a fit of jealousy or what he is pleased to call "a state of aberration." Death is by strangulation, the same method he used earlier to end the suffering of a wounded woodcock.

On a trip to Britain in 1929 Robinson Jeffers witnessed an English-style hunt and recorded his reaction in a poem, "Shooting Season," with the same point as Chekhov's and Colegate's respecting the sad deterioration of the upper class as it is evidenced in the hunt:

> The whole countryside deployed on the hills of heather, an
> army with banners,
> The beaters whoop the grouse to the butts.
> Three gentlemen fling up their guns and the frightened covey is
> a few wings fewer;
> Then grooms approach with the panniered horses.

The scene, as in Colegate's novel, is an old battleground, and the soldiers buried there speak:

> We dead that handled weapons and hunted in earnest, we old
> dead have watched
> Three little living gentlemen yonder
> With a bitter flavor in the grin of amusement, uneasily
> remembering our own
> Old sports and delights. It is better to be dust.[23]

A respectable defense of the individual hunter can be made, however, even in a time of diminishing wildlife. The expert hunter's considerable knowledge of animals and their habitats often inspires as much concern as the professional conservationist's for preserving wildlife. Thoreau attributed his "closest acquaintance with Nature" to hunting in his youth. Writers who still find favor in hunting draw upon the long literary tradition that portrays the hunt as an honorable trial of manly prowess and character, often resulting in momentous consequences for one or more of the participants. Ernest Hemingway did much to revive the theme of the hunt in twentieth-century writing—one of the elements in his writing that led Gertrude Stein to observe that he had too much of the "antique" in him. *Across the River and into the Trees* begins and ends with a scene in which Colonel Cantwell goes on his last duck hunt before his impending death. It is therefore important that the hunt should go well for him, but it starts badly, with the lagoon around his blind frozen and his Italian boatman acting sullen and uncooperative. The hunt ends well, however, as we return to it at the close of the novel by way of the colonel's recollections. In spite of the poor conditions the colonel brings down four ducks; the boatman commends him for his expert shooting and accepts the proffered wine at the end of the hunt. The boatman's earlier behavior is honorably accounted for: he reacts hostilely toward anyone wearing the Allied uniform because his wife and daughter had been raped by Allied soldiers. This makes him a war casualty like the colonel. The mildly successful outcome of the morning's hunt is enough to restore Cantwell's self-esteem. The beauty of the ducks he kills puts him in mind of Renata, the woman in Venice he has come to see for the last time: "I'd like to give her a vest made of the whole plumage the way the old Mexicans used to ornament their gods. . . . It could be beautiful . . . with Mallard drake skins for the back and sprig for the front with two longitudinal stripes of teal. One coming down over each breast."[24] The duck hunt is the last pleasant memory Colonel Cantwell enjoys before his death in the back seat of his command car. Shooting ducks and making love to a beautiful woman serve a purpose that is extremely important for the Hemingway hero: to help keep him from thinking about war and his imminent death.

In *The Heron* Giorgio Bassani makes a hunting episode like Hemingway's the central incident of his novel. The scene is again a marsh near Venice, and the hunter, Edgardo Limentano, is a war veteran suffering from postwar malaise. His guide, Gavino, is scornful of his client's prowess and resentful of his being a landowner. Edgardo never gets off a single shot, and he is further humiliated when he is forced to accept the forty ducks Gavino bags. Most of his time in the duck blind is spent watching a heron that Gavino has wounded. He cannot keep himself from observing in the minutest detail the pitiful efforts of the bird to escape, yet he cannot bring himself to put it out of its misery because he sees his own helplessness in the heron's desperate plight: "If he hadn't felt that shooting at it would seem, to him, shooting in a sense at himself, he would have fired at once." Instead, he watches the poor bird die. Unlike Colonel Cantwell, Edgardo has not been revived by his morning hunt; his manhood, like the colonel's impaired by the war, has not been restored to him. On his way home he meets a number of acquaintances whose scorn and abuse he weakly accepts. His final encounter with wild ducks is not at the marsh but in the display window of a taxidermist's shop he happens to pass in the street:

> The ducks, at least a dozen, filled in a compact group the proscenium of the little theater: so close you thought you could touch them, and calm, finally, not frightened, not forced to keep aloft, suspended on their short, fluttering wings, in the mobile and treacherous air. . . . In any case, the birds . . . were alive, with a life that no longer ran the risk of deteriorating; polished to a high gloss; but made beautiful, above all, surely more beautiful, and by a good deal, than when they were breathing and the blood ran swiftly through their veins: only he, perhaps, he thought, was able really to *understand* it, the perfection of this beauty of theirs, final and imperishable, to appreciate it fully.[25]

The beauty of Hemingway's dead ducks is offered up to love, Edgardo's, to death. Enthralled by his vision, Edgardo imagines himself inside that "sun-filled universe" behind the glass that reflects his face. At that moment he "felt slowly approaching, within him, vague as yet, but rich in mysterious promises, a secret thought that would free him, save him." The thought is his suicide, which would free him from a life of ugliness and shame, magnified by the incident of the heron, that he can no longer bear. We do not learn the details, but we can be sure that his death does not have the heroic decorum of the colonel's.

A duck-hunting scene makes the catastrophic climax of Lawrence Durrell's *Justine.* One of the party is killed, by accident or intention, by a shot from another hunter, possibly Justine's lover, Nessim. The result is that Justine feels she can no longer stay in Alexandria; she disappears, leaving Nessim and the narrator desolate: "It was as if she had removed the keystone to an arch: Nessim and I, left among the ruins." The tragic hunt had revealed to Justine the enormity of the way of life the three of them had shared.[26]

three. Killing the Sacred Bird

"Shoot all the birds you want, if you can hit 'em, but remember it's a sin to kill a mockingbird," a father advises his son upon presenting him with his first rifle in Harper Lee's *To Kill a Mockingbird.* An old peasant in Ivan Turgenev's "Kassyan of Fair Springs," from *A Sportsman's Sketches,* bitterly disapproves of the gentleman shooting a corncrake, and yet he himself traps nightingales. He explains the difference: "We must not kill them, of a certainty; death will take its own without that. . . . Death does not hasten, nor is there any escaping it; but we must not aid death. . . . And I do not kill nightingales—God forbid! I do not catch them to harm them, to spoil their lives, but for the pleasure of man, for their comfort and delight." When he is challenged with eating fowl he replies that geese and chickens "are provided by God for man, but the corncrake is a wild bird of the woods: and not he alone; many there are, the wild things of the woods and the fields, and the wild things of the rivers and marshes and moors, flying on high or creeping below; and sin it is to slay them: let them live their allotted life upon the earth."[27]

Taboos against the wanton killing of sacramental or totemic animals are common in primitive societies. The crew of Odysseus are all lost at sea as soon as their ship leaves the island of Thrinacia because they made the fatal mistake of slaughtering cattle sacred to the god Helios. Romantic writers revived the ancient taboo when they considered killing an animal a sin against nature. This is certainly one of the meanings of Coleridge's "Rime of the Ancient Mariner" as well as Melville's *Moby-Dick,* except that Ahab's motive is revenge against an animal that has injured him while the mariner's shooting of the albatross is without motive. The animal in each case is more than a mere natural phenomenon since it represents what might be called the life principle in nature, and so killing the animal is either the ultimate assertion of superiority over nature, as in *Moby-Dick,* or indifference to nature, as in Coleridge's poem. Melville very explicitly deifies the white whale, and Coleridge suggests that the albatross has "a Christian soul" and the crew "hailed it in God's name." (The albatross, in fact, was once regarded as sacred by Polynesians, since the god Kane, or Tane, sometimes took its form.) Killing the animal is therefore an act against God as well as nature, against the "sacramental unity" of all living things, as Robert Penn Warren puts it in his edition of Coleridge's poem.

The problem for all who participate in, or even witness, the killing of a sacramental or totemic animal then becomes a matter of atonement for sin. Ishmael is spared because of his instinctive love of nature and his ability to see beauty in all things, even the "poetry in blubber," while Ahab must die because of his hate and his vindictive assault on nature. Fellow crew members of the ancient mariner are doomed for holding a selfish view of the albatross, first as an omen of good luck for them ("the bird that made the breeze to blow"), then as a harbinger of bad luck ("the bird that brought the fog and mist"). The old sailor is close to perishing, too, until he learns, through dwelling on the matter anxiously and imaginatively, that everything in nature is of equal value and deserving of love. The principle is simply stated:

> He prayeth best, who loveth best
> All things both great and small;
> For the dear God who loveth us,
> He made and loveth all.
> (lines 614–17)

This appears to be too trite for some readers, who insist that the meaning of the poem is to be found in the mariner's experience and not in the moral he draws from it as an old man. But for the mariner, telling his story is as important for his redemption as the experience itself; it is a kind of ritual absolution in the presence of his fellows. As for his experience, it is a conversion that comes when he realizes that even seemingly ugly things, such as the water snakes he observes from the deck of the ship, are really beautiful:

> O happy living things! no tongue
> Their beauty might declare:
> A spring of love gushed from my heart,
> And I blessed them unaware.
> (lines 282–85)

At once he is released from the curse of the dead albatross drooped around his neck. Finding beauty and something to love in water snakes is the supreme trial for the ancient mariner, who has, presumably, the almost instinctive dread of serpents common to humankind; just as finding beauty in the fearsome white whale is a test of principle and imagination for the young schoolteacher Ishmael. Forced to live among men who are driven by greed and fear, and under the command of a man crazed by revenge, Ishmael separates himself from the crew's wholesale slaughter of whales by lovingly collecting and presenting to his readers the natural history of the whale species. This is his redemption; he alone is saved.

The point that nothing in nature can fail to "keep the heart / Awake to Love and Beauty!" is made again by Coleridge in "This Lime-Tree Bower My Prison," a poem written about the same time as "The Rime of the Ancient Mariner." Even the croaking of a crow flying overhead has charm: "No sound is dissonant which tells of Life." The poet reacts to the crow just as the mariner does when he sees the water snakes:

> when the last rook
> Beat its straight path along the dusky air
> Homewards, I blest it!
> (lines 68–70)

The same sentiment occurs earlier in these lines from Blake's "Visions of the Daughters of Albion":

> Arise, you little glancing wings, and sing your infant joy!
> Arise, and drink your bliss, for every thing that lives is holy!
> (195, 8.9–10)

A passage in Coleridge's *Notebooks* ten years after "The Rime of the Ancient Mariner" carries the principle of the indiscriminate love of all things in nature to an amazing, though for Coleridge not unusual, extreme.

> The soil that fell from the Hawk poised at the extreme bound-
> ary of Sight thro' a column of sunshine—a falling star, gem, the
> fixation, & chrystal of substantial Light, again dissolving & elon-
> gating like a liquid Drop—how altogether lovely this to the Eye,
> and to the Mind too while it remained its own self, all & only its
> very Self. . . . O many, many are the seeings, hearings, & tactual
> Impressions of pure Love, that have a being of their own—and
> to call them by the names of things unsouled and debased below
> even their own lowest nature by Associations accidental, and of
> vicious accidents, is *blasphemy*.[28]

Fifteen years later the poet was still haunted by the image, which appeared in an early draft of "Youth and Age" that speaks of the "mute" of a skylark shooting "downward in the sunshine like a falling star of silver" (no. 1085).

Both Coleridge and Melville are stating the ecological principle that our survival depends on our recognition of the worth and interrelatedness of all living things. Unfortunately one person's acting on this principle does not atone for the crime of all the others. In Coleridge's "Raven" a crime against nature occurs when woodsmen unwittingly cause the death of raven nestlings by cut-ting down a tree to be used as a ship's mast. When the ship sinks and the whole crew perishes, the parent ravens gloat in revenge. Neither the woodsmen nor the crew can be held responsible for the injury done to the ravens; Coleridge's point, however, has to do not with justice but with the unpredictable consequences of ignor-ing nature. It makes no difference if the assault against nature is willful, as in the case of Ahab, or unwitting, as with the ancient mariner and the woodsmen: the ship carrying humankind on the perilous sea of existence will inevitably meet with disaster, since our survival is subject to nature's laws.

The fateful killing of the albatross has some distant echoes. In a poem called "Snake" D. H. Lawrence recalls having once thrown a log at a snake that had come to his water trough, and although he fails to hit him he immediately regrets having scared him off:

> And I thought of the albatross,
> And I wished he would come back, my snake
> For he seemed to me again like a king . . .
> And so, I missed my chance with one of the lords
> Of life.
> And I have something to expiate;
> A pettiness.   (351)

Many years after writing an essay on Coleridge's poem, Robert Penn Warren tells the story of the wanton killing of a sacramental animal in "Red-Tail Hawk and the Pyre of Youth." As a boy stands on a high ridge a hawk suddenly appears out of the "convex perfection" of the sky, and though the bird is like a god with gold eyes that "see all," the boy shoots it. As in the case of the ancient mariner there is "no decision in the act . . . no choice in the act." When he stuffs the bird and places it on a shelf next to his favorite books, he is proud of his prowess as a hunter yet uncomfortably aware that the hawk is no longer "king of the air" but "forever earthbound, fit only / For dog tooth, not sky." After he leaves his boyhood home, he knows that wherever he goes "yellow eyes somewhere, unblinking, in vengeance stared." Upon his return years later he makes a pyre of his books and the stuffed bird. For the rest of his life he keeps reliving the moment he killed the bird, regretting that he had not known "that all is only / All, and part of all." Gwen Harwood reports a similar experience in "Father and Child." A child shoots an owl and is at once upset when she sees "those eyes that did not see / mirror my cruelty." Forty years later, walking with her eighty-year-old father,

> the child once quick
> to mischief, grown to learn
> what sorrows, in the end
> no words, no tears can mend.[29]

The duck in Ibsen's *Wild Duck* is even more central to the meaning of the play than the albatross in Coleridge's poem. Again, each person involved in the tragedy has a differing conception of the meaning of the wild duck kept by the Ekdal family in the attic of their house. The duck (a mallard in the English translation) had been given to the Ekdals by a servant of Hakon Werle, the hunter who had wounded it and the man responsible for having ruined Old Ekdal in a business transaction. To Ekdal the injured duck is a reminder of his ignominious dependence on Werle, who now employs him in a menial job, but it is also a pitiful symbol of the independence and vigor of his younger years when he was a big-game hunter and military officer. He has the illusion that the attic of his house, where he has assembled some rabbits, pigeons, and domestic fowl, the injured duck, and some old withered Christmas trees, is a wilderness where he and his son, Hjalmar, "go shooting." They spare the duck, however, because it represents the freedom they cherish but cannot actually possess.

Werle's son, Gregers, is mortified when he learns how his father has made the Ekdal family dependent upon his charity. He sets out to rescue them from the illusion of the duck, although he himself entertains the illusion that he is like the dog that retrieved the wild duck when it was shot and tried to escape by diving into the depths of the sea. He is convinced that the Ekdals must be disabused of the illusion they hold, and he plants this idea in the mind of Hedvig, Hjalmar's daughter. Together they plot to get Old Ekdal to kill the duck. When he refuses, Hedvig, who cannot bear to kill the animal she has grown to love and who is suffering from Hjalmar's rejection of her when he discovers that she is the daughter of his wife and Werle, kills herself instead of the duck. She sacrifices herself in a childish attempt to make things right for the family.

Unlike the ancient mariner, Hedvig has a regard for nature, even in the diminished form of an injured wild duck and tame animals kept in the attic of a city house. These animals and bits of dried vegetation are to her "a sort of world by itself," apart from the disappointing reality of her existence, a place, she confides to Gregers, that is like the "depths of the sea" where the duck had sought refuge when it was shot. Hedvig is caught up in the illusion of the wild duck even more than are Old Ekdal and Hjalmar. "My wild duck," she says. "It belongs to me." But she is a child, and her identification with an animal is innocent and in more normal circumstances would have formed an important part of the imaginative process of growing up. Old Ekdal's relation to the duck is that of a doddering old man who has never recovered from the wrong done to him. His son Hjalmar is most reprehensible, for he uses the illusion of the wild duck to avoid the responsibility of supporting his family, which he leaves to his wife and daughter. In his selfishness he is incapable of love, and this failing stands in contrast to Hedvig's deep love for the wild duck and for every person in her life, including her worthless father.

Hedvig has a right relation to nature that could have been a constructive influence on her development had she not been terribly abused by two adults, Hjalmar with his selfish rejection of her and Gregers with his well-meaning but dangerous suggestion that the wild duck must be destroyed in order to save the family from living with illusions. In some ways Nina in Chekhov's *Seagull* is an extension of the situation that Ibsen explored in his characterization of Hedvig. A lake is the focus of Nina's love of nature, and she too identifies with a bird, a gull that frequents the lake. Older than Hedvig, Nina has the ambition to be an actress and is caught in the dilemma of choosing a life close to nature at the lake or a life devoted to art. Two men obstruct the working out of her problem. Konstantin, her young admirer, shares her passion for the lake and the desire to be an artist. When a play of his is badly received, a play in which Nina has the chief part, he becomes enraged, kills the gull and lays it at Nina's feet. His act is a symbolic rejection of both art and love, too impetuous to be lasting, of course, but it offers Trigorin, an older and established author, the opportunity to make literary capital and a romantic conquest out of their quarrel. He finds a cue for a short story in the dead gull: "a young girl, such as you, has lived all her life beside a lake; she loves the lake like a seagull, and is as free and happy as a seagull. But a man comes by chance, sees her, and having nothing better to do, destroys her like the seagull here." He then plays out the story in actuality, seducing Nina and abandoning her after she bears a child. Forgotten is the romantic image of Nina as a seagull that so enchanted him at the start of their affair. Nina, however, does not play out the part written for her in his story; she rejects the idea of her destruction and comes to the mature realization that she is not the seagull but a person with a vocation to pursue. "I am not afraid of life," she tells Konstantin and refuses his belated offer of love. After Nina leaves to resume her career as an actress, Konstantin, now without love or vocation and "whirled about in a maze of dreams and images," destroys his manuscripts and kills himself, as he had predicted he would do when he killed the seagull two years before. In throwing off the negative influence of two men and seeing the symbolism of the bird for what it is, Nina succeeds in doing what the child Hedvig could not do. Central to the meaning of both plays is the idea that the fixation on personal symbols, symbols with which people identify themselves, may have tragic results when it blocks the will to live. The point is especially appropriate in Chekhov's play since it is an attack against the rage for symbolistic drama in his time.

In Boris Pasternak's *Doctor Zhivago* a wild duck, a gift to the doctor by the soldier who had shot it, becomes the choice dish at a family party. To dine on wild game was "an unheard of luxury" in Russia at the close of World War I, but Yuri finds that its "splendor was somehow pointless" because so many other good things are lacking and because no other families can dine so well: "And so it turned out that only a life similar to the life of those around us . . . is genuine life, and that an unshared happiness is not happiness, so that duck and vodka, when they seem to be the only ones in town, are not even duck and vodka." What appears to be the last wild duck is a symbol of the pall of deprivation and oppressive uniformity that was to settle over Russia after the Bolshevik Revolution, just as the killing of Coleridge's albatross and ravens spells disaster for the ship's crews. Ominous too is the singing of a nightingale described in one of Dr. Zhivago's poems:

> A nightingale raged in frantic song
> Like a church bell pealing forth a tocsin;
> He sang among branches interlaced and darkling
> Against the sunset's conflagration.[30]

The appalling mistreatment of birds in Jerzy Kosinski's *Painted Bird* is used as a symbol of man's inhumanity to man in Central Europe during World War II. In a key episode of the novel, or what has been called an "inverse fairy tale," we meet Lekh, a Slavic peasant who in his youth became familiar with the ways of the forest and birds.

> He observed the wondrous habits of quail and larks, could imitate the carefree call of the cuckoo, the screech of the magpie, the hooting of the owl. He knew the courting habits of the bullfinch; the jealous fury of the landrail, circling a nest abandoned by its female; and the sorrow of the swallow whose nesting place was wantonly destroyed by young boys.

Eventually he uses this knowledge to trap birds and exchange them for food among the villagers who value them as pets. Lekh finds a lover in Ludmila, a feeble-minded outcast who lives in the forest and is known for her insatiable sexual appetite and her power over animals. She brings out the better side of Lekh's crude nature.

> He made up tender songs for her in which she figured as a strange-colored bird flying to faraway worlds, free and quick, brighter and more beautiful than other creatures. To Lekh she seemed to belong to that pagan, primitive kingdom of birds and forests, where everything was infinitely abundant, wild, blooming, and royal in its perpetual decay, death, and rebirth; illicit and clashing with the human world.

The passionate affair of this strange couple, though it is carried on in a forest setting, is hardly idyllic in the pastoral tradition but violent and brutal. When Ludmila is unaccountably absent for a few days, Lekh rages (with the "fury of the landrail") and finds a fiendishly sadistic way to satisfy both his thwarted lust and momentary hatred of his missing lover. One after another he paints his caged birds in garish colors and turns them loose. We watch in horror this mockery of a bird's freedom:

> It would soar, happy and free, a spot of rainbow against the backdrop of clouds, and then plunge into the waiting brown flock. For an instant the birds were confounded. The painted bird circled from one end of the flock to the other, vainly trying to convince its kin that it was one of them. But, dazzled by its brilliant colors,

they flew around it unconvinced. The painted bird would be forced
farther and farther away as it zealously tried to enter the ranks
of the flock. We saw soon afterwards how one bird after another
would peel off in a fierce attack. Shortly the many-hued shape lost
its place in the sky and dropped to the ground. When we finally
found the painted bird it was usually dead. Lekh keenly examined the number of blows which the bird had received. Blood
seeped through its colored wings, diluting the paint and soiling
Lekh's hands.[31]

When there are no more birds to paint, Lekh leaves his hut. Ludmila returns to find him gone; in his absence she is violated by a
number of villagers and brutally killed by their jealous wives.

The painted bird of the title does not refer primarily to Ludmila,
however, but to the narrator, a young boy who has been separated
from his parents by the fortunes of war. Having dark skin, dark
hair, and dark eyes he is mistaken for a Jew or gypsy and must con-
stantly be on the alert whenever he encounters German soldiers
or the Slavic peasants among whom he seeks shelter. When Lekh
takes him in to be his helper, the boy sleeps in one of the larger
birdcages. Painted bird, outcast woman, or unattached boy—all
suffer terribly from the majority group's intolerance of difference.

Birds and the Erotic

> *Love is feathered like a bird*
>   *To keep him warm,*
>   *To keep him safe from harm,*
> *And by what winds or drafts his nest is stirred*
>   *They chill not Love.*
>   *Warm lives he:*
>   *No warmth gives off,*
>   *Or none to me.*
>
> Elizabeth Bishop, "Three Valentines"

Springtime is the season of heightened sexuality, and the universal tokens of spring are renewed vegetation and the return of bird song. Ancient tradition took early morning bird song to be the signal for lovers to rejoin their sweethearts for the day, as in the famous lover's plea from the Song of Solomon—

> The flowers appear on the earth;
> The time of the singing of birds is come,
> And the voice of the turtle[dove] is heard in the land.
>
> . . . .
>
> Arise, my love, my fair one, and come away.
>
> (2.12–14)

While this dates from the fourth century B.C., an Egyptian love song using the same imagery precedes it by fifteen hundred years:

> The voice of the dove calls:
> It says, "The earth is bright."
> What have I to do outside?
> Stop, thou birdling! Thou chidest me![1]

Poets as late as the Renaissance were still writing matin songs, such as Shakespeare's "Hark, Hark, the Lark," in which a bird bids the lover's sweet lady to arise, and Robert Herrick's "Corinna's Going A-Maying":

> When all the birds have matins said
> And sung their thankful hymns, 'tis sin
>   Nay, profanation, to keep in.
>   (Hebel and Hudson, 655)

From ancient beginnings evolved the epithalamium, an elaborate song celebrating a particular marriage. In the one Edmund Spenser wrote for his own marriage, several birds besides the turtledove waken the bride on her wedding day:

> Hark how the cheerefull birds do chaunt their laies
> And carroll of loves praise.
> The merry Larke hir mattins sings aloft,
> The thrush replyes, the Mavis [thrush] descant playes,
> The Ouzell [blackbird] shrills, the Ruddock [robin] warbles soft,
> So goodly all agree with sweet consent
> To this dayes merriment.
>   ("Epithalamion," lines 78–84)

From classical times birds were commonly associated with the "place fit for love" (*dignus amore locus*) as described by Petronius: "Witness the wood-haunting nightingale and the town-haunting swallow both, who, flitting over the grass and tender violets, beautified the place with their singing" (*Satyricon*, 131). The classical topos of the pleasant place (*locus amoenus*), consisting of shade trees, a meadow, a stream or fountain, flowers, and songbirds, continued into medieval and Renaissance rhetoric. Chaucer's *Parliament of Fowls*, for example, combines the pleasant place or "pleasance" with springtime, love, and birds:

> A gardyn saw I ful of blosmy bowes
> Upon a ryver, in a grene mede,
> There as swetnesse evermore inow is,
> With floures white, blewe, yelwe, and rede,
> And colde welle-stremes.
>   (lines 183–87)

On every bough a bird is singing "with voys of aungel in here armonye." In the garden is a temple where the goddess of nature is holding a convocation of birds on Saint Valentine's Day, the occasion "whan every foul cometh there to chese his make." February is too early for some birds to mate in England, but the poet is less interested in birds than the people they represent, and having birds speak like ladies and gentlemen is a literary convenience for the poet to handle a serious subject freely and amusingly. No matter that Chaucer and the literary convention behind him stretched the facts and indulged in fantasy; the significance for us is that birds are used to represent the harmonious operation of nature's laws that apply equally to humans as well as to animals, specifically the pairing of male and females "by evene acord" so that neither partner is wronged or forced. The center of attraction is a young female eagle whose request that she be allowed to delay her choice of a mate for another year is graciously granted by the goddess of nature.[2]

About 250 years after Chaucer's poem, John Donne used similar imagery in an epithalamium celebrating the marriage of one Lady Elizabeth and the Count Palatine. It begins with an invocation to the saint:

> Haile Bishop Valentine, whose day this is,
> > All the Aire is thy Diocis,
> > And all the chirping Choristers
> And other Birds are thy Parishioners,
> > Thou marryest every yeare
> The Lirique Larke, and the grave whispering Dove.[3]

The sorrow rather than the joy of love is the nightingale's special theme in the Philomela legend. There is a more general tradition, however, in which the nightingale has the happier role of being love's harbinger, most likely because its enchanting song is sung during the prime seasons of love, springtime and nighttime. In the medieval verse collection *Carmina Burana* the nightingale's song "incites to love," and in the more serious "literary debate" poems of the time, such as *The Owl and the Nightingale* and *The Cuckoo and the Nightingale,* in which speaking birds learnedly argue the merits of love versus religion, the nightingale is always cast as the advocate of love. From the latter poem John Milton may have learned the distinction he presents in a youthful sonnet, "O Nightingale," that it is most auspicious for lovers to hear a nightingale singing:

> Thy liquid notes that close the eye of Day,
>> First heard before the shallow Cuckoo's bill,
>> Portend success in love.

In *Romeo and Juliet* Shakespeare makes a similar distinction between birds. In order to keep Romeo at her side a little longer in the balcony scene of act 3, Juliet insists that the bird they hear is a nightingale and not a lark, "the herald of the morn," as Romeo fears. A little later they reverse sides, and Juliet urges him to go before he is caught in her presence:

> It is, it is! Hie hence, be gone, away!
> It is the lark that sings so out of tune,
> Straining harsh discords and unpleasing sharps.
> Some say the lark makes sweet division;
> This doth not so, for she divideth us.
>> (3.5.26–30)

The same situation occurs in a fourteenth-century B.C. Egyptian love poem:

> The voice of the swallow says:
> "It's light already. Mustn't you go now?"
> Don't, little bird. You bring dispute.

A humorous version of this motif appears in an English ballad, "The Grey Cock." The fair maiden in bed with her true love implores the "pretty feathered" not to crow until daylight:

> But him a-being young, he crowed very soon,
> He crowed two long hours before day;
> And she sent her love away, for she thought 'twas almost day,
> And 'twas all by the light of the moon.[4]

Shakespeare's distinction between the lark and the nightingale descends to Milton: in "L'Allegro" the song of the lark is said to "startle the dull night," while the nightingale's "even-song" in "Il Penseroso" is credited with "smoothing the rugged brow of Night." This figure comes out in Keats's "Ode to a Nightingale" as "tender is the night," a phrase borrowed by F. Scott Fitzgerald for the title of a novel. But its meaning in the novel is ironical, reverting to the tragic nightingale of the classical tradition. Fitzgerald's heroine, Nicole, is scarred for life by the sexual abuse she suffered from her father when she was a child. In one scene "this scarcely saved waif of disaster" comes out of the woods at night to sing to Dick Diver, her husband: "Minute by minute the sweetness drained down into her out of the willow trees, out of the dark world." In another scene a friend of theirs believes she hears the couple "singing faintly a song like rising smoke, like a hymn, very remote and far away."[5] Nicole and an "insistent bird" singing in the "erotic darkness" are descendants of Philomela, the classical symbol of love's tragic abuse. The night is not smoothed by their singing, not made tender for Nicole and Diver, whose marriage ends in bitterness and despair. As well as Keats's poem perhaps Fitzgerald recalled a passage from T. S. Eliot's *Waste Land* in which a painting in the home of a lady of high fashion portrays

> The change of Philomel, by the barbarous king
> So rudely forced; yet there the nightingale
> Filled all the desert with inviolable voice
> And still she cried, and still the world pursues,
> "Jug jug" to dirty ears.
>
> (40)

Fitzgerald's Nicole is indeed pursued by men, one, at the end of the novel, ominously named Tommy Barban.

Eliot's pun on *jug*, in the Elizabethan sense of copulation, emphasizes one of his important themes, that lust and the sexual abuse of innocents are signs of the present world's decadence. Eliot uses the Philomela motif for the same purpose in "Sweeney among the Nightingales." The poem draws a parallel between the gross sexuality of a contemporary man visiting a brothel and Agamemnon, the Greek king who was murdered by his wife for having been unfaithful to her while he was away at the Trojan War, and, more immediately, for bringing back with him his latest concubine. The poem closes with this striking juxtaposition of a patron departing the brothel and Agamemnon being murdered:

> The host with someone indistinct
> Converses at the door apart,
> The nightingales are singing near
> The Convent of the Sacred Heart,
>
> And sang within the bloody wood
> When Agamemnon cried aloud,
> And let their liquid siftings fall
> To stain his stiff dishonoured shroud.
>
> (35)

It is grim poetic justice that nightingales, the bird of the ravished Philomela, should sing at the death of the unfaithful king and foul his burial shroud in the manner of Harpies, the mythical bird-women. But poetic justice is out of the question in the contemporary scene; nightingales are singing at a convent but not at the brothel, where their significance would go unnoticed.

It may be that birds are perceived to be more erotic than other animals because their mating and nesting are often so easily observed by humans. One does not have to watch sparrows and doves very long to confirm the literary tradition that they are extremely active sexually. Both were the favorites of Aphrodite and Ishtar, goddesses of love and reproduction, and both have long been identified by male writers with the presumed lasciviousness of women. From an early time a popular subject in poetry was the description of a lady engaging in love play with a pet sparrow or dove, much to the envy of a would-be lover who never ceased hoping that her modesty in his company merely concealed her true desire. Thus the Roman poet Catullus on his friend Lesbia in "*Passer, deliciae maea puellae*":

> Little Sparrow, my lover's love
> with whom she plays, permits to lie
> within her lap to nip her fingers. . . .
> I should like to play with you
> as she, and soothe my troubled heart!

It is a fact, demonstrated by Konrad Lorenz in his study of greylag geese, that a bird raised from birth by a human will "tend to regard human beings, and human beings only, as potential partners in all reproductive activities," and for this reason "hand-raised male sparrows . . . enjoyed great popularity among loose-living ladies of Roman society."[6]

The lady with a sparrow nestling in her lap and bosom was a stock image in Renaissance poetry. Sir Philip Sidney's maid in "Lamon" puts the "happy wretch" between her breasts, "where snuggling well he appear'd content." In *Astrophel and Stella* the lover becomes impatient with the liberties that a pet sparrow, Philip, is taking with his mistress:

> I bare (with Envie) yet I bare your song,
>   When in her necke you did *Love* ditties peepe;
>   Nay, more foole I, oft suffered you to sleepe
> In Lillies' neast, where *Love's* selfe lies along.
>
> . . . .
>
> Leave that sir Phip, least off your necke be wroong.[7]

The innocent schoolgirl in John Skelton's "Philip Sparrow" takes her pet bird to bed with her:

> And on me it wolde leap
> Whan I was asleep,
> And his feathers shake,
> Wherewith he would make
> Me often for to wake,
> And for to take him in
> Upon my naked skin,
> God wot, we thought no sin:
> What though he crept so low?
> It was no hurt, I trow.
>   (64–65)

But later in the poem we are told that the bird would creep into the opening of her skirt where he set up a "flickering with his wings!"

Recent contributions to the tradition of the lecherous sparrow include William Carlos Williams's "Sparrow":

> Nothing even remotely
> subtle
>   about his love-making.
>   He crouches
> before the female,
>   drags his wings,
>   waltzing,
> throws back his head
>   and simply—
>   yells!

He pays a price for his lust when he is undone by an equally lustful mate; the poet sees

> the female of his species
>   clinging determinedly
>   to the edge of
> a waterpipe,
>   catch him
>   by his crown-feathers
> to hold him
>   silent,
>   subdued
> hanging above the city streets
>   until
>   she was through with him.[8]

In "Three Valentines" Elizabeth Bishop begins her playful disquisition on love with the amorous sparrow:

> Love with her gilded bow and crystal arrows
>   Has slain us all,
> Has pierced the English sparrows
> Who languish for each other in the dust
> While from their bosoms, puffed with hopeless lust,
>   The red drops fall;

then goes to the robin:

> The robins' wings fan fev'rish arcs and swirls
>   Attempting hugs;

and concludes with avian figures illustrating the tenaciousness of love:

> Claws he has like any hawk
>> To clutch and keep,
>> To clutch so he may sleep
> While round the red heart's perch his claws can lock
>> And fasten Love;

and love's tiresomeness:

> At nights the grackle Love will start
>> To shriek and shrill,
>> Nor will he once be still
> Till he has wide awake the backward heart.
>> (225)

The lustfulness of the domestic cock is even more flagrant than the sparrow's. In addition to its other symbolical burdens, the cock represents male sexuality, even lending its name to the phallus just as the swallow has been associated with the woman's pudendum.[9] To illustrate the cock's sexual prowess, Chaucer avows in "The Nun's Priest's Tale" that Chauntecleer "feathered" his favorite hen twenty times "er it was pryme" or before nine o'clock in the morning. And then "he looketh as it were a grym leoun, / And on his toos he rometh up and doun." The comparison with the lion may have come from the belief that cocks and lions are the only males that do not feel "dullness" after intercourse, a notion John Donne picks up in "Farewell to Love":

> Ah, cannot wee,
> As well as Cocks and Lyons jocund be,
>> After such pleasures.
>> (52)

A fifteenth-century English lyric opens with the familiar double meaning of *cock* and related terms such as *risen*—

> I have a gentil cock
>> Crowyth me day;
> He doth me rysyn erly,
>> My matynis for to say—

and closes with the offhand statement that "every nycht he per-chith him / In myn ladyis chaumbyr." [10]

In *The Man Who Died* D. H. Lawrence combines the traditional association of Jesus and the cock with the bird's erotic reputation in order to create an entirely new, and what to some Christians must be a sacrilegious, version of the resurrection. Lawrence's hero, never specifically named, awakes from death hearing "the shrill wild crowing" of a cock that corresponds to the legendary cockcrow at the birth of the Christ child, but this cock has quite a different message to bring. It is a "saucy, flamboyant bird" be-longing to a peasant who keeps him tethered so that he cannot escape. Seeing "not the bird alone, but the short, sharp wave of life of which the bird was the crest," the man buys the bird from the peasant and then releases it after it wins a harem of hens in a battle with another rooster at an inn. The cock, then, is the spur to his seeking an altogether new way of life, for, like the cock who "answers the lure of hens," the new Jesus sets out to find a "woman who can lure [his] risen body." He now realizes that he too was tethered, that in his former life he was wrong to deny the body when he asked his followers to serve him with "the corpse of their love," that "the body rises again to give and to take, to take and to give, ungreedily." The awakening of the man who died is a "full awakening" in the sense that it is a resurrection of the flesh as well as of the spirit. After the cock he hears "a nightingale winsomely, wistfully, coaxingly calling from the bushes beside a runnel of water, in the world, the natural world of morning and evening, forever undying, from which he had died." [11]

After much seeking the man who is determined to lead a new life finds a woman "with whom he can mingle his body." She is a priestess at a temple of Isis, the Egyptian goddess of "passionate fecundity," whose fate it is to search for the pieces of the dismem-bered body of her brother Osiris. When she finds the "final clue to him" (the phallus), she can become his bride and produce a son, Horus, a god associated with the sun and often shown in the form of a falcon. Lawrence transfers the role of the goddess Isis to the priestess, a twenty-seven-year-old woman whose father had been a captain in Mark Antony's army. "When she was young the girl had known Caesar, and had shrunk from his eagle-like rapacity.

The golden Antony had sat with her many a half-hour, in the splendour of his great limbs and glowing manhood, and talked with her of the philosophies and the gods" (*Man,* 189). Antony, in fact, had tried to seduce her, saying, "a maid should open to the sun, when the sun leans towards her to caress her." This could be the story of Cleopatra, but Lawrence's woman is destined to have a greater "sun" than Antony. The association Lawrence makes here between the woman in his story and Cleopatra (there is evidence that the queen actually did appear in public as a priestess of Isis) adds an interesting historical touch and further accentuates the close relation between Jesus and Osiris that characterized the early practice of Christianity in Egypt, where the fourth-century church celebrated the Feast of Epiphany on the same day as the festival of Isis.

The woman heals the wounds suffered by the stranger at his crucifixion, and they are now able to consummate their love. "I have sowed the seed of my life and my resurrection," he declares, and the woman bearing his child assures him that his resurrection will be in the person of the twice-born god Osiris. In leaving the woman to escape from the slaves of her vengeful mother, the stranger promises to return: "When the nightingale calls again from your valley-bed, I shall come again, sure as Spring" (*Man,* 210). The association of the woman with the nightingale, the pudendum in this context, balances the identification of her lover with the cock, the phallus. It has some precedent, too, in that the swallow was sacred to Isis and a 2700 B.C. bas-relief depicts Isis spreading winged arms over the coffin of Tutankhamen in her role as a guardian of the dead.[12]

For Lawrence the individual who has become stultified or "dead" must experience sex to the fullest in order to be revitalized. Sexual union is tantamount to spiritual union with life and reality. In *The Man Who Died* Lawrence adapts the story of the cock announcing Christ's birth and resurrection in order to advance the idea that sexual fulfillment is a necessary step in the process of both spiritual and physical renewal. Lawrence enforces his version of the story by using the reputation of the cock for sexual power and by constant and rather excessive punning on the terms *cock, risen,* and *coming.*

In *The Plumed Serpent* male sexuality is represented by a fabulous creature that Lawrence borrows from an ancient Aztec god, Quetzalcoatl, combining the features of a bird—a trogon and sometimes an eagle—with a snake. The snake is an earth figure and clearly phallic: "From the heart of the earth man feels his manhood rise up in him" (197). The bird is the divine representative of the sky and also phallic: "The bird of the sun treads the earth at the dawn of the day like a brown hen under his feet" (130). Don Ramon, a Mexican revolutionary, believes that he is the reincarnation of the bird-god, the "Living Quetzalcoatl." Although he and his chief associate, General Cipriano, seem to be sincere, it appears to Kate Leslie, the British woman who becomes personally involved with them, that they are really intent upon reviving a primitive religion as the means to establish an authoritarian government in Mexico and to assert male sexual superiority over women. Ramon's wife is terrified by her husband's principles—"I am not with you till my serpent has coiled his circle of rest in your belly," he tells her (344); and Kate shrinks from Cipriano, feeling "somewhat as the bird feels when the snake is watching it." She expresses her sense of being oppressed by both Mexico and Cipriano in a curious inversion of the supposed power of Quetzalcoatl worship to move one toward a new life: "And she had been beating her wings in an effort to get away. She felt like a bird round whose body a snake has coiled itself. . . . To pull one down. It was what the country wanted to do all the time, with a slow, reptilian insistence, to pull one down. To prevent the spirit from soaring. To take away the free, soaring sense of liberty" (72). Kate is speaking for Lawrence when she considers whether "the great death-continent," America, will one day "pull down the soul of the world." The image of the encircling snake is traditional; figurines dating from the sixth millenium picture snakes curled around goddesses having the form of waterfowl.[13] Lawrence may have found the image in Coleridges's *Christabel*, in which Bracy has a dream that he interprets as a premonition of Christabel's peril in associating with Geraldine:

> For in my sleep I saw that dove,
> That gentle bird, whom thou dost love,

> And call'st by thy own daughter's name—
> Sir Leoline! I saw the same
> Fluttering, and uttering fearful moan,
> Among the green herbs in the forest alone.
>
> . . . .
>
> I stooped, methought, the dove to take,
> When lo! I saw a bright green snake
> Coiled around its wings and neck.
>   (lines 531–50)

Kate's struggle is between the assertion of her ego and submission to male domination, between the individual will and the demands of the totalitarian community of Quetzalcoatl that Ramon and Cipriano want to establish. She recognizes the power Cipriano has to make her body flower. "But on the other hand, when she spread the wings of her own ego, and sent forth her own spirit, the world could look very wonderful to her, when she was alone" (*Serpent,* 439). This feeling does not prevail, however, and the book ends indecisively with Kate admitting to herself that "I must have both."

Kate Leslie does not want to be like the brown hen the sunbird treads, the branches of whose belly "droop with the apples of birth, with the eggs of gold." She is doubtful, as well she might be, of the overblown posturing of men who relate sexuality to primitive religious feeling. Anna Brangwen in *The Rainbow* is similarly put off when she witnesses her husband's almost sexual reaction to the architecture of Lincoln Cathedral and the religious feeling it represents:

> She wanted to get out of this fixed, leaping, forward-travelling movement, to rise from it as a bird rises with wet, limp feet from the sea, to lift herself as a bird lifts its breast and thrusts its body from the pulse and heave of a sea that bears it forward to an unwilling conclusion, tear herself away like a bird on wings, and in the open space where there is clarity, rise above the fixed, surcharged motion, a separate speck that hangs suspended, moves this way and that, seeing and answering before it sinks again, having chosen or found the direction in which it shall be carried forward.

Will Brangwen reluctantly comes around to her point of view by way of another impression of birds: "He listened to the thrushes in the gardens and heard a note which the cathedrals did not include: something free and careless and joyous."[14] (The effect of the thrushes on Will, turning him away from the cathedral, is like the effect of a flight of swallows on Stephen Dedalus, supporting his decision to reject the priesthood.) Thereafter the two learn to live together, but without passionate love; the direction Anna takes is to devote herself exclusively to the "little matriarchy" of her children.

In the last scene of *The Rainbow* Anna's daughter, Ursula, has an experience like her mother's in the cathedral. Pregnant and learning that she is now "bound" to live with Skrebensky, she flees the house and walks distractedly in the woods, becoming terrified when she loses her way and finds herself encircled by "myriads of tree-trunks, enormous and streaked black with water, thrust like stanchions upright. . . . She felt like a bird that has flown in through the window of a hall where vast warriors sit at the board. Between their grave, booming ranks she was hastening, assuming she was unnoticed, till she emerged, with beating heart, through the far window and out into the open, upon the vivid green, marshy meadow" (459). Again we have the image used by the Venerable Bede to describe the journey of the soul through this life, but here it seems to represent the flight of a woman from the phallic male.[15]

Lady Chatterley is more successful than any other heroine in fulfilling the sexual role Lawrence proposes for women. Her new life begins when she discovers the coops where the gamekeeper is breeding pheasants and becomes enthralled with the brooding hens, "the only things in the world that warmed her heart." She is especially moved when she sees one of the newborn chicks. "Pure, sparky, fearless new life!" she exclaims; "never had she felt so acutely the agony of her own female forlornness." She sees in the chicks the same assertion of life that the man who died sees in the cock, and shortly after this her body, like his, is resurrected, so to speak, when she becomes the gamekeeper's lover, choosing Mellors over her husband, Clifford. The two men are sharply contrasted on the basis of the sources from which they draw their feeling for life. Clifford, the industrialist, "simply felt life rush into him out of the coal, out of the pit," whereas Mellors is described as extracting something quite different from nature when he reaches under a setting hen to get a chick for Lady Chatterley to observe more closely: "And slowly, softly, with sure gentle fingers, he felt among the old bird's feathers and drew out a faintly-peeping chick in his closed hand."[16]

At the other extreme from Lady Chatterley is Lettie Tempest, the heroine of *The White Peacock,* who cannot bring herself to accept and return passionate love. She has what Lawrence defines, in "The Woman Who Rode Away," as the "sharpness and the quivering nervous consciousness of the highly-bred white woman." Consequently, the bird with which she is associated is not the brooding hen but the proud peacock. In a climactic scene she displays herself before the two men in her life, the upper-class husband she has trained "in the way he should go" and a handsome, manly farmer, George Saxton, to whom she is genuinely attracted.

> Lettie stood between the firelight and the dusky lamp glow, tall and warm between the lights. As she turned laughing to the two men, she let her cloak slide over her white shoulder and fall with silk splendour of a peacock's gorgeous blue over the arm of the large settee. There she stood, with her white hand upon the peacock of her cloak, where it tumbled against her dull orange dress. She knew her own splendour, and she drew up her throat laughing and brilliant with triumph. . . . she seemed to be moving in some alluring figure of a dance, her hair like a nimbus clouding the light, her bosom lit with wonder.
>
> (254–55)

The female peacock does not have the gorgeous plumage of the male and does not take the initiative in courting, but in giving Lettie the attributes of the male bird Lawrence is able to point up the irony of Lettie's failing femininity: she is a *white* (chaste) peacock, and her display is that of the magnificent male in appearance only. It is but a cloak she can lay aside, her true garment being a "dull orange dress," or the drab plumage of the indifferent peahen. No matter how moved her possible mates are, she cannot let herself go and delights only in false enticements. On a walk in the fields with George, she reveals the restraint she is under: "Don't you wish we were wild—hark, like wood-pigeons—or larks—or, look, like peewits! Shouldn't you love flying and wheeling and sparkling and—courting in the wind! . . . I wish we were free like that" (208). But this cannot be. "We have to consider things," she concludes. Whatever these are—her social position, her high-toned tastes, her fear of being passionate—Lettie gives up George and finds refuge in a loveless marriage.

The peacock, in its ugly rather than beautiful aspect, is associated with one other woman in the book, Lady Chrystabel, who is married to a man beneath her, Annable, a gamekeeper even more earthy than farmer George. At first they made a passionate couple (precursor to Lady Chatterley and her gamekeeper), but "she began to get souly" and Annable ran out on her. The experience has left him bitter about women. After her death Annable compares her to a peacock he sees perched on the statue of an angel in a churchyard: "The bird bent its voluptuous neck and peered about. Then it lifted up its head and yelled. The sound tore the dark sanctuary of twilight." Unusually perturbed, Annable reviles the bird: "That's the soul of a woman—or it's the devil . . . Just look! the dirty devil's run her muck over that angel. A woman to the end, I tell you, all vanity and screech and defilement" (*Peacock*, 148–49). For all its splendor he sees the peacock as behaving like a harpy. Later, however, at the funeral of the gamekeeper, who dies in an accident, other birds lament his death in the pastoral tradition of nature grieving over a deceased shepherd: "The heralds wave like shadows in the bright air, crying, lamenting, fretting forever. Rising and falling and circling round and round, the slow-waving peewits cry and complain, and lift their broad wings in sorrow. They stoop suddenly to the ground, the lapwings, then in another throb of anguish and protest, they swing up again, offering a glistening white breast to the sunlight, to deny it in black shadow, then a glisten of green, and all the time crying and crying in despair" (156). It is with an accurate eye that Lawrence observes the flight and call of the lapwings (plovers), also named peewits for their call. In this first of Lawrence's novels there is a greater abundance of closely observed birds and flowers than in any later novel.

Lawrence's peacocks may owe something to Poe's raven, the

bird that recalls to the unhappy lover in "The Raven" the painful
memory of the lost Lenore. The bird in the churchyard perches on
a statue, just as Poe's raven perches on the bust of Pallas Athene,
and is perceived by Annable to be either the devil or the soul of a
woman—that of his deceased wife, most likely. The original manu-
script has Annable saying that the appearance of the peacock is
"enough to make you believe in reincarnations" (*Peacock*, 379).
In an earlier scene "The Raven" is specifically mentioned when
Lettie and the narrator speculate on the "promise of sorrow" that
a single perched crow signifies. Like a "ghoul" the crow stays "on
the withered, silver-grey skeleton" of a holly-tree, on a "wet and
dreary" winter day, while his companions are swept away by the
wind "like souls hunting for a body to inhabit" (81–82).

The question Lawrence poses for his female characters is how
they will respond to male sexual passion. Bird imagery marks the
choices they have: compliance with the traditional role of breeder,
symbolized by the brown hen; escape from that role, represented
by visions of the free flight of birds; or absolute rejection of sex,
symbolized by a white bird. Their perplexity before these choices
reflects Lawrence's contribution to the assault on genteel standards of sexual behavior that began in the latter part of the nineteenth century and was completed in the twentieth century.

The white swans and doves of the past became less compelling
for many writers besides Lawrence, of course. The pure lady of
John Steinbeck's short story "The White Quail," for example, is
so intent on the ideal garden she wants to have someday that she
has but one qualification for a prospective husband: "Would the
garden like such a man?" Henry Teller seems to qualify, and on
the night he proposes marriage she tries writing out the name
"Mary Teller" using a peacock feather for pen. The garden is set
out exactly as she had planned it for many years. At the outer edge
a row of fuchsias, "like little symbolic trees," separates the garden from a hill "wild with cascara bushes and poison oak, with
dry grass and live oak." The fuchsias keep out the world beyond
the garden, "all rough and tangled and unkempt. The birds can
get in," Mary says. "They live out in the wild, but they come to
my garden for peace and for water." Within the garden itself all
precautions are taken to protect the plants; slugs and snails are

routinely killed, and Mr. Teller is forbidden to have a dog because it might "do things on the plants" and dig up the flower beds. When Mr. Teller tries Mary's bedroom door at night, he often finds it locked: "It was a signal. . . . He always tried the door silently. It seemed as though he didn't want her to know he had tried it." One of the birds attracted to the garden is a "dainty white hen quail," a bird Mary especially cherishes because she sees it as "the essence of me, an essence boiled down to utter purity. She must be the queen of the quail." A stray cat poses a threat not only to Mary's quail but to her own life in the Eden of her own making. Mr. Teller refuses to set out poison to kill the cat and proposes instead to give the cat a good scare by shooting at it with his air gun. His BB shot hits the white quail, however, and by chance enters the eye and kills it. He tells Mary that the cat will never come back.[17]

Mary's narcissism makes it impossible for her to have a normal sexual relationship with her husband. She identifies with the garden, a traditional symbol of the inviolate woman, and in protecting it from the intrusion of unruly forest plants, the slugs, the dog, and the cat she is subconsciously protecting herself from what she considers to be male defilement. Birds, another symbol of woman, are welcome in the garden, however, especially the white quail since it has escaped from the wild and preserved its "purity." Its whiteness distinguishes it from its brown-colored brethren and their leader, "a big fellow with a crest like a black question mark." Mr. Teller meekly accepts his wife's severe restraints; the only time he resists is when she asks him to use poison to rid the garden of the cat. At last the long-suffering husband finds a way to give vent to the feeling he must have had for a long time about his desperate marital situation when he says, "Dear, some dog might get it. Animals suffer terribly when they get poison." In defending the dog he is defending himself, and in killing the quail he is expressing his desire to remove what stands in the way of a normal marital relationship. Mary's identification with the quail is ironic in that the quail, like the dove, was once noted for its lasciviousness and was sacred to the Ephesian Artemis, an orgiastic Asian goddess, not to be confused with the chaste Artemis of the Greeks. As for poor Mr. Teller, he must suffer under the knowledge that some unfortunate Israelites were killed by the Lord for having "lusted" after the flesh of quails (Numbers 11.31–34). At the end of the story he exclaims, "Oh, Lord, I'm so lonely!"

The symbolical conflict of bird-woman and dog-man occurs in an earlier American story, done with a much finer touch than Steinbeck's, "A New England Nun" by Mary Wilkins Freeman. Louisa Ellis's home is as carefully shielded from male influence as Mary Teller's garden. All the "feminine appurtenances" she has gathered over the years—sewing utensils, china, linen, her many aprons variously designed for different tasks—"had become, from long use and constant association, a very part of her personality." The center of her maidenly activities is her sitting room. When Joe Dagget, the man to whom she is engaged, comes to visit in her "delicately sweet room, he felt as if surrounded by a hedge of lace." His presence there is terribly disturbing to both Louisa and her pet bird. On one occasion the "little yellow canary that had been asleep in his green cage at the south window woke up and fluttered wildly, beating his little yellow wings against the wires." Outside the house Louisa's "old yellow dog," Caesar, "dwelt in his secluded hut, shut out from the society of his kind and all innocent canine joys." Having once given her consent, Louisa feels bound to marry Joe Dagget: "No forebodings of Caesar on a rampage, no wild fluttering of her little yellow canary, were sufficient to turn her a hair's breadth." By chance, however, she learns that Joe would prefer to marry another woman, and the engagement is broken by mutual consent. Louisa "felt like a queen who, after fearing lest her domain be wrested away from her, sees it firmly insured in her possession." Now the canary "might turn itself into a peaceful yellow ball night after night, and have no need to wake and flutter with wild terror against its bars." [18]

Sylvia, in Sarah Orne Jewett's "A White Heron," is only nine years old, but "the woman's heart, asleep in the child, was vaguely thrilled by the dream of love" when she encounters a young man who is searching for a rare bird he has seen in the vicinity of the isolated farm where she lives with her grandmother. John James Audubon could have been the model for this character, who is quite knowledgeable about birds and is a collector of specimens. He boasts that he has "stuffed and preserved dozens and dozens" of birds he has "shot or snared." In one of his autobiographical

writings Audubon tells about staying with a country family, becoming "acquainted with my hostess and her sweet children," and
collecting (shooting) a "lovely Sylvia"—the name of an Old World
warbler that sometimes occurs in North America.[19]

The visitor in Jewett's "White Heron"—called an "ornithologist"—has reason to believe that Sylvia must know where the particular bird he is seeking has its nest, and he describes to her what
appears to be a heron or egret: "A queer tall white bird with soft
feathers and long thin legs. And it would have a nest perhaps in the
top of a high tree, made of sticks, something like a hawk's nest."
Sylvia indeed knows where the bird has its nest, but says nothing
even after spending a delightful day birding with the young man.
Early the next morning she visits the nest site alone and from the
top of a great pine tree sees the bird flying "with steady sweep of
wing and outstretched slender neck and crested head." Happily
she anticipates telling her secret to the visitor. But later that day,
even though she feels he "is so well worth making happy" and has
a childish notion that she "could have served and followed him
and loved him as a dog loves," she remains silent before him. "The
murmur of the pine's green branches is in her ears, she remem-
bers how the white heron came flying through the golden air and
how they watched the sea and the morning together, and Sylvia
cannot speak; she cannot tell the heron's secret and give its life
away" (161–71).

Sylvia is one of those rare spirits whose attachment to nature is
so intense that they avoid close contacts with people and transfer
their sexual feelings to natural phenomena, as, for example, James
Fenimore Cooper's virginal woodsman Natty Bumppo in *The Last
of the Mohicans,* who claims that his bride is "the dew on the open
grass—the clouds that float about in the blue heavens—the birds
that sing in the woods." When Sylvia lived in the city she had been
"afraid of folks," especially the "great red-faced boy who used to
chase and frighten her." She "never had been alive at all before
she came to live at the farm," and then within a year she gained
an intimate knowledge of all the places and living things in her
new environment. "There ain't a foot o' ground she don't know
her way over, and the wild creaturs counts her one o' themselves,"
her grandmother assures the visitor. In refusing to betray the white

heron to the collector's gun, Sylvia is rejecting love and the chance to take part in the "vast and awesome world" she has glimpsed from the top of the tree in favor of "an existence heart to heart with nature and the dumb life of the forest." Her virginity is surrendered, not to the young man but to the giant pine tree she climbs to find the heron's nest. She is the very opposite of the maiden in Elizabeth Barrett Browning's "Romance of the Swan's Nest" who dreams of showing her returning knight-errant a swan's nest, but upon checking it one day she discovers that "the wild swan had deserted— / And a rat had gnawed the reeds." Now she will never be able to show him "that swan's nest among the reeds!"

The year before "A White Heron" was published, the English writer W. H. Hudson told the story of a Uruguayan girl who spent her childhood, like Sylvia, in a "wild and solitary" place and had "only wild flowers, birds, and the ocean waves for playmates." When he was a boy of fifteen hunting ostriches, the narrator of *The Purple Land* encounters Transita and immediately falls in love. "I regarded her not as a mere human creature; she seemed more like some being from I know not what far-off celestial region who had strayed to earth, just as a bird of white and azure plumage and unknown to our woods, sometimes appears, blown hither from a distant tropical country or island, filling those who see it with wonder and delight."[20] Before the boy is old enough to propose marriage, however, the beautiful girl is carried off to Paris by a dissolute lover who soon abandons her, and she dies of tuberculosis.

Transita and her daughter Margarita are prototypes of Rima, the principal character in Hudson's best-known work, *Green Mansions*. The "bird-girl" is so close to nature that the young man who falls in love with her, Mr. Abel, mistakes her calls and songs for those of birds, and for the longest time he is unable to distinguish her from the green woods she inhabits. He can never quite understand her "bird-like warbling language." He had come to Venezuela looking for gold and instead falls in love with a purely natural creature, one "like all beautiful things in the wood—flower, and bird, and butterfly, and green leaf, and frond." Rima has the alertness of a wild animal, the "swiftness and grace and changeful brilliant color" of a hummingbird. As well as animal beauty she is endowed with a high degree of human spirituality, yet no more than Transita and Sylvia can she thrive in the company of humans. Abel's love for her does not complete her happiness, and she goes on a fruitless quest to find the place where her mother had once lived. Upon her return home, unaccompanied, she is attacked by the natives, who have always considered her a spirit hostile to their hunting in the woodlands she frequents. They set fire to the forest around the giant tree in which she has taken refuge: "The flames went up higher and higher with a great noise; and at last from the top of the tree, out of the green leaves came a great cry, like the cry of a bird, 'Abel! Abel!' and then looking we saw something fall; through leaves and smoke and flame it fell like a great white bird killed with an arrow and falling to the earth." In her treetop Rima suffers the fate that Jewett's Sylvia and her white heron had escaped, the ravishment of nature and innocence by men. The lush rain forest on the Orinoco River will now be abused by the natives and suffer the same fate as its presiding spirit. For Abel, losing the bird-girl means losing his tie with nature; he is left "dwelling alone on a vast stony plain in everlasting twilight."[21]

Hudson draws on the thoroughly romantic conception that nature is animated and may appear to us strikingly in animal personifications and, further, that an intense love of nature is akin to religious and even sexual feeling. Abel firmly believes that his bird-girl is "a being apart and sacred, and this feeling seemed to mix with my passion, to purify and exalt it and make it infinitely sweet and precious" (*Mansions*, 146). While Hudson admired Oliver Wendell Holmes's *Elsie Venner* for its snake-girl heroine, he was disappointed that the genteel Holmes did not take as romantic a view of animal nature as he had with his "double being," the bird-girl. Elsie had to be brought back to the human fold and purged of the snake poison, or original sin, she inherited from her mother. This is accomplished by her falling in love with a young man, on the assumption that love for fellow humans is the ultimate refinement. The animal in poor Elsie is extirpated but at the cost of her life, an ending Hudson deplored because "it is not in harmony with the conception of Elsie, of a being in whom the human and serpentine natures were indissolubly joined" (*Naturalist*, 164–65). Hudson could not go as far as Lawrence in his embrace of natural instincts in woman, but he could reject the hypocrisy of the genteel male who is attracted by the woman's natural instincts but yields to society's demand to restrain them.

To express the fear of menacing and intractable women there was once a great store of mythical female monsters whose contacts with men were motivated by hatred and revenge rather than submissiveness. Best known in Western literature as Harpies, Furies, and Sirens, they assumed various bizarre forms, but all at one time or another were conceived as having the body of a bird and the face and breasts of a woman. The Sirens described by Homer in book 12 of the *Odyssey* waylaid unsuspecting men and kept them from ever rejoining wife and family. Furies, or Erinyes in Greek, pursued men who were guilty of familial crimes. Harpies punished men who offended the gods; in their most famous assault, an appropriately domestic act, they starved Phineus almost to death by snatching food from his table and fouling what remained with their droppings, until Jason and his Argonauts drove them off.

Avenging bird-women continue to turn up in literature. One contemporary instance occurs even in the uncompromisingly naturalistic *Last Exit to Brooklyn* by Hubert Selby, Jr. Harry Black covers his latent homosexuality with the most extreme male vulgarity and violence imaginable. Hardly able to bear his oversexed wife's nightly advances, he feels guilty for rejecting her and suffers from a recurrent incubus:

> The Harpies swooped down on Harry and in the darkness under their wings he could see nothing but their eyes: small, and filled with hatred, their eyes laughing at him, mocking him as he tried to evade them, knowing he couldnt and that they could toy with him before they slowly destroyed him. He tried turning his head but it wouldnt move. He tried and tried until it rolled back and forth but still the eyes glared and mocked and the gigantic wings beat faster and faster and the wind whirled around Harry and his body chilled and he could sense their large sharp beaks and feel the tips of feathers as they brushed his face.[22]

It is in a dream, too, that three winged goddesses appear to a principal character in Salman Rushdie's *Satanic Verses,* a novel that amusingly mixes twentieth-century realism with the ancient origins of Islam. The pre-Islamic Al-Lat, Uzza, and Manat, who probably bear some relation to the three Greek Erinyes, afflict the Indian film star Gibreel Farishta because, in his dream-role as the angel Gibreel, he has denied their divinity: "They fall upon him from the night sky, the three winged creatures, flapping around his head, clawing at his eyes, biting, whipping him with their hair, their wings. He puts up his hands to protect himself, but their revenge is tireless, continuing whenever he rests, whenever he drops his guard. He struggles against them, but they are faster, nimbler, winged" (126). The title of the novel is related to the three goddesses: in order to win converts among those who believe in the old pre-Islamic religion, Mahound, Rushdie's name for the prophet Mohammed, declares that they are "exalted birds" acceptable to Allah. Later he disavows them, saying that it was Satan rather than the angel Gibreel who had put the words in his mouth.

A very extended adaptation of avenging birds is to be found in the concluding section of William Styron's *Lie Down In Darkness*. Just before her suicide Peyton Loftis, in an interior monologue somewhat like Molly's in James Joyce's *Ulysses*, dwells obsessively on all the sordid details of her misspent life. Various leitmotivs serve as indirect expressions of feelings deep in the unconscious of the troubled young woman. By far the most frequently recurring image has to do with a group of flightless birds that are always present "upon the boundaries" of her consciousness: "land-bound birds whirling about, dodos and penguins and cassowaries, ostriches befouling their lovely black plumes, and these seemed mixed up with Bunny." Bunny is Peyton's special name for her father, who has scarcely suppressed incestuous feelings for his daughter. Since flight is a well-known Freudian symbol of coitus, it is reasonable to interpret the flightless birds as representing Peyton's sexual failure with her many lovers, a failure caused by her passionate relationship with her father. To compensate for her frustration she is promiscuous with a number of men. "How many times have I lain down to sin out of vengeance, to say *so he doesn't love me, then here is one that will*, to sleep then and dream about the birds." Of course, the daughter of an upper-class Southern family suffers terrible guilt for having behaved so improperly. Can the guilt be from the accident when she "let Maudie fall"? No, "birds were for another time, another guilt, when I lay down with all the hostile men," she insists. "Guilt is the thing with feathers, they came back with a secret rustle, preening their flightless wings and I didn't want to think."[23] Possibly there is an ironical echo here of the opening line of a poem by Emily Dickinson: " 'Hope' is the thing with feathers— / That perches in the soul" (no. 254).

Guilt and sexual inadequacy inevitably lead to Peyton's preoccupation with the thought of death, and again the birds carry the theme. Flightless birds are especially appropriate here, for they have long been the earliest and easiest targets for extinction by hunters. Peyton lives in dread of a recurrent pain in her womb "like the claw of some bird waiting"; when she gets temporary relief from pills, the pain is "dormant, cautious, watchful, like that condor with one waking eye" (*Darkness*, 326). She has a sensation of drowning: "Then in my drowning soul the birds pranced solemnly across the plain and their feathers rustled flightless in the evening" (345). The plain is the land of the dead, where she imagines herself to be: "Across the margin of my mind they came, the wingless birds, the emus and dodos and ostriches and moas, preening their wings in the desert light: a land of slumber, frightening me, where I lay forever dozing in the sands" (363). Yet at the end of her ordeal, just as she is about to leap from the twelfth floor of a building in Harlem, the image of the birds in her consciousness undergoes a radical change. If before they had haunted her like the winged Erinyes, the mythical avengers of domestic wrongs, they are changed now into the Eumenides or Kindly Ones, releasing her as they finally released Oedipus, another victim of sexual tragedy. If before they horrified her with the Dantean vision of a hopeless condition of death in a desert, now they are supplanted by the phoenix suggested in the line from Sir Thomas Browne from which the title of the novel is taken—"It cannot be long before we lie down in darkness, and have our light in ashes." No longer flightless, the birds are now seen as ascending to paradise while Peyton prepares to jump to her death and purgatory in the street below:

Myself all shattered, this lovely shell? Perhaps I shall rise at another time, though I lie down in darkness and have my light in ashes. I turn in the room, see them come across the tiles, dimly prancing, fluffing up their wings, I think: my poor flightless birds, have you suffered without soaring on this earth? Come then and fly. And they move on past me through the darkening sands, awkward and gentle, rustling their feathers; come then and fly. And so it happens treading past to touch my boiling skin—one whisper of feathers is all—and so I see them go—oh my Christ!—one by one ascending my flightless birds through the suffocating night, toward paradise.   (368)

Actually the line from Browne's *Urn Burial* does not refer to the legend of the phoenix: his marginal note ascribes it to the "custom of the Jews, who place a lighted wax-candle in a pot of ashes by the corpse" (1:168).

Peyton Loftis is the very opposite of Hilda in Hawthorne's *Marble Faun,* though not unlike Hilda's sinful friend Miriam, who bears a remarkable resemblance to a painting of Beatrice Cenci, the notorious parricide suspected of having incestuous relations with her father. The doves sharing a tower with Hilda do not abandon her when she feels tainted with the knowledge of her friend Miriam's sin; Peyton suffers under the impression that her ugly birds haunt her for her promiscuity. The virginal Hilda is so happy in her innocence that she is "half inclined to attempt a flight from the top of my tower, in the faith that I should float upward" like one of her doves (chap. 7). Peyton can only wish that her birds will ascend to paradise as she plunges to her death from the washroom of a high loft building in Harlem.

Caged birds, doves, and the swan in its gentler aspect have represented the feminine ideal for male writers. The brooding hen, as we have already noted, has been the model for the protected and protecting mother. The plight of the caged bird has also served as a common metaphor to represent the dependent position of women. The Victorian lady in Mrs. Browning's *Aurora Leigh* is described as living

> A sort of cage-bird life, born in a cage,
> Accounting that to leap from perch to perch
> Was act and joy enough for any bird.
> (1.304)

The spirited woman, like Jane Eyre, tries to break out of the cage, much to the dismay of Rochester in Charlotte Brontë's novel, who "finds it impossible to be conventional" with the new governess: "I see at intervals a glance of a curious sort of bird through the close-set bars of a cage; a vivid, restless, resolute captive is there; were it but free it would soar cloud-high." The caged bird is but one more image in a succession of confining places and would-be jailers that Jane has had to deal with, such as Mrs. Reed at Gateshead and Reverend Brocklehurst at Lowood, but there is no restraint that can crush Jane's spirit, as Rochester learns. "Whatever I do with its cage, I cannot get at it—the savage, beautiful creature! If I tear, if I rend the slight prison, my outrage will only let the captive loose." At the end of the novel their positions are reversed: the blinded Rochester is like a "caged eagle, whose gold-ringed eyes cruelty has extinguished," and Jane must now look after him, "just as if a royal eagle, chained to a perch, should be forced to entreat a sparrow to become its purveyor."[24]

Jane is more successful in gaining freedom than are some of her successors. Throughout *Tess of the D'Urbervilles* Hardy's heroine is compared to a bird that is trapped, caged, and finally destroyed.[25] She begins like Wordsworth's Lucy or Hudson's Rima, "a fresh and virginal daughter of Nature"; her buoyant walk is "like the skim of a bird which has not quite alighted" (*Tess*, 249). All this changes when she is tricked by her cousin Alec into making love with him in a "sort of couch or nest" that he has prepared for her in a natural forest setting, ironically, where all about her "were poised gentle roosting birds in their last nap" (88–90). Tess has been caught "like a bird in a springe." She is attracted to the next man in her life when, "like a fascinated bird," she stops to listen to Angel Clare playing a harp. When he deserts her for her single transgression, the bird imagery changes. No longer does she walk with a "quiescent glide . . . of a piece with the element she moved in"; instead she trudges the countryside looking for work, each place becoming more dreadful than the last, until she reaches Flintcomb-Ash, "a starve-acre place." The winter season there brings strange migrant birds from the North Pole, "gaunt spectral creatures with tragical eyes—eyes which had witnessed scenes of cataclysmal horror" (367). In all her suffering Tess does not blame Clare; like the bird in Hardy's poem that does not resent having been blinded, she "was not provoked, thought no evil of his treatment of her." Yet, like a trapped animal, "a caged wretch," she is finally provoked into killing Alec after he comes back into her life and makes her his mistress. To the end she is still associated with birds, her dressing-gown having "a frill of down" and her street hat a gathering of black feathers. At Stonehenge, weary with fleeing from the police, she falls asleep on the Stone of Sacrifice: "Her breathing now was quick and small, like that of a lesser creature than a woman" (505).

Even female characters who anticipate the new feminism of the second half of the twentieth century accede to literary attitudes created by the preponderance of male writers over the centuries. Lara, in Pasternak's *Doctor Zhivago*, accepts the male stereotype when she says to Yuri, " 'You were given wings to fly above the clouds, but I'm a woman, mine are given me to stay close to the ground and to shelter my young.' He was deeply moved by everything she said" (362). Edna, in Kate Chopin's *Awakening*, vows not to be one of the mothers who "esteemed it a holy privilege to efface themselves as individuals and grow wings as ministering angels." [26] She is warned by Mademoiselle Reisz, an older woman who has won her freedom, that "the bird that would soar above the level plain of tradition and prejudice must have strong wings. It is a sad spectacle to see the weaklings bruised, exhausted, fluttering back to earth." Edna, as it turns out, is one who fails; Lawrence's Kate Leslie, in *The Plumed Serpent*, may be another.

Ultimate failure following the assertion of independence seems to be the inevitable result for female characters who attempt to break literary tradition. [27] Throughout Tennessee Williams's *Roman Spring of Mrs. Stone*, the heroine is compared to a hawk because in her prime she had been a forceful, grasping person, with the look of "a rapacious bird" in her eyes. But age is beginning to tell: "Her body had flown like a powerful bird through and above the entangling branches of the past few years, but her face now exhibited the record of the flight." To escape attention in Rome she has taken an apartment that "stood like the solitary eyrie of a bird above the roofs of the city." Mrs. Stone presents an appearance quite different from Hawthorne's saintly Hilda in her bell tower. To an Italian waif in the street below, Mrs. Stone and a friend, standing on the terrace, appear to be "two exotic giant birds that were commanding a precipice." To the reader it is reported that "her frightened and aging face had the look of an embattled hawk peering from the edge of a cliff in a storm." What supports her spirit now is an affair she is having with an Italian prince who supports himself being a *marchetta*, or gigolo. In making love with him she likes to think she is "a bird that sprang skyward." Finally, however, she must face up to the fact that her lover stays only to be kept in luxury. When he accuses her rather than himself of being "someone who is interested only in the golden excrement of the American Eagle," she dismisses him angrily, "rushed past him with the rapidity of a great-winged bird." [28] But this is her last hawklike act, for she immediately feels that she is now "drifting" into a state of nothingness, and to stop the drift she goes out on the terrace and signals the ominous figure below to come up, an invitation that will surely end in her degradation if not mortal harm.

Frau Rosalie von Tümmler in Thomas Mann's *Black Swan* is another lovesick, aging widow, who like Mrs. Stone feels rejuvenated when she falls in love with an American half her age. The mother of a grown daughter and a young son, she justifies the liaison with the romantic notion that in surrendering to her feelings—"the flowering spring of pain in my soul"—she is merely following a law of nature. But on the very day when she reveals her passion to Keaton she is taught a hard lesson by nature. On a springtime outing to Holterhof Castle with Keaton and her children, she removes from Keaton's pocket some bread he had brought to feed the resident swans and begins to eat it, "warm from his body." One of the swans angrily hisses at her. It appears that Rosalie hungers for love as swans hunger for food, though they "disguised their appetite," and when finally given the bread they "accepted with unperturbable dignity," as she clearly does not when she eats the bread out of Keaton's pocket and later when she makes up to Keaton on the same occasion.[29] That night she is taken ill and cannot meet her would-be lover. Nature had "reappeared calamitously": her illness is diagnosed as cancer of the ovary and uterus. In the few weeks of life remaining to her she is haunted by the memory of the hissing swan, "his blood-red bill, the black beating of the wings."

There are exceptions to the rule of submissive female birds. When King Lear finally comes to realize the evil his daughter Regan has done him, he exclaims, beating his breast, "O Regan, she hath tied / Sharp-toothed unkindness, like a vulture, here" (2.4.132). Ruth Rendell borrows the line to make a collective noun of multitude for the title of her mystery novel *An Unkindness of Ravens*, in which about five hundred unmarried women over sixteen form an organization "designed to give men no quarter," that is, groups of three or four members are expected to kill a man to prove they are "true feminists." The group is named ARRIA after a brave Roman matron who showed her convicted husband how to commit suicide; ARRIA also stands for "Action for the Radical Reform of Intersexual Attitudes," and the acronym is printed on members' t-shirts along with a drawing of a bird having a woman's head. One teenager has "felt-tipped pen drawings on her arms and hands . . . [of] a raven woman with aggressive breasts and erect wings, somehow obscene on those smooth golden arms, childish and rounded." In Hildegarde Flanner's "Hawk Is a Woman" the horrible terms describing a hawk's devouring a lark compare with those used by male writers:

> Into the winsome breast she plied her beak,
> Took at a gulp the rosy heart, a pinch
> Of too great innocence, drank the whole lark
> Down, the inmost blood down, licked the lark down
> With vicious dainty pick, oh the damned thief!

Revenge is called for—to be performed by another female hawk— "May hawk be hawked upon, I say." [30]

Men in literature often conceive of their sexual role in terms of the violent and rapacious traits of birds. If from the male point of view of her husband's boon companions, Mrs. Ramsay, in Virginia Woolf's *To the Lighthouse*, is like a "hen straddling her wings out in protection of a covey of little chicks," from the point of view of her youngest son Mr. Ramsay is a sterile "beak of brass, the arid scimitar of the male, which smote mercilessly, again and again, demanding sympathy." [31] Ambiguity being the rule for all imagery, especially imagery drawn from nature, birds may serve opposite symbolical purposes. Monks in their paintings "plucked the wings of birds to make angels of men, and the claws of birds, to make devils of men," John Ruskin writes (15:25). The traditional association of the swan is with purity and beauty, as Edmund Spenser so well expresses in "Prothalamion," a "spousal verse" in which two brides are compared to a pair of swans on the Thames:

> So purely white they were,
> That even the gentle streame, the which them bare,
> Seem'd foule to them, and bad his billowes spare
> To wet their silken feathers, least they might
> Soyle their fayre plumes with water not so fayre,
> And marre their beauties bright,
> That shone as heavens light,
> Against their Brydale day.
> (lines 46–53)

But the swan is hermaphroditic, writes Gaston Bachelard, feminine in its contemplation of water, masculine in action.[32] Its form and whiteness suggest the dazzling beauty and purity of a nude woman bathing, while the violence and the phallicism of the male, we might add, are clearly indicated by the swan's neck and bill and the powerful blows it is capable of delivering with its wings. To illustrate his point Bachelard cites the scene in *Faust* (Part Two), "On the Lower Peneios," in which "the prince of swans" assaults Leda while she is bathing with her attendants. Better examples would be Yeats's "Leda and the Swan," in which appears the assault of the bird that staggers the girl by the "sudden blow" of its "great wings beating," or this from Lawrence's "Leda":

> Come not with kisses
> not with caresses
> of hands and lips and murmurings;
> come with a hiss of wings
> and sea-touch tip of beak
> and treading of wet, webbed, wave working feet
> into the marsh-soft belly.
> (436)

Wooing might inspire the poet with gentle bird imagery, but lovemaking did not. Andrew Marvell's lover in "To His Coy Mistress" imagines himself and his reluctant mistress making love "like amorous birds of prey" that "devour" their time together and "tear [their] pleasures with rough strife." Walt Whitman's male lovers in "Children of Adam" are "free and lawless" like "two hawks in the air," and in "The Dalliance of Eagles" the violence of mating occurs in flight:

> The rushing amorous contact high in space together,
> The clinching interlocking claws, a living, fierce,
>   gyrating wheel,
> Four beating wings, two beaks, a swirling mass
>   tight grappling,
> In tumbling turning clustering loops, straight downward falling.
>
> (412)

Whitman's daring eroticism—at least for his time—may be better appreciated when we compare his lines with the genteel description by his friend John Burroughs, to whom a pair of eagles "appeared to clasp claws, then swing round and round several times, like school-girls a-hold of hands"; or with this description of the nuptial flight by Edwin Way Teale, a professional naturalist: "A pair of bald eagles grasp talons in mid-air and come cart-wheeling down through the sky, turning over and over in a wild plunge that carried them earthward for hundreds of feet." Drawing on the tradition that expresses religious devotion through sexual imagery, William Everson makes the "mate-flight" of eagles a symbol of the union of the soul with God as they

> Climb the pouring up-shaft of air;
> And high where the thunderheads mushroom and coil
> Turn to; and in the gyre and sweep
> That is a tremendous strength of wings,
> Clutch claw to claw and the beaks clash;
> And in that high instantaneity
> The skyborne join is made,
> And all passion poured—
> So is the grappling of the soul in its God.
>
> (100)

All three descriptions include the wheeling flight and clenched claws, suggesting a direct line of descent from Burroughs. It is not likely that eagles ever mate in flight, however, as Everson suggests; Whitman's "dalliance" is nearer to the facts of courtship behavior of tumbling eagles. About the only bird in North America that copulates in flight is the white-throated swift. Lewis Nkosi makes use of this phenomenon when the hero of his *Mating Birds,* an African black man convicted for making love to a white woman, observes from his prison cell a pair of birds "clinging to each other joyfully . . . up there in freedom and open space." [33]

There are exceptions to the sexually dominant male, of course. One is the narrator in Glenway Wescott's *Pilgrim Hawk,* a novelette with the distinction of having a bird as the central image over an extended narrative. What holds the interest of Alwyn Tower one eventful afternoon is a trained peregrine falcon that is brought by visitors into the house of his lady friend, Alexandra Henry. First it is the bird's look that fascinates Tower, a professional writer from whose point of view the entire story is conveyed: "It was like a little flame; it caught and compelled your attention like that, although it did not flicker and there was nothing bright about it nor any warmth in it. It is a look that men sometimes have; men of great energy, whose appetite or vocation has kept them absorbed every instant of their lives." [34] It is not only the presence and behavior of the bird that fascinates him but the expert knowledge of falcons conveyed to him by its owner, Mrs. Cullen, who is always ready to talk about "the dear theme of the hawk." Intrigued by Mrs. Cullen's facility of combining knowledge with imagination, of making easy "transitions from hawk to human and objective to subjective," Tower amuses himself with speculations about the bird as the center of a set of symbolical meanings. He proceeds in a manner somewhat like Ishmael's factual and fanciful manipulation of the white whale in *Moby-Dick,* though Tower's absorbing interest is to plumb the depths of personal relations rather than metaphysical problems. The "all-embracing symbolic bird" comes to represent for him the various kinds of behavior of the company of people gathered that day at his friend's house. He begins with Madeleine and Larry Cullen and speculates that the hawk has come between them, since she makes a "loving fuss" over the bird and her husband is jealous and even attempts to set it free. Both are like the hawk in some ways, Madeleine in her beauty and primitive force, Larry in his attempt to "bate," or escape his wife's control. Counterpointed against the wealthy Cullens and their hawk is another love triangle consisting of their chauffeur, Ricketts, and their host's servants, Jean and Eva. Jean is jealous of his wife's flirtatious manner with Ricketts, who is described as "a fine Cockney, bright-eyed and sharp-nosed." The upshot of the Cullen affair is tragicomedy with Mr. Cullen pulling a gun on someone—his wife, Ricketts, the hawk, or himself—and being disarmed by his domineering wife.

Less dramatic but more important than any of these is the relation Tower sees between himself and the hawk. The bird's aspect, the "solemn glance of its maniacal eyes," somehow helps Tower to concentrate his attention on a number of disturbing things in his own life. He is especially attracted by the falcon's rapacious hunger, "an image of amorous appetite" as well as "other human hungers, mental and sentimental," by which he means his own ambition to be a writer and the lover of Alexandra, his hostess. Yet he cannot help admitting that the bird's hunger is satisfied in a praiseworthy way; he learns what Frau von Tümmler had also discovered, that the satisfaction of hunger in animals has none of the ugliness and foolhardiness of appetite in humans: "I had been hearing so much and thinking so romantically of hawk-hunger, that I expected a lunge and a grab, like a wolf or a cat; it was not so at all. It took two or three minutes for Lucy's appetite to accumulate. . . . When Lucy paused and raised her weird face between mouthfuls, it seemed spiritual rather than sensual; a bigoted face. There was no histrionic angry temper, no showing off. Thoroughly and slowly it went on to the end, with meditation upon every feather, every crumb of meat, every sip of blood—sacramental" (*Hawk*, 654). But he learns from Mrs. Cullen that old hawks eventually starve to death because failing eyesight, damaged feathers, and dulled talons make it hard for them to hunt successfully. (Aristotle observed that when the eagle's beak became crooked and lengthened with age the bird starved to death [9.619a15].) This information leads Tower to a comparison of the falcon's tragic fate and his own aging: "The old bachelor is like

an old hawk." The desire to love is still sharp, but there is "less
and less likelihood of being loved, less and less ability to love."
The early hope of becoming a good writer turns bitter when the
middle-aged man finally discovers he has not enough talent: "The
unsuccessful artist also ends in an apathy, too proud and vexed to
fly again, waiting upon withheld inspiration, bored to death." (One
recalls Eliot's "aged eagle," in "Ash-Wednesday," whose "wings
are no longer wings to fly.") When Tower is given the falcon to hold
for a few minutes, he has the feeling that death, "concentrated and
embodied," is perching on his gauntleted hand. At the close of the
story, when he is forced to face the ugly facts of human behavior,
such as Larry Cullen's frustration and his own failures, Tower rejects the image of the noble hawk he has created and concludes
that the bird has been "trapped out of the real wind and rock,
and perverted rather than domesticated, kept blind and childish,
at the mercy of every human absurdity," and this is precisely the
"absurd position of the artist in the midst of the disorders of those
who honor and support him" (677). Tower's failure to understand
the domestic problem of the Cullens seems to discredit the whole
attempt of the artist to explore the mysteries of human affairs by
means of symbolical analogies. The falcon has sharpened his sense
of inadequacy in both his craft of writing and his relation to Alexandra.[35]

The South African hero of Alan Paton's *Too Late the Phalarope*
is also unable to satisfy his sexual desires in an acceptable manner, but instead of merely contemplating his failure like Tower in
The Pilgrim Hawk, Pietr van Vlaanderen willfully acts upon his
feelings even though he knows that he risks bringing ruin upon
himself and his family. Whereas the relation between human and
falcon is exhaustively explored by Tower himself, only the reader
can be aware of similarities between Pietr and the bird he resembles. In his case it is not the predatory falcon but the phalarope,
a shorebird species distinguished for its reversal of sexual roles.
The female, larger and more brilliantly plumaged than the male, is
the pursuer in courtship, while the male holds back until aroused,
and then he may try any female, though he is only successful with
his own mate. She, however, sometimes practices sequential poly-
andry; the male incubates the eggs and cares for the young.

A well-known athlete, war hero, and police lieutenant, Pietr is nonetheless feminine in nature. In his childhood Pietr grows to be "like his mother, tender and gentle," largely as a reaction against his tyrannical father, a fanatical champion of Afrikaner religious, political, and racial ideology. Serious trouble originates in his marriage. His "long and shy and protracted" courtship is finally brought to an end only when his fiancée takes the lead, and when her ardor is cooled by the respectability marriage and children entail in Afrikaner society, Pietr is too gentle to bring her to an understanding of his needs. To satisfy these he is drawn into an affair with a streetwise black woman, Stephanie, who works at odd jobs and makes some money on the side by brewing and selling illegal beer. She has had white men come after her before, and she soon discovers that by playing on the lieutenant's sympathy for her and her fatherless child she can get him to help her out of her many scrapes with the police and her employers. She easily dominates him in their brief conversations and even dares to smile at him, and of course "no such girl might look in such a way at such a man," and no such man may consort with such a woman. But Pietr finally does succumb to passion and is soon discovered by a jealous subordinate.

Pietr well knows the terrible consequences of violating the Immorality Act of 1927—utter disgrace for himself and his entire family and the ruin of his career. Overly diffident, he is alone in his struggle, first in resisting temptation and then in dealing with the consequences; for he cannot reveal his torment to anyone, especially his father, who disapproved of everything he had ever done. The single break in the old man's steely armor is his love of birds, which he shares with his son, and this bond leads to some rare moments of tenderness. One is occasioned by a birthday gift Pietr gives him, *The Birds of South Africa*. A man of one book only, his family Bible in Dutch, "he was astonished that there was such a book, and by the numbers of the plates, and their colours also. His eyes went from one bird to another, and you knew that he was feeling under some kind of power of the book, and did not wish to fall under it openly, but being a clean man and honest, he did not wish to hide it altogether." Later, to disprove a statement by the English author of the book that the phalarope is a coastal bird only, he takes his son on a bird walk. The old man sees the bird first:

> Then because the son could not see, the father went and stood behind him, rested his arm on the son's shoulder, and pointed at the bird. But the son could see no bird, for he was again moved in some deep place within, and something welled up within him that if not mastered could have burst out of his throat and mouth, making him a girl or child. Therefore he could neither see nor speak.
> Then his father said in excitement, look son, it runs.
> But when his son made no answer, he said, can't you see?
> And the son said in a low voice, I cannot see.

The scene is full of the most poignant ironies. The father sees the phalarope, probably knows about the female characteristics of the male bird, but remains blind to his son's exceptional tenderness. The son is so deeply moved by the touch of his father on his shoulder that he is afraid to seize this moment to confess his transgression for fear that he may break down in a way unbecoming a grown male. If only the phalarope had brought them together long ago! "The boy Pietr had something of the woman in him," observes the narrator of the novel, Tante Sophie, "and the father none at all until it was too late." For the father the presence of a phalarope at an inland site helps support his tremendous pride in his homeland; it is of a piece with his fierce nationalism and racism. In an earlier scene the son has a strong emotional response to the red-cheeked cuckoo (with the suggestive scientific name *cuculus solitarius*), a bird whose cry suggests for him the pity and tragedy of the human predicament in a fallen world:

> like a hand suddenly plucking at the strings of the heart, so that your whole being shook and trembled; and why and why, why no one knew, it was the nature of man and the creation, that some sound, long remembered from the days of innocence before the world's corruption, could open the door of the soul, flooding it with a sudden knowledge of the sadness and terror and beauty of man's home and the earth. But you could not keep such knowledge, you could not hold it in your hand like a flower or a book,

for it came and went like the wind; and the door of the soul would not stay open, for maybe it was too great joy and sorrow for a man and meant only for angels. Yet you could ride again in the rain, in the *piet-my-vrou's* season, and he would call again, and catch you again by the throat and make you tremble.[36]

In *Flaubert's Parrot* Julian Barnes cites a newspaper story that had attracted Flaubert's attention at the time he was working on "A Simple Heart." A man who had taught his pet parrot to utter the name of his lost love became so fond of the bird that upon its death he began to think that he too was a parrot and started to move about and flap his arms like a bird. His family committed him to a *maison de santé;* he escaped, was found perched in a tree, and was returned to the hospital (57–58). A man's neurotic identification with a bird is also the subject of a novel by William Wharton, an American writer who makes his home in Paris. *Birdy* is a narrative that somehow manages to combine a case history of schizophrenia with an authoritative account of the process of breeding canaries. The balancing of fantasy with the detailed knowledge of animals calls to mind Melville's combining Ahab's madness with the process of whaling in *Moby-Dick*. In Wharton's novel a teenager nicknamed Birdy records his daily and purely factual observations of the birds he is raising and at the same time incidentally records his gradual slipping into a mental condition in which he believes he is a bird. To fly like a bird, to be "practically free from gravity and friction," was Birdy's original motivation, and to this end he undertakes a number of strenuous exercises to develop the muscles he considers necessary for flight. Could the young boy have read "The Spirit of Gravity" in *Thus Spake Zarathustra?* "Bird-nature," Nietzsche wrote there, is "hostile to the spirit of gravity," and he gave instructions that he "who would become light and be a bird . . . must first learn standing and walking and running and climbing and dancing" (3.55).

Of course Birdy eventually learns that a human being cannot fly, but by this time he has become so intent on his close observation of his canaries that he begins to think of himself as one of them. "With the binoculars I can concentrate on one bird and watch it. I'm trying to find out what it's thinking, I can get the feeling I'm a bird after a while." The final transition from human to bird, however, is in his dreams, for in his dreamlife he is able to fly at last. And flying, he discovers, is like bird song, like poetry: "In the dream, I sing. I can never remember singing like a boy, but singing as a bird is completely different from anything I've ever known. . . . I sound like a roller canary singing, but the words I'm hearing are in English and sound almost like poetry."[37]

"In my sleep I continually dream of birds," John James Audubon admitted. Night after night Birdy dreams not only that he flies like a bird but that he has fallen in love with a bird, an association that is in accord with the Freudian idea that the dream of flying is a subconscious expression of sexual desire. Birdy calls his dream-bird Perta—"because that's the closest word I can think of for the sound I know her by," he says, though it calls to mind Pertelote, the favorite hen of the rooster Chauntecleer in Chaucer's "The Nun's Priest's Tale." One night Birdy consummates his love for Perta, discovering upon awakening that he has had a "wet dream." Among the canaries of the breeder he deals with he finds a bird he believes is actually the bird of his dream and he brings her home. Being Perta's mate is now just as important as flying, and being a bird in his dream more important than being human in his waking life. "I let go. I settle deeply into the life I've always wanted. I become, re-become, a bird in this world of dream" (*Birdy*, 261). But he never goes so far into his dream that he neglects reality altogether (any more than the mad Ahab ever loses his skill as a navigator and whaler). It is avian reality for Birdy, of course: "The realest thing is the dream and the next real thing is watching my birds." His imagination is exercised on himself and not on the birds, who are always described in the most factual way. Here is Perta, for example, bathing:

> Perta hops onto the side of the dish and puts her beak into the clear, cold water. She lets it run back down her throat, tipping her head back and thrusting her breast forward, stretching upward on her thin legs. She does this again. I watch. Then, she pushes her face into the water and splashes back under her wings. She flaps her wings to capture the cold water under the warmest part of her wings, inside where the down of softest feathers is. She does this

two or three times before she lightly springs into the water, arches her back, tilts her head and starts throwing the clean water onto the feathers between her wings on her back.   (235)

Eventually Birdy, like Alwyn Tower, must deal with the world of reality, which comes in the form of a cat that is stalking Perta. Birdy is aware of the cat in his dream but is unable to "move" himself out of his dream to save Perta. In his last dream he releases all his "free fliers," the birds he has trained to fly free out of doors and return to their cages, and he joins them in their flight to freedom until he can no longer keep up: "I find myself getting heavier, falling, gliding down to the earth. . . . I flap my arms as I fall and I just manage to get back into my sleep under the empty sky" (299–300). This marks the final collapse of his dream life, and from that point on Birdy suffers a complete breakdown and is in and out of hospitals, like the French parrot-lover. No longer able to dream, he must surrender the life of perfect freedom and love that birds enjoy. Birdy cannot be like the "successful schizophrenic" in another Wharton novel, *Dad* (1981), in which the hero manages to remain functional in real life while still enjoying a mental vision of the life he prefers.

Alwyn Tower's brief encounter with a falcon confirms the doubts he has had about his sexual and artistic failings; Birdy's love of birds draws him into a fantasy world; George Gattling, the hero of Harry Crews's *The Hawk Is Dying* finds the reality of love and beauty in training a wild hawk. Like Birdy, he is an ordinary American youth with an extraordinary passion for birds; he, too, dreams of being a bird: "He took wing. Was a hawk. Wheeled under a diamond sky. He knew he was dreaming, but he was a hawk, with a hawk's eyes, and a hawk's mouth and a hawk's hunger and he flew on in a bright depthless sky where nothing else moved."[38] He has an obsession for something rare that no one around him can begin to understand or appreciate, falconry. It begins with his meeting a university professor who raises fighting cocks and was once an *austringer*, a hawk trainer. He introduces George to *The Art of Falconry* (*De arte venandi cum avibus*), the thirteenth-century classic by Frederick II of Hohenstaufen, Holy

Roman Emperor and King of Sicily and Jerusalem from 1212 to 1250, and this becomes the novice's guide for the trapping and training of wild hawks. But someone raised in Bacon County, Georgia, and now the operator of an automobile upholstery shop in Gainesville, Florida, cannot be expected to subscribe to all of the fine principles of a medieval nobleman, the grandson of the great Barbarossa. To "man" his hawks George uses a method that true falconers would consider "slovenly": he withholds food and rest until the bird either dies or is willing to perch quietly on his hand so that further training can proceed. Emperor Frederick, however, allows reduced rations only "to insure the progressive taming of the wild bird without starving her too much; otherwise one might reduce unduly the courage, activity, and other qualities necessary in a good hunting falcon," and he disapproves of those falconers "who attempt, through emaciation and extreme hunger, to reduce their birds to obedience in a very short time."[39] George has already had two kestrels die on him, but he insists to all who object to his treatment that the birds have a "choice" between submission and death. "All he had to do was hop on my hand and eat," he says of the last one, whose corpse—no bigger than a mockingbird, his horrified girlfriend observes—he stuffs down the kitchen disposal.

George follows the same crude countryman's method to tame a red-tailed hawk he illegally traps at Paynes Prairie, a wildlife refuge just south of Gainesville. Since the red-tailed hawk is not a particularly good candidate for falconry, the training period becomes quite an ordeal. For several days George keeps the bird leashed to a block in the back yard or to his gloved hand, withholds food, and keeps her awake by stroking her with a feather. All through this the bird is damaging herself by continually bating, flying off the perch and getting jerked short by the jesses on her legs, thus striking the ground or wildly dangling upside-down. George suffers along with the bird, his constant vigil leaving him exhausted and subject to wild dreams in the few moments when he dozes off. In one he dreams he is a hawk driving his talons into the back of his nephew. George's fate is tied to the bird's: "He knew he would not feel good until *she* ate, until he saw her step to his glove and eat and knew she was not going to die, until he knew that she had chosen him over death" (*Dying*, 199). And there are moments of relief in the painful process, once when he observes the hawk preening herself: "No longer flying against the leash, or pecking at the jesses, she was now cleaning and stroking each long flight feather individually. She bent to the oil gland under her tail and then came back to draw a single feather through her crooked mandible in a long, gracefully sensuous sweep of her head. Joy, sharp and great as pain, moved in him. He turned to the others, and the joy was instantly dead. Nobody was watching the hawk" (55). There are moments, too, when the hawk stays calm, when George is lifted out of his sordid surroundings and experiences religious feelings under the spell of the bird:

> He lifted the hawk to his wrist. She made no angry ruffle of her feathers, but took his glove quickly and—it seemed to him— gratefully. . . . the longer he stood, the more sharply he became aware of a strange, and to his mind, ridiculous desire to abase himself, to shed his *self* before something that was not human. Very quietly in an effort to keep the hawk steady and calm, he knelt there among the trees. He felt the heavy wall of indifferent woods, and above it the blank face of the sky. He remembered the preacher and thought to pray.
>
> (150)

Finally the hawk is manned; the break occurs when George and Betty are making love, high on marijuana, the hawk perched above them on a fake arm improvised from newspapers stuffed into a sock. It is the first time George had ever achieved a feeling of true love for someone. "He had always known if he waited long enough and tried hard enough that he would get there"—just as he had known that he could man the hawk.

Having manned the hawk, George begins to feed her biddies, makes a hood according to the directions in Emperor Frederick's book, spends twelve days accustoming her to the hood and flying her to the lure. Her docility under the hood bothers him, though: "There was something about the hood that was disgusting. . . . To put a hood on the biggest, strongest, and most magnificent raptor in the world was to reduce it to something any child could carry." That cannot be helped, however, and the hawk is in a sense re- turned to the wild, for on the thirteenth day she is allowed to "fly free at something with blood in it." George releases a rabbit in the required open ground, which happens to be a cemetery called the Meadow of Perpetual Care. "The hawk left its perch in a surge of power that never saw a wing stroke the air, as though the air itself were sucking her toward her prey. As the hawk drove her talons through its back, the rabbit squealed in short startled bursts like metal cutting metal, and squealed and kept squealing (*Dying*, 226). Betty, who just a few moments before pleaded with George to let the hawk go free, exclaims, "It's the most *beautiful* thing in the world!" George has succeeded in making a convert of at least one person whose life had been empty and whose relations with people had been faked. And George himself has been saved; through the ancient art of falconry, however imperfectly practiced, he has escaped the pervading falseness of his time, what he calls living by a "code" in a world grown ugly and almost insane. His experience with the hawk has made him face reality and respect its most elemental forms. George has succeeded where Alwyn Tower and Birdy failed, finding a way to relate to nature and his fellow humans by means of a concrete contact with a bird. His success is summarized in the simple process of getting the bird to perch on his glove:

> He pressed the glove against the back of the hawk's legs and she stepped back and up, just the way Emperor Frederick had promised she would. It seemed to George an awesome mystery that any hooded hawk anywhere in the world would step in precisely the same way if the back of her legs were touched. It was true in the days of Frederick, and it was still true. Presumably, it would be forever. For the first time in his life George felt himself part of some immutable continuity.
>
> (221)

Love is a part of that continuity, and it is a bird in the ancient tradition that clears the way for love.

Literature and the Future of Birds

The question that he frames in all but words
Is what to make of a diminished thing.
    Robert Frost, "The Oven Bird"

In ancient times birds had the honor of being considered the world's first inhabitants, existing even before the gods. Early writers were impressed with the sheer abundance of birds. One of Homer's frequent similes compares the flocking of birds with the massing of armies, and a favorite literary device from antiquity to the Renaissance was the catalog of birds, or the listing and brief description of as many different species as a writer could muster from his own observation and from the works of his predecessors. Aristophanes mentions about sixty species in *The Birds*, Virgil a dozen in book 1 of the *Georgics*, Chaucer thirty-six in *Parliament of Fowls*, John Skelton seventy-five in "Philip Sparrow." The abundance of birds confirmed a natural law the Creator had established for humankind's benefit, the plenitude and diversity of nature. Chaucer was delighted to see so many birds at one time and place:

> That erthe, and eyre, and tre, and every lake
> So ful was, that unethe was there space
> For me to stonde, so ful was al the place.
>   (lines 313–15)

The tradition of the catalog of birds is still alive—Louis Untermeyer outdoes Chaucer by one species for a total of thirty-seven in "Return to Birds," and William Everson and Theodore Roethke accumulate numerous birds in their poems—but the modern writer is more likely to notice the depletion than the munificence of nature. Our tender feelings for birds are expended now on the killing and dying of birds, their loss, their silencing. The death of a bird is somehow terribly affecting. No doubt it is our familiarity with the bird's animated movements and lively sounds that make its decease all the more shocking. Typical of the modern sensibility are these lines from Emily Dickinson:

> His Bill is clasped—his Eye forsook—
> His Feathers wilted low—
> The Claws that clung, like lifeless Gloves
> Indifferent hanging now—
> The Joy that in his happy Throat
> Was waiting to be poured
> Gored through and through with Death.
>   (no. 1102)

Or these from Robinson Jeffers's "Hurt Hawks":

> The broken pillar of the wing jags from the clotted shoulder,
> The wing trails like a banner in defeat,
> No more to use the sky forever but live with famine
> And pain a few days.
>   (97)

Instead of rejoicing in nature's liberal hand, as their predecessors did, writers in our time express grief and guilt over the destruction of wildlife, a theme, as we have noted, emphatically stated by Coleridge and Melville. Growing out of the general romantic sensitivity to nature, *Moby-Dick* and *The Rime of the Ancient Mariner* have special relevance now, not only because of their eloquent renewal of the primitive's respect for the animal and appreciation of the interdependence of human and animal, but because of their forceful statement of the consequences of our turning our hand, whether purposefully or carelessly, against the animal, the prime symbol of nature. We are now more receptive to such warnings because we have finally come to realize that since the eighteenth century we have radically changed the face of the earth in ways that may not be altogether desirable. Egalitarian idealism freed us from the authoritarian restraints of earlier societies that were committed to steady-state economies of scarcity, and the demands we now make on natural resources seem quite justified to supply the more and more elaborate needs and desires of an expanding population. Individuals have certainly benefited from this release of human energy, but it has subjected the environment to a degree of exploitation that we now recognize as having many bad results. Political freedom created a will to consume the world's goods and forced the collaboration of science, technology, and business enterprise to support an unprecedented degree of industrial activity. Especially since World War II the extent and speed of change have been so great and the proliferation of earth-changing substances and processes so numerous that we are losing control over the harmful and possibly irreversible effects they may have. We do know, however, that there has been a reduction of both the quality and quantity of natural biosphere resulting in the extinction of untold species of fauna and flora.

Of course, there are vast numbers of animals in existence, probably more than at any time in the history of the world, but these are the individuals among a few species that can be domesticated to serve as pets or processed to supply food and other practical needs. They can hardly fill the gap left by creatures that live in a state of nature, the numbers and diversity of which contribute so much to the health of the planet and the spiritual health of humankind. Breeding captive wild birds, when it is possible, is not an altogether satisfactory solution for replenishing depleted populations because the artificially bred birds lose some of the traits of their species, often including the crucial one of breeding in the wild after they are released. Indeed, experts are finding that when zoo-bred birds are released they spread new diseases that their fellows in the wild cannot withstand.

A number of wild bird species do manage to survive because they are able to adjust to man-made environments. Their simplified and generalized adaptability to all sorts of conditions gives them a better chance than more highly specialized species to thrive in the environmentally uniform world that we are so busily making. Unfortunately, it is the high degree of specialization that creates the beauty we see in animal and plant forms, and many of the birds we prize are being supplanted by less appealing, if more opportunistic, species, the Snopeses of the bird world. Such is the gull, for instance; it is ironical that gulls in their thousands have learned to thrive on pickings from landfills, the detritus of a civilization that is characterized by its wasteful consumption of the world's goods. At the close of Eliot's "Cape Ann" it is the gull that takes over from the "delectable" birds—among them four species of sparrow, the Blackburnian warbler, and the bobwhite: "But resign this land at the end, resign it / To its true owner, the tough one, the seagull." The gull does not happen to be in competition with the species named by the poet, but there is no question among ornithologists that gulls are a serious threat to the continued breeding of a number of "delectable" water birds like the tern and the loon. The crow is another spoiler that has learned to survive in degraded environments. In Ted Hughes's "Crow and the Birds," the soaring eagle, the swooping swallow, the bullfinch "plumped in the apple bud," and the goldfinch "bulbed in the sun" are overshadowed by Crow, "spraddled head-down in the beach-garbage, guzzling a dropped ice-cream."

Although we cannot fail to notice the deterioration of our natural surroundings, few people are aware of the loss of many little-known forms of wildlife that depend on special habitats for their survival. Sentimental as well as practical demands obstruct the preservation of natural areas. The diminishing wilderness has become so rare that there is now an unhealthy competition among more and more people to consume it while it lasts, and the majority of these have no real respect for wilderness and only the shallowest notion how to treat it with care. If the wilderness was a temple to the romantic and a workshop to the practical-minded, since Victorian times it has become a playground. For many males it is a place to exercise macho instincts, a means of enjoying cheap kicks, a new toy to be used up and discarded. Unfortunately, their power to do harm is increased by the new technologies of transportation and hunting at everyone's disposal.

Margaret Atwood is especially sensitive to the new breed of

nature lovers. In *Surfacing* her heroine is appalled by the "cause-less, undiluted" killing of a heron by two shooters she believes are Americans:

> To prove they could do it, they had the power to kill. Otherwise it was valueless; beautiful from a distance but it couldn't be tamed or cooked or trained to talk, the only relation they could have to a thing like that was to destroy it. . . . I imagined the surge of elec-tricity, nerve juice, as they hit it, brought it down, flapping like a crippled plane. . . . It would have been different in those countries where an animal is the soul of an ancestor or the child of a god, at least they would have felt guilt. . . . It doesn't matter what country they're from, my head said, they're still Americans, they're what's in store for us, what we are turning into. . . . I felt a sickening complicity.

Another type Atwood finds reprehensible is the tourist who has no special regard for wilderness but, out of boredom and a feeble desire to do the things recommended in the travel brochures, must have a wilderness experience. For something to do the heroine of "Scarlet Ibis," a short story in *Bluebeard's Egg*, drags her hus-band and daughter on an afternoon trip to the Caroni Swamp in Trinidad to take in the return of the scarlet ibises to roost at sunset. But the birds do not seem as real to her as the unpleasant-ness of the swamp, the leaking boat, and the antics of her fellow passengers. There is no wilderness experience, only something to talk about: "When she told about this later, after they were safely home, Christine put in the swamp and the awful boat, and the men singing and the suspicious smell of the water. . . . She ended with the birds, which were worth every minute of it, she said. She pre-sented them as a form of entertainment, like the Grand Canyon: something that really ought to be seen, if you liked birds, and if you should happen to be in that part of the world."[1] Ironically, Christine's husband, who had not been eager to visit a swamp "probably crawling with mosquitoes," seems to be moved by the beautiful spectacle of the birds: "Don took hold of Christine's hand, a thing he had not done for some time; but Christine, watch-ing the birds, noticed this only afterwards." Coming many years after *Surfacing*, "Scarlet Ibis" reflects Atwood's sharpened view of the unsettled attitudes people still have regarding wilderness. In his conversion Don makes amends for the destructiveness of the thoughtless shooters that drew the author's rage in the early novel, while Christine's seemingly commendable interest in wilderness proves to be but shallow curiosity.

With appreciation comes the desire to save wildlife. But efforts to prevent the extinction of any great number of animal species are not likely to succeed in the long run because it may never be possible to protect their habitats from the growing variety and number of harmful human encroachments. Even though conservationists for many years have made heroic efforts to preserve wildlife, we must recognize that because of the demand to press almost every patch of the earth's surface into human service, including even the frozen poles, it is no longer possible to save large enough tracts to make any difference to endangered species. It is difficult to stop the destruction of remaining unspoiled wilderness areas in the Third World, whose people merely want to share the higher standard of living of those who preceded them in the extraction of wealth from the earth. The fate of Rima the bird-girl, killed by her neighbors, was W. H. Hudson's symbol of this process, which he foresaw as early as 1874 when he left South America. As for land already in use, the extirpation of lingering wildlife still continues. Even in conservation-minded America there is an Animal Damage Control agency of the federal government that systematically destroys animals guilty of feeding on livestock and crops or simply trespassing on cultivated sites (6,729 egrets in 1988 for raiding fish ponds and disturbing gardens), even ravens making off with golf balls on fairways.

Some hope for wildlife may lie in the new techniques of restoring degraded environments such as wetlands or in "mitigating" the harmful effects of highways, power plants, and dams. Most such efforts are quite pitiful, and it is too soon to judge their success. The sincerity of the motive behind them is sharply questioned in Richard Wilbur's "In a Bird Sanctuary":

> Because they could not give it too much ground
> they closely planted it with fir and shrub.

A plan of pathways, voted by the Club,
contrived to lead the respiter around
a mildly wandering wood, still at no cost
to get him lost.

Now over dear Miss Drury's favored trees
they flutter (birds) and either stop or not,
as if they were unconscious that the spot
is planned for them, and meant to buy release
for one restrained department of the soul,
to "make men whole."
                                    (354)

Mary McCarthy goes much further in questioning the successful coexistence of wildlife and humans in the modern age. Her young hero in the novel *Birds of America* is wise beyond his years when he is struck with the idea that "the closer Nature got to the human, the uglier it could be." He and his mother flee the desert of California, which he regarded as "the product of some nuclear catastrophe that had befallen an earlier race of scientists," and return to "Nature's bosom," an isolated New England village where they had lived before. But after an absence of four years they found things had changed there. A new superhighway has obliterated all traces of a beautiful waterfall, and the great horned owl at the local wildlife sanctuary has died; also missing were the offshore cormorants, whose "stillness and fixity made them seem so horribly ancient, Peter thought, as though they had preceded time." The degradation of nature awaits Peter wherever he goes. In Paris he is at first encouraged by the unusual number of birds pointed out to him by a group of enthusiastic French *ornithologistes.*

Migrating birds were stopping off more and more in the city as the city spread; they were seeing certain birds this morning that had not been sighted in Paris in fifty years. The idea gave Peter a ray of hope: one of the side-benefits of megalopolis would be that if you lived long enough you could see flocks of evening grosbeaks in the Christmas tree at Rockefeller Center. Every cloud had a silver lining. As the old haunts of birds were transformed into sinister housing developments, linked by murderous highways, the city would become an aviary.

But Peter's hope is short-lived. In a street accident the Fatshedera plant on which he has been lavishing the most loving care is destroyed; he finds it in the gutter, "its whitish root system exposed" and its "crown of pale leaves lying a yard away like a severed head, near the Metro entrance."[2]

The climax of this train of disillusionment comes for Peter on a visit to the Jardin des Plantes in Paris. He is horrified to find that "the botanical garden had a derelict, desolate appearance, and the rows on rows of denuded plants with their pale-green identifying markers reminded him of a cemetery" (*Birds*, 332). The visit ends in a violent encounter—a black swan gashes his hand and forearm when he tries to feed the bird. It is ironical that a swan turns on the well-meaning boy, for the swan is one avian species that is amenable to life in an artificial environment. Hospitalized and delirious from an antibiotic to which he is allergic, he has "imaginary visitors," one of whom, "a small man, scarcely five feet high, in an unbuttoned twill jacket with a white stock," had traveled "all the way from Königsberg" to say "something important." Peter at first thinks the little man says "God is dead," but it is worse than that: "Mankind can live without God. . . . Nature is dead, *mein kind.*" The novel ends on this note. The choice of Immanuel Kant to deliver this grim message was appropriate. In *Critique of Judgment* Kant insists that what we do to make life worthwhile must be done "in accordance with the purpose that nature has along with us." Even though man may be independent of nature by virtue of reason and understanding, "nature has not in the least excepted him from its destructive or its productive powers," the equilibrium of which he must be careful to preserve. Therefore, man is foolish when he destroys the "advantageousness of certain natural things" just to satisfy "arbitrary fancies for which he was not at all predestined by nature," such as "using the variegated plumage of birds to adorn his clothes." McCarthy saw that the process of destruction had come a long way since Kant's time. "Nature is no longer the human home," she wrote in an essay at the time she was working on her novel. "Technology, originally associated with the civilizing arts of building and weaving, has replaced Nature as the Number One opponent of human society." Ironically, the tool we used to master nature is now turned against us.[3]

The twentieth-century anxiety over the health of the environment is nothing new, of course. We have always exacted a costly toll from every environment in which we have lived, and sensitive observers have always perceived the earth to be on a downward ecological course. As early as the first century B.C. the Roman poet Lucretius noted the decline of the earth's reproductive powers: "Yes and even now the age is enfeebled and the earth exhausted by bearing scarce produces little living creatures, she who produced all races and gave birth to the huge bodies of wild beasts. . . . The sorrowful planter too of the exhausted and shriveled vine impeaches the march of time and wearies heaven, and comprehends not that all things are gradually wasting away and passing to the grave, quite forspent by age and length of days."[4] The philosopher-poet did not despair, for he believed that the atoms dispersed from one dying form will someday combine to make another living thing. Western religious thought has eschewed natural cycles, however, and has interpreted ecological disaster as retribution for offenses against God. Birds were seen as an ambivalent symbol standing at the close as well as at the beginning of life on earth, at the destruction as well as at the creation of the world. The "day of the Lord's vengeance," when the streams and the land "shall become burning pitch," is presided over by the cormorant, the bittern, the raven, and the owl: "There shall the great owl make her nest, and lay, and hatch, and gather under her shadow: there shall the vultures also be gathered, every one with her mate" (Isa. 34.8–15). In the Revelation of Saint John the fallen Babylon becomes the "habitation of devils, and the hold of every foul spirit, and a cage of every unclean and hateful bird"; birds are summoned to gorge themselves on the corpses of the slain (18.2, 19.17–18).

Apocalyptic imagery of this sort has persisted. Over the supine figures of Albion and England in Blake's *Jerusalem* the "famish'd Eagle screams on boney wings" (4.94.15). England's war making had ravished the land: "The corn is turn'd to thistles & the apples into poison, / The birds of song to murderous crows, his joys to bitter groans" (1.19.10–11). Crows also figure in Carl Sandburg's description of a fallen city:

> And there are black crows
> crying "Caw, caw,"
> bringing mud and sticks
> building a nest
> over the words carved
> on the door where the panels were cedar
> and the strips on the panels were gold
> and the golden girls came singing:
>> We are the greatest city,
>> and the greatest nation:
>> nothing like us ever was.[5]

This is a renewal of the prophet Zephaniah's account of the desolation visited upon Nineveh by the Lord:

> Both the cormorant and the bittern shall lodge in the
>> upper lintels of it;
> their voice shall sing in the windows;
> desolation shall be in the threshold:
> for he shall uncover the cedar work.
> This is the rejoicing city that dwelt carelessly,
> that said in her heart, I am, and there is none beside me.
>
> (2.14–15)

Herman Melville's model of the world's end in *The Encantadas* was the Galapagos Islands, "looking much as the world at large might, after a penal conflagration." Dominating the scene of utter desolation is Rock Rodondo, the "aviary of Ocean," where "innumerable sea-fowl" gather from miles around and take up positions according to their several species, like the fallen angels in Milton's hell. Some are outlandishly ugly, misshapen—penguins, pelicans, gray albatrosses; all are murderous—gannets, shearwaters, sperm-whale birds (seagoing phalaropes), and gulls. "Fancy a red-robin or a canary there! What a falling into the hands of the Philistines, when the poor warbler should be surrounded by such locust-flights of strong bandit birds, with long bills cruel as daggers" (69). For this grim picture Melville took his cue from Spenser's *Faerie Queene*, in particular the description of Sir Guyon's peril when his ship is lost in a "grosse fog" just as it approaches land and "this great Universe seed one confused mass":

> Even all the nation of unfortunate
>> And fatal birds about them flocked were,
>> Such as by nature men abhor and hate,
>> The ill-faste [ill-faced] Owle, deaths dreadfull messengere,
>> The hoars Night-raven, trump of dolefull drere,
>> The lether-winged Bat, dayes enimy,
>> The ruefull Strich [screech owl], still waiting on the bere,
>> The Whistler [plover] shrill, that whoso heares, doth dy,
> The hellish Harpies, prophets of sad destiny.
>
> (2.12.36)

Birds have long been the measure of our fate, their extinction portending disaster for humankind. The caged canary in the coal mine performs the same service as the dove that in the story of the Golden Fleece was sent out by the Argonauts before they risked losing their ship in the narrow passage of the Clashing Rocks. The trial doves sent out by Noah in the Bible and Utnapishtim in *Gilgamesh* to determine whether the earth could support life after the Flood prefigure the actual birds of our own time that serve as measures of the ecological health of the entire world. The ultimate irony is that the pollution of the earth's atmosphere with carbon dioxide and chlorofluorocarbons may destroy the life-supporting functions of the sun, the natural phenomenon with which so many birds have been identified in the myths of people all over the world. In the beginning the eagle and the falcon were sun-birds; in the end the kingdom that Ted Hughes's Crow comes to rule over is one of darkness and silence, which Crow himself finally leaves:

> The empty world, from which the last cry
> Flapped hugely, hopelessly away
> Into the blindness and dumbness and deafness of the gulf.
>
> (*Crow*, 81)

The "sick world" pictured in Harlan Ellison's *Deathbird Stories* is not nursed back to health under the wings of a bird but dies there:

The Deathbird closed its wings over the Earth until at last, at the end, there was only the great bird crouched over the dead cinder. Then the Deathbird raised its head to the star-filled sky and repeated the sigh of loss the Earth had felt at the end. Then its eyes closed, it tucked its head carefully under its wing, and all was night.

Far away, the stars waited for the cry of the Deathbird to reach them so final moments could be observed at last, at the end, for the race of Men.[6]

As well as being witnesses and omens of evil, birds themselves are thought to bring death and destruction to humankind. Ancient myths make use of the fact that there is something preternaturally terrifying about the wild beating of wings about the heads of people. In their most primitive forms Harpies, Sirens, and Furies were all winged monsters that mercilessly pursued their victims. From their stronghold in a marsh the Stymphalian birds in the Greek myth killed men with their brazen beaks and claws, and from the sky they rained down death with sharp feathers and poisonous feces. A modern version of world-destroying birds is Daphne du Maurier's story "The Birds," in which a pesky attack of ordinary backyard birds against two neighboring families in a small English village gradually gathers more and more force until we are left with the impression that the whole world is subjected to an assault for which there is no defense. Birds suddenly display an "instinct to destroy mankind with all the deft precision of machines." In Michael Crichton's *Andromeda Strain* the fatal virus from a fallen satellite is spread by vultures feeding on the corpses of already stricken victims.[7]

The world returned to chaos when "there was no man, and all the birds of heaven were fled" (Jer. 4.25). The total disappearance of birds and bird song is a favorite sign of cosmic desolation in the dystopias, or negative utopias, pictured by writers who foresee the end of our civilization, if not of the human race itself. It is only outside of the official borders of George Orwell's totalitarian state in *Nineteen Eighty-Four*, in the forbidden Golden Country, that the rebellious Winston encounters a single forlorn thrush: "For whom, for what, was that bird singing? No mate, no rival was watching it. What made it sit at the edge of the lonely wood and pour its music into nothingness?" The song inspires momentary passion for the woman he loves, and this constitutes "a blow struck against the Party," but it can have no lasting result in a world from which instinct and passion have been eradicated. In Eugene Zamiatin's *We* a Green Wall separates a "machine-like, perfect world from the irrational, ugly world of trees, birds, and beasts." When the Wall is breached by dissidents, the "sterile, faultless sky" swarms with a great horde of birds. "The city seemed foreign, wild, filled with the ceaseless, triumphant hubbub of the birds. It seemed like the end of the world, *Doomsday*." This, ironically, is the reaction of the loyal inhabitants, and to their relief the birds are soon zapped by high-voltage electrocutors: "On the west side the sky was twitching every second in a pale blue, electric convulsion; a subdued, heavy roar could be heard from that direction. The roofs were covered with black, charred sticks—birds." The Wall is restored, "for Reason must prevail." Electrified wires similarly destroy the wild animals that try to cross the frontier between the Savage Reservation in New Mexico and the civilized world in Aldous Huxley's *Brave New World*. Love of nature is abolished in this purely utilitarian society—"A love of nature keeps no factories busy"—and infants are conditioned to be horrified "at the mere sight of those gaily-coloured images of pussy and cock-a-doodle-doo and baa-baa black sheep." Privileged visitors to the Savage Reservation are appalled by the survival of primitive customs among the Indians, customs that D. H. Lawrence had celebrated earlier in *The Plumed Serpent*. They wear "cloaks of turkey feathers" and "huge feather diadems"; they worship painted images of an eagle and a naked man "nailed to a cross."[8]

The leaders of these countries cannot tolerate an appreciation of nature because they fear it may create in some people a mood of revolt from the constraints that a totally mechanized society requires to operate efficiently. The incipient doubters in *Nineteen Eighty-Four*, *We*, and *Brave New World* are crushed, but a happier fate may await the dissidents in Walter Tevis's *Mockingbird*. The humanity of a single couple, Mary Lou and Paul Bentley, is renewed in the year 2467 when they rediscover the long lost ability to read, starting with a line Paul has seen in an old silent film:

"Only the mockingbird sings at the edge of the woods." Through-out the rest of the book this reference to the song of a bird is associated with the feelings and spiritual values of the "ancient" world, especially with the heritage of poetry and religion. Mary Lou is delighted to find that the bird's song is "like the words [of poetry] I just read, isn't it? It makes you feel something and you don't know what it is."[9] Rediscovering the past means survival in a moribund world for this devoted couple as well as the possible renewal of the human race. Mary Lou and Paul are able to have a child because with their new knowledge they can avoid the tran-quilizing drugs, laced with sterility-causing agents, to which the rest of the population has become addicted. The couple also learns how to be self-sufficient and no longer needs the support of the technological infrastructure operated by robots. The world's chief robot, Robert Spofforth, weary of his long service, can now cease to function since there is no need for him to assure the continued life of the people in his charge. His demise is associated with a passage from Eliot's "Song for Simeon": "My life is light, waiting for the death wind, / Like a feather on the back of my hand." Like Simeon, who resigned himself to die after he saw the infant Jesus in the temple (Luke 2.25–35), Spofforth has seen the child, also miraculous, of Mary Lou and is ready to die. His bird is not the mockingbird but a sparrow that lights on his arm as he stands on the top of the Empire State Building: "And then from nowhere and darkness there is a fluttering in the wind, and a small dark presence settles on Spofforth's motionless right forearm and be-comes, in abruptly frozen silhouette, a bird. Perched on his arm a sparrow, a city sparrow—tough and anxious and far too high. And it stays there with him, waiting for dawn" (246). The sparrow is like Simeon's feather, or death, in Eliot's poem. But it is also the survival of nature; for, as dawn breaks over the city, where hubris has led to disaster for the human race, the sparrow "flicks its head and flies away from Spofforth's bare arm, holding its tiny life to itself."

We may share Tevis's hope for the future because it is quite probable that in spite of the continuing loss of healthy environ-ments some wild birds will be tenacious enough of life to survive in sufficient numbers to remain ubiquitous and observable, close at hand but untamed. This is the kind of view Wordsworth was able to take in "To the Cuckoo":

> The lordly eagle-race through hostile search
> May perish; time may come when never more
> The wilderness shall hear the lion roar;
> But, long as cock shall crow from household perch
> To rouse the dawn, soft gales shall speed thy wing,
> And thy erratic voice be faithful to the Spring!
> (Misc. Sonnets, 3.14)

We must commend the sensitivity that was concerned about the survival of the eagle as early as 1827, though we cannot be quite as confident as Wordsworth that birds such as the cuckoo will thrive as long as domestic fowl. The opportunity to hear the "first summons" of the cuckoo, "with its twin notes inseparably paired," is less likely with every passing year. Resident rather than migratory birds will stand a better chance to survive, species that have accommodated themselves to wilderness pockets and artificial habitats and do not run the terrible risks of traveling long distances from one part of the world to another in search of breeding as well as wintering habitats. Only a few migrant species appear to have no trouble surviving, those that have found safe niches in city and town—the robin getting his living on suburban lawns, the phoebe nesting over the doorway, the swallow under the eaves.

The loss of the great wilderness areas of the past may not be as hard to take as we now imagine. People have never felt comfortable with stark wilderness unmitigated by conditions permitting human habitation. Even the most primitive people require a foothold, a clearing, in the forest. To grieve over the sacrifice of wilderness to commercial exploitation is understandable but a sentimental indulgence nonetheless. James Dickey addresses this problem in *Deliverance*, a moving account of a trip taken by four ordinary suburban males on one of the few remaining wild rivers in America. They are especially anxious to see and enjoy the river before it is dammed and its rugged gorge covered with a lake. For their adventure they affect the primitivistic, macho style of outdoor sport, carrying bows instead of firearms and using canoes to journey down the river. They are tested by a variety of traditional wilderness perils that include the physical obstacles of the river gorge and a deadly encounter with depraved human denizens of the forest. The most memorable encounter of the narrator is with a wild animal, an owl that perches on the ridgepole of his tent:

> Something hit the top of the tent. . . . The canvas was punctured there, and through it came one knuckle of a deformed fist, a long curving of claws that turned on themselves. . . .
>
> I lay with the sweat ready to break, looking up through almost-closed lids, full now of a dread that was at least partly humorous. . . . I pulled one hand out of the sleeping bag and saw it wander fraily up through the thin light until a finger touched the cold reptilian nail of one talon below the leg-scales. . . . I slipped my forefinger between the claw and the tent, and half around the stony toe. The claw tightened; the strength had something nervous and tentative about it. It tightened more, very strongly but not painfully. . . .
>
> All night the owl kept coming back to hunt from the top of the tent. I not only saw his feet when he came to us; I imagined what he was doing while he was gone, floating through the trees, seeing everything. I hunted with him as well as I could, there in my weightlessness. The woods burned in my head. Toward morning I could reach up and touch the claw without turning on the light.

We have here a progression from the initial dread of the wild animal to the full awareness of its magical presence and complete identification with the owl as the epitome of terror and beauty in nature. After the narrator's return to his ordinary middle-class existence, the events of the wilderness experience are transformed into permanent meaning: "The river and everything I remembered about it became a possession to me, a personal, private possession, as nothing else in my life ever had. . . . It pleases me in some curious way that the river does not exist, and that I have it. In me it still is, and will be until I die, green, rocky, deep, fast, slow, and beautiful beyond reality." [10]

What began as an actual experience of wilderness ends as a memory. The implication is that remaining wild places such as the river gorge will soon become "what the real estate people call an unspoiled location [where] perhaps only the unkillable tribe of rabbits will be left" (*Deliverance*, 278). Will there ever come a time when birds will live on only in our hearts as a memory preserved in literature? D. H. Lawrence seems to be saying this in "The Triumph of the Machine" when he predicts that birds will never be quite removed from human consciousness even though machines will have stripped them from the earth, for "in the hearts of some men there still is sanctuary / where the lark nests safely." But Lawrence cannot leave it there: the machines will eventually break down, and "all the creatures that were driven back into the uttermost corners of the soul / they will peep forth" (957–58). In "God's Grandeur" Gerard Manley Hopkins expresses the same hope: even though "generations have trod . . . bleared, smeared" the soil, "nature is never spent" (66).

The more likely possibility is that with the growing public, political, and even economic awareness of the importance of wilderness some habitats for wildlife will be preserved. In anticipation and support of this outcome, Thoreau teaches us that neighboring pockets of woodland and wetland can serve our need for the primitive and the wild as long as we lend them a little of our subjectivity: "It is in vain to dream of a wilderness distant from ourselves. There is none such. It is the bog in our brains and bowels, the primitive vigor of Nature in us, that inspires that dream. I shall never find in the wilds of Labrador any greater wildness than in some recess in Concord, *i.e.* than I import into it" (August 30, 1856).

"I rejoice that there are owls," writes Thoreau in the chapter called "Sounds" in *Walden.* "Let them do the idiotic and maniacal hooting for men. It is a sound admirably suited to swamps and twilight woods which no day illustrates, suggesting a vast and undeveloped nature which men have not recognized" (328). But Thoreau, like Cooper and Audubon before him, was well aware that nature even in a newly settled country like America was no longer what it used to be. Even his beloved Walden Pond had suffered from the depravations of earlier settlers; a *Journal* entry reminds us that it is a "maimed and imperfect nature" that all of us inherit no matter when we live:

When I think what were the various sounds and notes, the migrations and works, and changes of fur and plumage which ushered in the spring and marked the other seasons of the year, I am re-minded that this my life in nature, this particular round of natural phenomena which I call a year, is lamentably incomplete. . . . I take infinite pains to know all the phenomena of the spring, for instance, thinking that I have here the entire poem, and then, to my chagrin, I hear that it is but an imperfect copy that I possess and have read, that my ancestors have torn out many of the first leaves and grandest passages, and mutilated it in many places.

(March 23, 1856)

In the entry for April 11, 1857, he notes that the Concord River is dead: "The very fishes in countless schools are driven out of a river by the *improvement* of the civilized man, as the pigeon and other fowls out of the air. . . . We are reduced to a few migrating suckers, perchance."

What it comes down to is that Thoreau learned to be satisfied with less and less wilderness. "When I have only a rustling oak leaf or the faint metallic cheep of a tree sparrow, for variety in my winter walk, my life becomes continent and sweet as the kernel of a nut" (February 8, 1857). He was content to limit his wilderness experience to the study of undeveloped pockets of land in the vicinity of Concord. "What's the need of visiting far-off mountains and bogs, if a half-hour's walk will carry me into such wilderness and novelty? . . . I see there are some square rods within twenty miles of Boston just as wild as a square rod in Labrador, as unaltered by man" (August 30, 1856). His "brute neighbors" in *Walden* are the phoebe that builds a nest in his shed, the robin that seeks "protection in a pine which grew against the house," and the partridge that leads "her brood past my windows, from the woods in the rear to the front of my house, clucking and calling to them like a hen, and in all her behavior proving herself the hen of the woods." His ideal singing bird would be the "once wild Indian pheasant," or barnyard fowl; if only it "could be naturalized without being domesticated, it would soon become the most famous sound in our woods, surpassing the clangor of the goose and the hooting of the owl" (329).

These are Thoreau's familiar birds; his mystery bird is the loon.

The "Brute Neighbors" chapter closes with a long passage describing his pursuit of a loon on Walden Pond:

> As I was paddling along the north shore one very calm afternoon . . . having looked in vain over the pond for a loon, suddenly one, sailing out from the shore toward the middle a few rods in front of me, set up his wild laugh and betrayed himself. I pursued with a paddle and he dived, but when he came up I was nearer than before. He dived again, but I miscalculated the direction he would take, and we were fifty yards apart when he came to the surface this time, for I had helped to widen the interval; and again he laughed long and loud, and with more reason than before. He manoeuvred so cunningly that I could not get within half a dozen rods of him. . . . It was a pretty game, played on the smooth surface of the pond, a man against a loon.
>
> (400–401)

The loon's "demoniac laughter" Thoreau accounted "perhaps the wildest sound that is ever heard here, making the woods ring far and wide. I concluded that he laughed in derision of my efforts, confident of his own resources." Or perhaps the call of the loon summoned the god of the loons for help, for after "one of those prolonged howls . . . immediately there came a wind from the east and rippled the surface, and filled the whole air with misty rain, and I was impressed as if it were the prayer of the loon answered, and his god was angry with me; and so I left him disappearing far away on the tumultuous surface" (402). Like Melville's white whale, Thoreau's loon is the ungraspable essence of nature's wildness. Yet, like Ishmael, at the risk of being intrusive, Thoreau felt he must devote himself to the study of nature, as though to make amends for the sins against nature committed by his ancestors and neighbors.

The inescapable impression we get from "Brute Neighbors" is that Thoreau actually preferred to spend his time in a modified, pastoral landscape than cope with the terrifying chaos of Mt. Katahdin, the scary owls of the night, and the hopeless pursuit of the loon. His example may help to teach us how to accept and yet make the most of a diminishing wilderness and declining variety of wildlife. Our pastoral scene is more limited than his, of course, but we may take some comfort in the fact that our cities and their suburbs support greater numbers of birds than do agricultural and wooded areas, and in time the varied biomass of the suburbs may attract as many different species as the remaining forests. The hope of young Peter in Mary McCarthy's novel that "the city would become an aviary" is not entirely impossible. As Coleridge writes in "This Lime-Tree Bower My Prison," when an accident kept him in his garden while others went on a walk,

> No plot so narrow, be but Nature there
> No waste so vacant, but may well employ
> Each faculty of sense, and keep the heart
> Awake to Love and Beauty!
> (181, lines 61–64)

Restoring to the animal the significance it once had for humans is one of the needs of an advanced civilization to regain a necessary relation to nature. Natural places alone do not inspire us nearly as much as wild animal life; the Endangered Species Act has been the prime mover of public sentiment in our present conservation efforts. Some kind of animal presence is required to endear us to the sense of wildness that Thoreau expressed in his axiom that "in Wildness is the preservation of the World." And the development of this sense, as Thoreau divined, must be served by increasingly symbolical means, for there is no returning now to the primitive conditions that once gave animals their original significance. We are practically reduced to the cultivation of attitudes concerning nature rather than actual experiences of nature. We must accept finally the truth that the human being has developed in such a way that we must move always from matter to spirit, from things to the ideas of things. Through the new disciplines of ecology and ethology, science, as though to make amends for its past omissions, is doing its part to rehumanize our perception of nature by studying the precise effects of our use of nature and paying more attention to animal behavior in the wild. But new facts must be supplemented with a renewal of humanity's past deep-seated responses to nature, and these are the prime materials of the arts. The kind of literature we have been dealing with, literature stimulated by that most animated and communicative animal, the bird, is especially suited to keep those feelings alive. As Charlton Ogburn reminds us, "Birds account for a disproportionate amount of our perception of nature."[11] True, and their role may become greater in the future, for it appears likely that as well as having been one of our earliest links to nature the bird may prove to be our last and best remaining contact with wildlife.

"Poetry is connate with the origins of man," declared Shelley in "A Defence of Poetry." As a repository of all modes of feeling and seeing, those of the deep past as well as the present, literature may be counted on to continue expressing the powerful impressions birds make on mankind. Ancient myths are never quite lost to poetry, and centuries after Aristophanes poets still celebrate the primacy of birds and give affirmative answers to the rhetorical question asked by Matthew Arnold in "Poor Mathias":

> Was it, as the Grecian sings,
> Birds were born the first of things,
> Before the sun, before the wind,
> Before the gods, before mankind,
> Airy, ante-mundane throng—
> Witness their unworldly song!
> (606, lines 131–36)

D. H. Lawrence imagines a time "before anything had a soul" when the hummingbird was a bit of matter that "flashed ahead of creation" ("Humming-Bird," 372). Being first inhabitants, "ante-mundane," birds enjoyed earth in its paradisal state, the "golden time" that Wordsworth hears in bird song and Hopkins calls "a strain of earth's sweet being in the beginning / In Eden garden" (67). Thoreau wrote in his journal (March 4, 1840) of birds that "sang as freshly as if it had been the first morning of creation," and in the call of a cuckoo the hero of Alan Paton's *Too Late the Phalarope* hears "that same sound, long remembered from the days of innocence before the world's corruption" (47). Jeffers notes the antiquity of pelicans:

> And the wings torn with old storms remember
> The cone that the oldest redwood dropped from, the tilting
>   of the continents,
> The dinosaur's day, the lift of new sea-lines.
> The omnisecular spirit keeps the old with the new also.
> Nothing at all has suffered erasure,
> There is life not of our time.
>   ("Pelicans," 66)

The awe with which the wild animal was once reverenced can be revived, especially the awe in which birds were once held, for, as Jane Harrison observes, "of all living creatures, birds longest keep their sanctity." The same point is made by Denise Levertov in "Come into Animal Presence"—

> Those who were sacred have remained so,
> holiness does not dissolve, it is a presence
> of bronze, only the sight that saw it
> faltered and turned from it.
> And old joy returns in holy presence.[12]

The challenge to literature is to continue finding significance in "animal presence," and fortunately we can expect the presence of many birds to continue, though diminished in the variety of species. Ubiquitous and insistent, birds occupy every corner of our world: its sky, and the land's vegetation from treetops to the bush underfoot; its seas, lakes, rivers, and their shores; its swamps, mountains, woodlands. Most fortunately, birds are still the persistent users or actual residents of seemingly uncongenial places and facilities: town, city, suburb, and cultivated countryside; house and high-rise tower, bridge and roadway; fence and strung wire. As long as they are with us birds will remain the steadfast harbingers of daylight and darkness, if not of the seasons, and the mysterious prompters of our inmost feelings. Writers will not lack actual contact with birds for inspiration.

One example of dealing with birds dwelling in unlikely places may be found in the poetry of Theodore Roethke, who was brought up in heavily industrialized Saginaw, Michigan. In "The Far Field" we have the blue jay "rasping from the stunted pine," the whippoorwill moving "along the smoky ridges," and the gulls wheeling "over their singular garbage." Yet he does not despair:

> Among the tin cans, tires, rusted pipes, broken machinery,—
> One learned of the eternal;
>
> . . . .
>
> I suffered for birds, for young rabbits caught in the mower,
> My grief was not excessive.
> For to come upon warblers in early May
> Was to forget time and death.
>   (199)

Roethke even does a poem in the ancient tradition of the bird catalogue; in "All Morning" twenty-three species are named and briefly characterized—"A delirium of birds!" And if some are now extinct, that is still all right:

> It is neither spring nor summer: it is Always.
> With towhees, finches, chickadees, California
>   quail, wood doves,
> With wrens, sparrows, juncos, cedar waxwings, flickers,
> With Baltimore orioles, Michigan bobolinks,
> And those birds forever dead,
> The passenger pigeon, the great auk, the Carolina paroquet,
> All birds remembered, O never forgotten.
> All in my yard, of a perpetual Sunday,
> All morning! All morning!
>   (235)

Learning to deal with a diminished natural world is our inevitable lot. Can literature be of help in that process? Henry David Thoreau and Robert Frost believed they could help in some small way, Thoreau by writing about the way he chose to live his life, Frost by the meanings he was able to extract from slight materials—the way an ovenbird continues to sing even when "leaves are old" and "highway dust is over all." John James Audubon had a grander notion, that Sir Walter Scott could use his literary talents to stop the degradation of the natural environment in North America. He never ventured to make such a proposal to the great man, but he confided to his journal that often when he was traversing the wilds of America he would shout to himself,

> Oh Walter Scott, where art thou? Wilt thou not come to my country? Wrestle with mankind and stop their increasing ravages on Nature, and describe her now for the sake of future ages. Neither this little stream, this swamp, this grand sheet of flowing water, nor these mountains will be seen in a century hence as I see them now. Nature will have been robbed of her brilliant charms. The currents will be tormented and turned away from their primitive courses. The hills will be levelled with the swamp. . . . Fishes will no longer bask on the surface, the eagle scarce ever alight, and these millions of songsters will be drove away by man. Oh Walter Scott, come, come to America! Set thee hence, look upon her, and see her grandeur. Nature still nurses her, cherishes her. But a tear flows in her eye. Her cheek has already changed from the peach blossom to sallow hue. Her frame inclines to emaciation. Her step is arrested. Without thee, Walter Scott, she must die, unknown to the world.[13]

No doubt literature cannot do as much as Audubon wanted from his idol, but creative writers drawing on a rich store of literary antecedents, as well as adding new insights to meet present needs, may help to keep alive the sensitivity that is absolutely essential in the conservation of wildlife and natural beauty.

Preface

1. John Ruskin, *Love's Meinie*, in *The Works of John Ruskin*, 25:76 (unless otherwise stated, Ruskin quotations are from this collection); Henry David Thoreau, *The Journal of Henry D. Thoreau*, December 14, 1855 (Thoreau's *Journal* entries will be designated by date only in the text); Loren Eiseley, *The Immense Journey* (New York: Vintage, 1959), 168–69.

2. Saint-John Perse, "Oiseaux, No. 1," in *Collected Poems* (unless otherwise stated, Perse quotations are from this collection); Charlton Ogburn, *The Adventure of Birds*, 16–17.

3. Emily Dickinson, *The Complete Poems of Emily Dickinson*, no. 266 (Dickinson's poems will be cited by number in the text); Izaak Walton, *The Compleat Angler*, 14.

4. Caroline Spurgeon, *Shakespeare's Imagery* (Cambridge: Cambridge University Press, 1961), 48; Samuel Taylor Coleridge, "Shakespeare Lectures," in *The Great Critics*, ed. James Harry Smith and Edd Winfield Parks, 3d rev. ed. (New York: Norton, 1951), 545.

5. Salman Rushdie, *The Satanic Verses*, 397.

Chapter 1: Birds, Poetry, and the Poet

1. *Sophocles: Oedipus at Colonus*, trans. Robert Fitzgerald (New York: Harcourt Brace, 1941), ll. 673–77.

2. Lawrence Millman, "Neskapi Folktales," *Boston Globe*, July 30, 1989.

3. John Lydgate, "A Seying of the Nightingale," in *The Minor Poems of John Lydgate*, ed. Henry Noble MacCrachen (London: Oxford University

Press, 1962); *The Works of Sir Thomas Browne*, 2:268. Subsequent quotations from Browne are from this collection.

4. Richard Barnefield, "An Ode," in *Poetry of the English Renaissance*, ed. J. William Hebel and Hoyt H. Hudson, 241. Selections from this work will be cited in the text as Hebel and Hudson.

5. Wallace Stevens, "The Man with the Blue Guitar," in *The Collected Poems of Wallace Stevens*, 168. Unless otherwise stated, Stevens's poetry is quoted from this work.

6. For an account of Ovid's influence on subsequent versions of the Philomela story, see Wilmon Brewer, *Ovid's Metamorphoses in European Culture*, vol. 2 (Boston: Marshall Jones, 1941).

7. See J. R. T. Pollard, "The Birds of Aristophanes: A Source Book for Old Beliefs," *American Journal of Philology* 69 (1948): 353–76; D'Arcy W. Thompson, *A Glossary of Greek Birds* (Hildesheim: Olms, 1966).

8. Aristophanes, *The Birds*, in *Four Greek Plays*, ed. and trans. Dudley Fitts (New York: Harcourt Brace, 1960), 241, 243 (Parabasis 1.676–82, 736–46).

9. *George Gascoigne's "The Steele Glas" and "The Complaynt of Phylomene": A Critical Introduction*, ed. William Wallace, Elizabethan and Renaissance Studies no. 24 (Salzburg: Institut für Englische Sprache und Literatur, 1975).

10. Pliny, *Natural History*, 10.81–82; Walton, *Compleat Angler*, 16; Gerard Manley Hopkins, "The Nightingale," in *The Poems of Gerard Manley Hopkins*, 30 (unless otherwise stated, quotations from Hopkins are from this collection).

11. Homer, *The Homeric Hymns*, trans. Apostolos N. Ahanassahis (Baltimore: Johns Hopkins University Press, 1976), 62.

12. John Clare, "Natural History Letters," in *The Poetry of Earth*, ed. E. D. H. Johnson (New York: Atheneum, 1974), 175.

13. Charles Hartshorne, *Born to Sing: An Interpretation and World Survey of Bird Song* (Bloomington: Indiana University Press, 1973), 88; William H. Thorpe, *Bird-Song* (Cambridge: Cambridge University Press, 1961); Louis J. Halle, *The Storm Petrel and the Owl of Athena* (Princeton, N.J.: Princeton University Press, 1970), 134, 153–54. See also Edward A. Armstrong, "Aspects of the Evolution of Man's Appreciation of Bird Song," in *Bird Vocalization*, ed. R. A. Hinde (Cambridge: Cambridge University Press, 1969), 343–65.

14. Thomas Hardy, "The Spring Call," in *The Complete Poems of Thomas Hardy*, 244–45 (unless otherwise stated, quotations from Hardy's poetry are from this collection); E. B. White, "A Listener's Guide to the Birds," in *Poems and Sketches* (New York: Harper & Row, n.d.), 62.

15. H. W. Garrod, *The Profession of Poetry* (Oxford: Oxford University Press, 1929), 145; Samuel Taylor Coleridge, "The Nightingale," in *The Poems of Samuel Taylor Coleridge*, 264 (unless otherwise stated, Coleridge quotations are from this collection); D. H. Lawrence, "The Nightingale," in *Phoenix: The Posthumous Papers of D. H. Lawrence*, (hereafter cited in the

text as *Phoenix*); Plato, *Phaedo*, in *The Dialogues of Plato*, 85a (all references to the *Dialogues* will be given in the text with the traditional marginal page numbers and subsections); A. R. Chandler, "The Nightingale in Greek and Latin Poetry," *Classical Journal* 30 (October 1934): 78–84. See also Chandler's *Larks, Nightingales, and Poetry* (Columbus: Ohio State University Press, 1958) for another account of the nightingale in literature and a short anthology of European poetry dealing with the nightingale and the skylark.

16. Ralph Waldo Emerson, "The Miracle," *Poems*, in *Emerson's Complete Works*, 9:306 (unless otherwise stated, quotations from Emerson are from this collection); Richard Wilbur, "All These Birds," *New and Collected Poems*, 269 (unless otherwise stated, quotations from Wilbur are from this collection); John Ciardi, "No White Bird Sings," *Selected Poems*, 50–51 (poems from this collection will be cited in the text as *Selected Poems*); Wallace Stevens, "Of Mere Being," in *Opus Posthumous*, ed. Milton J. Bates (New York: Knopf, 1989), 141; Ciardi, "Yet Not to Listen to that Sung Nothing," in *Person to Person* (New Brunswick, N.J.: Rutgers University Press, 1964).

17. John Burroughs, *The Writings of John Burroughs*, 14:31, 35; Louis Halle, *Spring in Washington* (1947; repr., Baltimore: Johns Hopkins University Press, 1988), 71; Walt Whitman, *Specimen Days* (1882), in *Walt Whitman: Complete Poetry and Collected Prose*, 850 (unless otherwise stated, Whitman quotations are from this collection).

18. Matthew Arnold, "Philomela," in *The Poems of Matthew Arnold*, 374 (unless otherwise stated, Arnold quotations are from this collection); Robert Penn Warren, "Ornithology in a World of Flux," in *Selected Poems: New and Old, 1923–1966* (New York: Random House, 1966), 119.

19. C. M. Bowra, *Primitive Song* (New York: New American Library, 1963), 164; Oscar Wilde, letter of January 1889 to W. H. Pollack, editor, *Saturday Review*, in *The Letters of Oscar Wilde*, 236 (quotations from this collection will be cited in the text as *Letters*); Burroughs, *Writings*, 5:85, 93; Natalie Angier, Science Times section of the *New York Times*, Aug. 21, 1990.

20. Sir A. Landsborough Thomson, ed., *A New Dictionary of Birds* (New York: McGraw-Hill, 1964), 652; Whitman, *Specimen Days*, 905.

21. Ezra Pound, "A Retrospect," in *Literary Essays of Ezra Pound* (New York: New Directions, 1968), 9; Ernest Hemingway, "The Snows of Kilimanjaro," in *The Short Stories of Ernest Hemingway* (New York: Scribner's, 1938), 52–53).

22. Robert Penn Warren, "Sunset Scrupulously Observed," in *Rumor Verified: Poems 1979–1980* (New York: Random House, 1980), 31.

23. John Clare, *John Clare: Selected Poems and Prose*, ed. Eric Robinson and Geoffrey Summerfield (Oxford: Oxford University Press, 1966), 19; Theodore Roethke, "The Heron," in *The Collected Poems of Theodore Roethke*, 15 (unless otherwise stated, Roethke quotations are from this collection); T. S. Eliot, "Cape Ann," in *The Complete Poems and Plays*, 95; Marianne Moore, "No Swan So Fine," *The Complete Poems of Marianne*

Moore, 19 (unless otherwise stated, Eliot and Moore quotations are from these collections).

24. Geffrey Whitney, *A Choice of Emblemes,* 54 (hereafter cited in the text as *Emblemes*).

25. Robert Frost, "Our Singing Strength," *Complete Poems of Robert Frost,* 297 (unless otherwise stated, Frost quotations are from this collection). W. S. Merwin, "Birds Waking," in *Green with Beasts* (unless otherwise stated, Merwin quotations are from this collection).

26. James Thomson, "Spring," in *The Seasons,* in *Poetical Works,* 26, ll. 614–17, 620–30, 751–54 (unless otherwise stated, Thomson quotations are from this collection). For an excellent discussion of Thomson's birds and beasts see Ralph Cohen, *The Unfolding of "The Seasons"* (Baltimore: Johns Hopkins University Press, 1970).

27. Edna St. Vincent Millay, "Spring," in *Collected Lyrics of Edna St. Vincent Millay* (New York: Harper, 1939), 53.

28. A. R. Ammons, "Saliences," in *Collected Poems* (New York: Norton, 1972).

29. William Carlos Williams, "To Waken an Old Lady," *The Collected Earlier Poems of William Carlos Williams* (New York: New Directions, 1951), 200.

30. George Meredith, "Hard Weather," *The Poetical Works of George Meredith,* 320–21 (unless otherwise stated, Meredith quotations are from this collection). Emerson's poem is called "The Titmouse," the British name for the American chickadee. Emerson's expert knowledge of birds is in evidence here when he distinguishes for the general reader the seasonal change in the chickadee's call:

> For men mis-hear thy call in Spring,
> As 't would accost some frivolous wing,
> Crying out of the hazel copse, *Phe-be*
> And, in winter, *Chic-a-dee-dee!*

E. B. White gives the distinction a humorous flip in "A Listener's Guide to the Birds," from *Poems and Sketches:*

> in spring you can get the heebie-jeebies
> Untangling chickadees from phoebes.
> The chickadee, when he's all afire,
> Whistles, "Fee-bee," to express desire.
> He should be arrested and thrown in jail
> For impersonating another male.
>
> (62)

31. Sylvia Plath, "Black Rook in Rainy Weather," in *The Collected Poems,* 57.

32. Charles W. Kennedy, trans., *An Anthology of Old English Poetry.* Com-

pare Ezra Pound's translation of "The Seafarer" in *Personae* (New York: Boni & Liveright, 1926), 64.

> There I heard naught save the harsh sea
> And ice-cold wave, at whiles the swan cries,
> Did for my games the gannet's clamour,
> Sea-fowls' loudness was for me laughter,
> The mews' singing all my mead-drink.
> Storms, on the stone-cliffs beaten, fell on the stern
> In icy feathers; full oft the eagle screamed
> With spray of his pinion.

33. Thomas Hardy, *Tess of the D'Urbervilles*, 367 (hereafter cited in the text as *Tess*).

34. William Blake, "Visions of the Daughters of Albion," in *Blake: Complete Writings*, 195 (unless otherwise stated, all Blake quotations are from this collection).

35. Whitman, "Of That Blithe Throat of Thine," *Leaves of Grass*, in *Complete Poetry*, 623. Greely's *Three Years of Arctic Service* (New York, 1886) is an account of the Lady Franklin Bay expedition of 1881–84. On an Easter Sunday Greely and his crew, some of whom were dying of starvation, heard "a snow-bird chirping loudly"; it was taken as "a good omen, and did much to cheer us through the day" (2:289). Greely's feet were in "horrible condition." From 1873 Whitman suffered from paralysis.

36. Robert Penn Warren, "Evening Hawk," in *New and Selected Poems, 1923–1985*, 167 (unless otherwise stated, quotations from Warren's poetry are from this collection), and *Audubon: A Vision* (New York: Random House, 1969), ll. 250–53. For discussions of Warren's hawks and images of light, see Leonard Casper, *Robert Penn Warren: The Dark and Bloody Ground* (Seattle: University of Washington Press, 1960).

37. T. H. White, ed., *The Bestiary: A Book of Beasts*, 142–43.

38. William Cullen Bryant, "To a Waterfowl," in *American Poetry*, ed. Gay Wilson Allen, Walter B. Rideout, and James K. Robinson, 593; Robert Browning, *Paracelsus* (1835), in *The Complete Works of Robert Browning*, ed. Roma A. King, Jr. (Athens: Ohio University Press, 1969), 1:565–70.

39. John Ciardi, "Small Elegy," *The Strangest Everything* (New Brunswick, N.J.: Rutgers University Press, 1966), 31.

40. Sidney Lanier, "The Marshes of Glynn," in Allen, Rideout, and Robinson, *American Poetry*, 596; William Everson, "A Canticle of Waterbirds," in *The Veritable Years*, 83–85 (unless otherwise stated, quotations from Everson are from this collection).

41. William Everson, *On the Writing of Waterbirds*, ed. Lee Bartlett (Metuchen, N.J.: Scarecrow, 1983), 59.

42. For a discussion of shamanism with special emphasis on birds, see Mircea Eliade, *Shamanism: Archaic Techniques of Ecstasy* (New York: Pan-

theon, 1964). David M. Guss, ed., *The Language of Birds* (San Francisco: North Point, 1985) is a wide-ranging collection of "Tales, Texts, & Poems of Interspecies Communication."

43. Aristotle, *Historia Animalium*, 9.615b1.

44. Horace, *The Complete Works of Horace*, ed. Caspar J. Kraemer, Jr., trans. Warren H. Cudworth (New York: Book League of America, 1938), ode 2, 201.

45. Edmund Spenser, "Ruines of Time," *The Poetical Works of Edmund Spenser*, 599–602. Unless otherwise stated, Spenser quotations are from this collection.

46. Included in Orlando Gibbons, *First Set of Madrigals and Motets* (1612).

47. William Wordsworth, "To the Cuckoo" (1802), *Wordsworth: Poetical Works*, 146.

48. Johann Wolfgang Goethe, *Goethe's Faust*, 39, ll. 1090–99. Subsequent quotations are cited in the text as *Faust*.

49. George Santayana, "Skylarks," from *Soliloquies in England*, in *The Philosophy of Santayana*, ed. Irwin Edman (New York: Scribner's, 1953), 340; Richard Holmes, *Coleridge: Early Visions* (New York: Viking, 1990), 80n, 254.

50. Charles Baudelaire, "Élévation." My translation: "Happy the one who can with strong wing leap up toward bright and serene fields, he whose thoughts, like skylarks, take free flight each morning toward the skies."

51. Oscar Wilde, "The Burden of Itys," in *Complete Works of Oscar Wilde* (New York: Harper & Row, 1989), 740, 744.

52. William Butler Yeats, "Sailing to Byzantium," in *The Collected Poems of W. B. Yeats*, 192 (unless otherwise stated, quotations from Yeats's poetry are from this collection); Sir John Mandeville, *Mandeville's Travels*.

53. Ted Hughes, "Skylarks," *Wodwo* (London: Faber & Faber, 1967); James Wright, "A Presentation of Two Birds to My Son," in *The Green Wall* (New Haven, Conn.: Yale University Press, 1957).

54. Vladimir Nabokov, *Pale Fire* (New York: Putnam, 1962), 133, 292.

55. William Henry Venable, "My Catbird," in *The Bird-Lovers' Anthology*, comp. Clinton Scollard and Jessie B. Rittenhouse, 138–39; Henry Van Dyke, "The Veery," in *The Poems of Henry Van Dyke* (New York: Scribner, 1921); John Crowe Ransom, "Philomela," in *Selected Poems* (New York: Knopf, 1969) 63.

56. Henry David Thoreau, "Upon the Lofty Elm Tree Sprays," in *Collected Poems of Henry Thoreau*, 7 (unless otherwise stated, quotations from Thoreau's poetry are from this collection). See also Thoreau's *Journal* for August 5, 1842. Theodore Roethke in "Infirmity" reports being cheered by a vireo singing "deep in the greens of summer." For a good discussion of Thoreau's birds in both Walden and the journals, see Charles R. Anderson, *The Magic Circle of Walden* (New York: Holt, Rinehart, 1968).

57. Jefferson to his daughter Martha on May 21, 1787, *The Family Let-*

ters of Thomas Jefferson, ed. Edwin Morris Betts and James Adam Bear, Jr. (Columbia: University of Missouri Press, 1966), 41.

58. Ogburn, *Adventure of Birds*, 174; Louis Untermeyer, "Return to Birds," in Scollard and Rittenhouse, *Bird-Lovers' Anthology*, 10. The hermit thrush was once popularly called "swamp angel" (Jack Wennerstrom, "Antique Bird Names," *Bird Watcher's Digest* [Jan.–Feb. 1990], 47).

59. Burroughs, "The Return of the Birds" (1865), in *Writings* 1:26–27, 6:88. See also Clara Barrus, *Whitman and Burroughs, Comrades* (Boston: Houghton Mifflin, 1931), 24. Robert Henry Welker, *Birds and Man: American Birds in Science, Art, Literature, and Conservation 1800–1900* (Cambridge, Mass.: Harvard University Press, 1955), discusses Burroughs's influence on Whitman as well as Whitman's use of J. P. Giraud's *The Birds of Long Island* (1844). In his notes on *The Waste Land* Eliot credits Frank Chapman's *Handbook of Birds of Eastern North America* (1895) for information on the hermit thrush.

60. Whitman, "To Soar in Freedom and in Fullness of Power," from *Old Age Echoes* [posthumous], in James E. Miller, Jr., ed., *Walt Whitman: Complete Poetry and Selected Prose* (Boston: Houghton Mifflin, 1959), 386.

61. Leo Spitzer, "*Explication de Texte* Applied to Walt Whitman's Poem 'Out of the Cradle Endlessly Rocking,'" *English Literary History* 16 (1949): 238.

62. Stephen Vincent Benét, "Ode to Walt Whitman," in *Selected Works of Stephen Vincent Benét* (New York: Rinehart, 1942), 439.

63. "The Deserted Home," trans. Kuno Meyer, in *Selections from Ancient Irish Poetry* (London: Constable, 1911), 92.

64. Ovid, "Metamorphosis of Alcyone," in *Metamorphoses*, trans. Horace Gregory (New York: New American Library, 1960), 319; Euripides, *Iphigenia in Tauris*, in *Greek Tragedies*, 2.1089–96; Herman Melville, *Billy Budd*, in *The Great Short Works of Herman Melville*, 421–22 (unless otherwise stated, Melville quotations are from this collection).

65. James Joyce, *A Portrait of the Artist as a Young Man*, 168–69 (hereafter cited in the text as *Portrait*).

66. Thoth, inventor of writing in letters, is pictured in the Egyptian Book of the Dead with the head of an ibis and crescent moon. In the Hermetic tradition he is the patron of the imagination. Joyce refers to him in *Ulysses* as "Thoth, god of libraries, a birdgod, moony-crowned."

Chapter 2. Birds and the Supernatural

1. Neolithic period figurines of the "cosmic egg laid by a bird" are shown in Marija Gimbutas, *The Gods and Goddesses of Old Europe* (Berkeley: University of California, 1974), 101–7. For discussions of the cosmogonic egg see Mircea Eliade, *Patterns in Comparative Religion* (1958; repr., Cleveland:

World, 1968), 413–16; Joseph Campbell, *The Hero with a Thousand Faces* (1949; repr., New York: World, 1964), 274–78; Harold Bailey, *The Lost Language of Symbolism* (1912; repr., New York: Barnes and Noble, 1957), 94, 210–11.

2. Algernon Swinburne, trans., "Chorus of the Birds," in *Swinburne's Collected Poetical Works*, vol. 2 (New York: Harper, 1926), 457; *Kalevala*, trans. W. F. Kirby (New York: Everyman's Library, 1951), 1.177–244.

3. For a brief history of the use of the eagle as a national emblem, see Ernest Ingersoll, *Birds in Legend and Folklore*, chap. 2. The eagle in U.S. military insignia is discussed by Duncan Campbell, "The Eagle Militant," *Early American Life*, Aug. 1978, 32–35. The eagle remains the most popular symbol of war-making power, particularly since the airplane became the premier weapon in World War II. *Adlertag* ("Eagle Day") was the name given to August 15, 1940, at the start of the German air attack on England. An interesting example of the confusion of the eagle symbol is the title of a book about World War II by Ronald Spector, *Eagle Against the Sun: America's War with Japan* (1985). Far from being at war with the sun, the eagle in ancient tradition revived itself in the sun, and in some beliefs was the sun itself. In a poem entitled "The American Eagle" D. H. Lawrence sets the eagle, representing U.S. imperialism, against the dove, America's "protestations of love and liberty." America's is the only eagle left, he declares, since those of European powers are "reeling from their perches" (*The Complete Poems of D. H. Lawrence*, 413; unless otherwise stated, quotations from Lawrence's poetry are from this collection).

4. Aquinas, *"Rhythmus ad SS. Sacramentum,"* trans. Gerard Manley Hopkins, in Hopkins, *Poems*, 212; Philippe de Thaun, "The Pelican," trans. Richard Wilbur, in Wilbur, *Poems*, 259–60; Whitman, "Trickle Drops," in *Complete Poetry*, 278; Thornton Wilder, *The Cabala and the Woman of Andros* (New York: Harper & Row, 1958), 37–38.

5. See Ingersoll, "Birds in Christian Tradition and Festival," in *Birds in Legend and Folklore*, chap. 6.

6. For an exhaustive account of the goldfinch in art, see Herbert Friedmann, *The Symbolic Goldfinch* (New York: Pantheon, 1946).

7. Saint Ambrose, *"Aeterne Rerum Conditor,"* trans. J. V. Cunningham, in *Latin Poetry in Verse Translation*, ed. L. R. Lind, 325; White, *Bestiary*, 151; Henry Vaughan, "Cock-Crowing," in *The Complete Poetry of Henry Vaughan*, ed. French Fogle (New York: Norton, 1969), 276–77.

8. Elizabeth Bishop, "Roosters," in *The Complete Poems: 1927–1979* (unless otherwise stated, Bishop quotations are from this collection). See Anne R. Newman, "Elizabeth Bishop's 'Rooster,' " in *Elizabeth Bishop: Modern Critical Views*, ed. Harold Bloom (New York: Chelsea House, 1985).

9. Melville's story has been the subject of considerable speculation, the most comprehensive discussions being those by William B. Dillingham, *Melville's Short Fiction* (Athens: University of Georgia Press, 1977), and Sidney P.

Moss, " 'Cock-A-Doodle-Doo!' and Some Legends in Melville Scholarship," *American Literature* 40 (1968): 198–210.

10. Henry David Thoreau, "Walking," in *The Selected Works of Henry D. Thoreau*, 685 (unless otherwise stated, prose quotations from Thoreau are from this collection).

11. Sean O'Casey, *Cock-a-Doodle Dandy*, in *Collected Plays*, vol. 4 (London: Macmillan, 1967), 122, 132.

12. William Butler Yeats, *Calvary*, in *The Collected Plays of W. B. Yeats*, 290–92 (hereafter cited in the text as *Collected Plays*), and *Four Plays for Dancers* (1921), 135–37.

13. The descent of the cosmogonic egg from Basil through Jerome, Augustine, and Du Bartas to Milton is traced by Frank Egleston Robbins, *The Hexaemeral Literature* (Chicago: University of Chicago Press, 1912).

14. Matt. 3.16, Mark 1.10, John 1.32, Luke 3.22. The dove was accepted as a symbol of the Holy Spirit by a local council at Constantinople in A.D. 536.

15. "The Three Languages," in *Grimm's German Folk Tales*, trans. Francis P. Magoun, Jr., and Alexander H. Krappe (Carbondale: Southern Illinois University Press, 1960), 126; Sir Walter Raleigh, *The History of the World* (New York: Burt Franklin, 1964), 398–99, bk. 1.11.6.

16. John Pielmeier, *Agnes of God* (New York: New American Library, 1985), vii.

17. Saint Teresa, *The Complete Works of St. Teresa*, trans. and ed. E. Allison Peers (New York: Sheed & Ward, n.d.), 1:271.

18. Gertrude Stein, *Four Saints in Three Acts*, in *Selected Operas and Plays of Gertrude Stein*, ed. Malcolm Brinnin (Pittsburgh: University of Pittsburgh Press), 72–73; *Lectures in America* (1935; repr., Boston: Beacon, 1957), 129.

19. Gustave Flaubert, "A Simple Heart," in *Three Tales*, trans. Arthur McDowell (New York: New Directions, 1924), 64, 72.

20. Julian Barnes, *Flaubert's Parrot*, 182–83.

21. Henry James, *The Wings of the Dove*, vols. 19 and 20 of *The Novels and Tales of Henry James* (New York: Scribner, 1937), bk. 2:143.

22. Dorothea Krook, *The Ordeal of Consciousness in Henry James* (London: Cambridge University Press, 1962), 229; Peter K. Garrett, *Scene and Symbol from George Eliot to James Joyce* (New Haven, Conn.: Yale University Press, 1969), 134.

23. Isaac Rosenberg, Walter Benton, Earle Birney, and Dunstan Thompson in Oscar Williams, *The War Poets* (New York: Day, 1945).

24. "The Story of the Magpie," in *Le Livre du Chevalier de la Tour-Landry* (1371–72), in *A Literary Middle English Reader*, ed. Arthur Stanburrough Cook, 311; John Collier, "Bird of Prey," in *The John Collier Reader* (New York: Knopf, 1972).

25. "The Twa Corbies" and "The Three Ravens," in *English and Scottish Popular Ballads*, ed. Helen Child Sargent and George Lyman Kittredge (Boston: Houghton Mifflin, 1932), 45; Alexander Pushkin, "Raven Doth to Raven

Fly," in *Alexander Pushkin: Collected Narrative and Lyrical Poetry*, trans. Walter Arndt (Ann Arbor, Mich.: Ardis, 1984); Thomas Lovell Beddoes, "Old Adam, the Carrion Crow," in *English Poetry and Prose of the Romantic Movement*, ed. George Benjamin Woods (New York: Scott Foresman, 1929), 1131; Anthony Hecht, "Birdwatchers of America," in *The Hard Hours: Poems By Anthony Hecht* (New York: Atheneum, 1967).

26. Patrick F. Houlihan, *The Birds of Ancient Egypt*, 132.

27. *Beowulf*, in *Old English Poetry*, trans. J. Duncan Spaeth (Princeton, N.J.: Princeton University Press, 1921), 41.17–21.

28. Peter S. Beagle, *A Fine and Private Place* (1960; repr., New York: Ballantine, 1969), 13, 61.

29. Robinson Jeffers, "Vulture," in *Rock and Hawk*. Unless otherwise stated, Jeffers quotations are from this collection.

30. James Thurber, "Whip-Poor-Will," in *My World—and Welcome to It* (New York: Harcourt Brace Jovanovich, 1969), 27–32; Patrick Süskind, *The Pigeon* (New York: Knopf, 1988), 14–15.

31. Theodore Dreiser, *An American Tragedy* (1925; repr., New York: Dell, 1959), 490, 527. I have been unable to find a source Dreiser may have used in his description of the "weir-weir" bird uttering its "ouphe and barghest cry." I can only deduce from the circumstances that it is a bittern. It is tempting to speculate that he had seen an article on the bittern suggesting that its three-note call is "accompanied by a peculiar undertone like a choking person gasping for breath" (Frederick Hermann, *Bird Lore* 26 [Nov.–Dec. 1924]: 441.)

32. Homer, *The Iliad of Homer*, trans. Richmond Lattimore (Chicago: University of Chicago Press, 1951), 12.237–40; Euripides, *The Bacchae*, in *Three Plays of Euripides*, trans. Paul Roche (New York: Norton, 1974), 87, ll. 256–57.

33. D. H. Lawrence, *The White Peacock*, 81 (hereafter cited in the text as *Peacock*).

34. "The Phoenix," in Kennedy, *Old English Poetry*. For a detailed appreciation of the Old English version, see Gilbert Highet, *The Classical Tradition*, rev. ed. (New York: Oxford University Press, 1957), 32–35.

35. *The Epic of Gilgamesh*, trans. N. K. Sanders (Baltimore: Penguin, 1967), 89. For a discussion of the claim made by some scholars that the Bible also describes the dead as being clad in feathers, see Alexander Heidel, *The Gilgamesh Epic and Old Testament Parallels* (Chicago: University of Chicago Press, 1946), 199–200.

36. W. S. DiPiero, "Thrasher," *New Yorker*, May 8, 1989, 76.

37. C. Day Lewis, "Buzzards over Castle Hill," in *Collected Poems of C. Day Lewis* (London: Cape, 1954), 285–86.

38. Beryl Rowland, *Birds with Human Souls: A Guide to Bird Symbolism*, 144; Edgar Allan Poe, "The Philosophy of Composition," in *Edgar Allan Poe: Essays and Reviews*, ed. G. R. Thompson (New York: Library of America, 1984), 25 (subsequent quotations are cited in the text as *Essays*).

39. Allen, Rideout, and Robinson, *American Poetry*, 341.

40. For possible sources of "The Raven" see William Gravely, "Christopher North and the Genesis of 'The Raven,'" PMLA 66 (Mar. 1951): 149–61; for parodies of the poem see Kenneth Silverman, *Edgar A. Poe: Mournful and Never-Ending Remembrance* (New York: HarperCollins, 1991), 238.

41. Odo of Cluny, *Occupatio*, cited in D. W. Robertson, *A Preface to Chaucer* (Princeton, N.J.: Princeton University Press, 1963), 94; Geoffrey Chaucer, *Legend of Good Women*, ll. 136–39. For a study of the soul-snatching fowler, especially in Chaucer, see B. G. Koonce, "Satan the Fowler," *Mediaeval Studies* 21 (1959): 176–84.

42. Herman Melville, *Moby-Dick*, chap. 130:678; Melville, *Clarel*, ed. Walter E. Bezanson (New York: Hendricks House, 1960), 382.

43. Wallace Stegner, *The Spectator Bird* (New York: Doubleday, 1976).

44. Hilda Doolittle, "Leda," in *Collected Poems, 1912–1944*, ed. Louis Martz (New York: New Directions, 1983), 120.

45. Rainer Maria Rilke, Sonnet 6 from "Nine Sonnets from the Thematic Material of the 'Sonnets to Orpheus,'" in *Rainer Maria Rilke: Poems 1906 to 1926*, trans. J. B. Leishman (New York: New Directions, 1957), 178. The epigraph I use at the head of this section also comes from Leishman, 265.

46. Leo Spitzer, "Leda and the Swan," *Modern Philology* 51 (May 1954): 271–76.

47. Dante, *The Divine Comedy*, trans. Dorothy Sayers (London: Penguin, 1950), Inferno 17.130–32.

48. Giorgio Melchior, *The Whole Mystery of Art: Pattern into Poetry in the Works of W. B. Yeats* (London: Routledge & Kegan Paul, 1960), 78.

49. Oliver St. John Gogarty, "Leda and the Swan," in *The Collected Poems of St. John Gogarty* (New York: Devin-Adair, 1954), 176–77.

50. Bassus, from Norman Douglas, *Birds and Beasts of the Greek Anthology* (London: Chapman & Hall, 1928) 6.125; Pamela Hansford Johnson, *The Unspeakable Skipton* (New York: Harcourt Brace, 1959).

51. Mona Van Duyn, "Leda Reconsidered," in *To See, To Take* (New York: Atheneum, 1971), 79–80.

52. D. H. Lawrence, "The Crown," in *Reflections on the Death of a Porcupine and Other Essays* (Bloomington: Indiana University Press, 1963), 75–78.

53. D. H. Lawrence on *Moby-Dick*, in *Studies in Classic American Literature* (1922; repr., New York: Doubleday, 1953), 172–73; Lawrence, *The Plumed Serpent*, ed. L. D. Clark (Cambridge: Cambridge University Press, 1987), 58 (hereafter cited in the text as *Serpent*).

54. Saul Bellow, *The Adventures of Augie March* (New York: Viking, 1960), 338.

55. Aristotle noted the enmity between eagle and serpent because the eagle "lives on snakes" (9.609a50). For discussions of the association of bird and serpent, see Edward A. Armstrong, *The Folklore of Birds*; Mircea Eliade, ed., *Encyclopedia of Religion* (New York: Macmillan, 1987), 13:372. For discus-

sions of Lawrence's use of the image, see Alice Baldwin, "The Structure of the Coatl Symbol in *The Plumed Serpent*," *Style*, 5 (Spring 1971): 138–50, and Ross Parmenter, *Lawrence in Oaxaca* (Salt Lake City: Peregrine Smith, 1984). Background material on the god figure Quetzalcoatl may be found in Jacques Soustelle, *The Daily Life of the Aztecs* (New York: Macmillan, 1962).

56. Friedrich Nietzsche, *Thus Spake Zarathustra*, 8 (prologue 4), 322 (part 4.74).

57. Emanuel Swedenborg, *The True Christian Religion*, trans. John C. Ager (New York: Swedenborg Foundation, 1906), 1:64–65.

58. Ted Hughes, "Crow and the Birds," in *Crow*, 26 (hereafter cited in the text as *Crow*).

59. Ted Hughes, "Hawk Roosting," in *Selected Poems, 1957–1967* (New York: Harper & Row, 1973).

60. For a close analysis of "The Bird with the Coppery, Keen Claws," see Barbara M. Fisher, *Wallace Stevens: The Intensest Rendezvous* (Charlottesville: University Press of Virginia, 1990), 25–27.

61. Mordecai Richler, *Solomon Gursky Was Here* (New York: Knopf, 1990), 143, 62, 408.

Chapter 3. Birds Caged, Hunted, and Killed

1. See Lee R. Johnson, "Aviaries and Aviculture in Ancient Rome" (Ph.D. diss., University of Maryland, 1968).

2. Hardy letter cited in Hal Orel, *The Final Years of Thomas Hardy, 1912–1928* (Lawrence: University of Kansas Press, 1976). For a discussion of birds in Hardy, see J. O. Bailey, *The Poetry of Thomas Hardy* (Chapel Hill: University of North Carolina Press, 1970).

3. Maya Angelou, *I Know Why the Caged Bird Sings* (New York: Random House, 1969).

4. May Sarton, *Selected Poems of May Sarton*, ed. Serena Sue Hilsinger and Lois Bryner (New York: Norton, 1978), 93.

5. Sally Carrighar, *Wild Heritage* (Boston: Houghton Mifflin, 1965), 63.

6. Konrad Lorenz, *King Solomon's Ring*, 75, 173.

7. Roger Welch, "A Song for the Pioneers," *Audubon*, Nov.–Dec. 1992, 112–15.

8. Peter Green, *Ovid: The Erotic Poems* (New York: Penguin, 1982), 291; Dorothy Parker, "From a Letter from Lesbia," *Collected Poetry of Dorothy Parker* (New York: Modern Library, 1936), 181.

9. John Skelton, *The Complete Poems of John Skelton*, 60–73. Unless otherwise stated, Skelton quotations are from this collection.

10. Theodore Howard Banks, *Milton's Imagery* (New York: Columbia University Press, 1950), 154.

11. Homer, *The Odyssey*, trans. Albert Cook (New York: Norton, 1967), 22.468–70.

12. Plautus, *Asinaria*, in *Three Roman Poets*, trans. F. A. Wright (London: Routledge & Kegan Paul, 1938), 215–16.

13. Alexander Pope, "Windsor-Forest," in *The Poems of Alexander Pope*, ed. John Butt (New Haven, Conn.: Yale University Press, 1963), 199, ll. 125–34, 111–18, 371–74.

14. Aeschylus, *Agamemnon*, in *Three Greek Plays*, trans. Edith Hamilton (New York: Norton, 1937).

15. Cited from Audubon's *Ornithological Biography* (1831–39) by Alexander B. Adams, *John James Audubon: A Biography* (1966; repr., New York: Putnam, 1976).

16. It was in Maine that Thoreau dined on the red-headed woodpecker—duly noted in his appendix to *Maine Woods* (New York: Crowell, 1966), 415. For Thoreau's observations on birds' nests see *Journal*, June 6 and 12, 1856.

17. W. H. Hudson, *The Book of a Naturalist*, 79 (hereafter cited in the text as *Naturalist*).

18. Geoffrey Ward, "FDR Birdwatcher," *Audubon*, Jan. 1990, 55; Burroughs, "Bird Enemies," in *Writings*, vol. 3.

19. Peter Matthiessen, *Killing Mister Watson* (New York: Random House, 1990), 47.

20. In another Ruskin lecture series we have this: "And very earnestly I ask you, have English gentlemen as a class, any other real object in their lives than killing birds?" (*The Eagle's Nest*, in *Works*, 22:243). Ruskin was very disturbed about killing birds for feathers to be used in women's fashions and the "merciless abstraction" of eiderdown. He quotes a long passage from William John Courthope's *Paradise of Birds* (1870) on these abuses. Ruskin said he gave up completing *Love's Meinie* because of the "distress and disgust of what I had read of bird-slaughter" (25:xxxi).

21. Rebecca West, *The Birds Fall Down* (New York: Viking, 1966), 76.

22. Isabel Colegate, *The Shooting Party* (New York: Viking, 1980), 136.

23. Jeffers, "Shooting Season," first published in *Descent to the Dead* (1931) and reprinted in *A Selection of Shorter Poems by Robinson Jeffers*, ed. Robert Haas (New York: Random House, 1987), 137.

24. Ernest Hemingway, *Across the River and into the Trees* (New York: Scribner, 1950), 282.

25. Giorgio Bassani, *The Heron* (New York: Harcourt Brace, 1968), 91, 158–59.

26. Lawrence Durrell, *Justine* (New York: Dutton, 1957), 225.

27. Ivan Turgenev, "Kassyan of Fair Springs," in *A Sportsman's Sketches*, trans. Constance Garnett (1902; repr., New York: AMS Press, 1970), 1:182–84.

28. Samuel Taylor Coleridge, *The Notebooks of Samuel Taylor Coleridge*,

ed. Kathleen Coburn, vol. 3 (Princeton, N.J.: Princeton Univ. Press, 1973), no. 3401.

29. Gwen Harwood, "Father and Child," in *The Women Poets in English*, ed. Ann Stanford, 295.

30. Boris Pasternak, *Doctor Zhivago*, 148, 436.

31. Jerzy Kosinski, *The Painted Bird* (1965; repr., New York: Modern Library, 1970), 42–43, 49, 51.

Chapter 4. Birds and the Erotic

1. Cited in Hugh J. Schonfield, *The Song of Songs* (New York: New American Library, 1959), 41.

2. For a detailed discussion of the birds in Chaucer's *Parliament of Fowls*, see J. A. W. Bennett, *The Parlement of Foules, An Interpretation* (Oxford: Oxford University Press, 1957).

3. John Donne, *The Complete Poetry and Selected Prose of John Donne*, 171. Unless otherwise stated, Donne quotations are from this collection.

4. Houlihan, *Birds of Ancient Egypt*, 124. Originally in Child's *English and Scottish Popular Ballads*, the American version of "The Gray Cock" cited here is from Olive Diane Campbell and Cecil J. Sharpe, *English Folk Songs from the Southern Appalachians* (New York: Putnam, 1917), 128.

5. F. Scott Fitzgerald, *Tender Is the Night* (1933; repr., New York: Scribner, 1962), 136, 40. For the relation with Keats see William E. Doherty, " '*Tender Is the Night*' and 'Ode to a Nightingale,' " in *Tender Is the Night: Essays in Criticism*, ed. Marvin J. LaHood (Bloomington: Indiana University Press, 1969).

6. Catullus, "*Passer, deliciae maea puellae*," in *Odi et Amo: The Complete Poetry of Catullus*, trans. Roy Arthur Swanson (New York: Liberal Arts Press, 1959), no. 2. The wide influence of Catullus's two bird poems is studied by Karl Pomeroy Harrington, *Catullus and His Influence* (New York: Cooper Square, 1969). Lorenz, *King Solomon's Ring*, 133.

7. Sir Philip Sidney, *The Poems of Sir Philip Sidney*, 208, no. 83.

8. William Carlos Williams, "The Sparrow," in *Pictures from Brueghel and Other Poems* (Norfolk, Conn.: New Directions, 1962), 131–32.

9. In his *Lexicon* the tenth-century lexicographer Suidas based his analogy of the swallow (*chelidon*) and the vulva on a verse from Sappho, though this identification does not hold with modern scholarship. The bird's nest still has a similar application, however. In *Romeo and Juliet* the Nurse tells Juliet that she will go to "fetch a ladder, by the which your love / Must climb a bird's nest soon when it is dark" (2.5.73–75). In Thomas Mann's *Doctor Faustus*, Adrian foolishly commissions his best friend to speak on his behalf to the woman he wants to marry, and when he learns that his friend had also made known his own love for her, resulting in their engagement, Adrian says, "It reminds one of a schoolboy who finds a bird's nest and out of sheer joy shows it to another boy who then goes and steals it" (chap. 42). In "The Uncon-

scious Bird Symbol in Literature" (*American Imago* 7 [1950]: 173–82) Arthur Wormhoudt offers evidence, often not very convincing, of the association of birds with the breast and penis.

10. Cook, *Middle English Reader*, 429.

11. D. H. Lawrence, *St. Mawr and the Man Who Died*, 163–78 (hereafter cited in the text as *Man*).

12. Reproduced in *Man, Myth, and Magic*, ed. Richard Cavendish (New York: Cavendish, 1955), 3:786. The goddess Nekhbet in the form of a griffin vulture is similarly poised in the mortuary temple of Queen Hatshepshut (Houlihan, *Birds of Ancient Egypt*, 40–41). In a volume of poems titled *Cave Birds* Ted Hughes adapts, more obscurely than Lawrence, some motifs of the Osiris legend: the initial affront against woman, the death of the transgressor, the reassembling of the body parts, and the rebirth in the form of a hawk. A winged Isis was sometimes represented as reviving Osiris with the beating of her wings.

13. Gimbutas, *Gods and Goddesses*, 144–46.

14. D. H. Lawrence, *The Rainbow* (1915; repr., New York: Modern Library, 1927), 191, 193.

15. For discussions of Lawrence's use of Bede's sparrow, see E. L. Nicholes, "The 'Simile of the Sparrow' in *The Rainbow*," *Modern Language Notes* 64 (1949): 171; Patricia Abel and Robert Hogan, "Lawrence's Singing Birds," in *A D. H. Lawrence Miscellany*, ed. Harry T. Moore (Carbondale: Southern Illinois University Press, 1959), 204–11.

16. D. H. Lawrence, *Lady Chatterley's Lover* (1928; repr., New York: Modern Library, 1959), 121–26.

17. John Steinbeck, "The White Quail," in *American Short Stories*, ed. Eugene Current-Garcia and Walton R. Patrick, 535–40.

18. Mary Wilkins Freeman, "A New England Nun," ibid., 268–79.

19. Sarah Orne Jewett, "A White Heron," in *The Country of the Pointed Firs and Other Stories*, sel. Willa Cather (1925; repr., New York: Doubleday, 1956); John James Audubon, *Audubon Reader: The Best Writings of John James Audubon*, ed. Scott Russell Sanders (Bloomington: Indiana University Press, 1986), 65.

20. W. H. Hudson, *The Purple Land* (1885; repr., New York: Modern Library, 1926), 182.

21. W. H. Hudson, *Green Mansions* (1904; repr., New York: Random House, 1944), 218, 240 (hereafter cited in the text as *Mansions*).

22. Hubert Selby, Jr., *Last Exit to Brooklyn* (1957; repr., New York: Grove, 1965), 126.

23. William Styron, *Lie Down in Darkness* (New York: New American Library, 1951), 325, 351, 355–56 (hereafter cited in the text as *Darkness*).

24. Charlotte Brontë, *Jane Eyre* (London: Penguin, 1953), 140, 314–15, 434.

25. See Philip Mahone Griffith, "The Image of the Trapped Animal in Hardy's *Tess of the D'Urbervilles*," *Tulane Studies in English* 13 (1963): 85–94.

26. Kate Chopin, *The Awakening*, introd. Kenneth Eble (1899; repr., New York: Capricorn, 1964), 19.

27. Birds in fiction about women is the subject of an early discussion by Ellen Moers, *Literary Women* (New York: Doubleday, 1976), 245–51.

28. Tennessee Williams, *The Roman Spring of Mrs. Stone* (New York: New Directions, 1950), 115, 11, 70.

29. Thomas Mann, *The Black Swan*, trans. Willard Trask (New York: Knopf, 1976), 75, 116–25.

30. Ruth Rendell, *An Unkindness of Ravens* (New York: Pantheon, 1985), 125–27, 70–71; Hildegarde Flanner, "Hawk Is a Woman," in *Women Poets*, ed. Stanford, 223.

31. Virginia Woolf, *To The Lighthouse* (New York: Harcourt Brace, 1927), 34, 59.

32. Gaston Bachelard, *L'eau et les rêves* (Paris: Libraire Jose Costi, 1942), 52.

33. John Burroughs, in *The Heart of Burroughs's Journals*, ed. Clara Barrus (Boston: Houghton Mifflin, 1928), 72; Edwin Way Teale, *North with the Spring* (New York: Dodd, Mead, 1951), 54; Lewis Nkosi, *Mating Birds* (New York: St. Martin's, 1986), 27.

34. Glenway Wescott, *The Pilgrim Hawk* (1940), in *Great American Short Novels*, ed. William Phillips (New York: Dial, 1957), 634 (hereafter cited in the text as *Hawk*).

35. On Wescott's use of the falcon to symbolize the writer's problems, see Ira Johnson, *Glenway Wescott: The Paradox* (Port Washington, N.Y.: Kennikat, 1971), and William H. Rueckert, *Glenway Wescott* (New York: Twayne, 1965).

36. Alan Paton, *Too Late the Phalarope*, 95, 213, 47. Austin Roberts was the author of *The Birds of South Africa*, first published in 1940 and revised in 1957 by G. R. McLachan and R. Liversidge.

37. William Wharton, *Birdy* (1978; repr., New York: Avon, 1980), 186, 231 (hereafter cited in the text as *Birdy*).

38. Harry Crews, *The Hawk Is Dying* (New York: Knopf, 1973), 55 (hereafter cited in the text as *Dying*).

39. *The Art of Falconry*, trans. Casey A. Wood and F. Marjorie Fyfe (Stanford, Calif.: Stanford University Press, 1943), 160.

Chapter 5. Literature and the Future of Birds

1. Margaret Atwood, *Surfacing* (New York: Simon and Schuster, 1972), 134–50, and "Scarlet Ibis," *Bluebeard's Egg* (Boston: Houghton Mifflin, 1986), 198–99.

2. Mary McCarthy, *Birds of America* (New York: Harcourt Brace, 1971), 162, 183 (hereafter cited in the text as *Birds*).

3. Immanuel Kant, *Critique of Judgment*, in *Kant: Selections*, ed. Theodore

Meyer Greene, trans. Max Muller (New York: Scribner, 1929), 491 (sec. 82), 462–63 (sec. 63); Mary McCarthy, "One Touch of Nature," in *The Writing on the Wall and Other Literary Essays* (New York: Harcourt Brace, 1970), 212. In the same essay she refers to the influence of Kant on Wordsworth's criticism of industrial progress (196).

4. Lucretius, *On the Nature of Things*, in *The Stoic and Epicurean Philosophers*, ed. Whitney J. Oates, trans. H. A. J. Munro (New York: Random House, 1940), 113, bk. 2.

5. Carl Sandburg, *The Complete Poems of Carl Sandburg*, rev. ed. (New York: Harcourt Brace Jovanovich, 1986), 184–85.

6. Harlan Ellison, *Deathbird Stories* (New York: Harper & Row, 1975), 334.

7. Daphne du Maurier, "The Birds," in *Echoes from the Macabre* (New York: Doubleday, 1977); Michael Crichton, *The Andromeda Strain* (New York: Random House, 1969).

8. George Orwell, *Nineteen Eighty-Four* (1949; repr., New York: New American Library, 1961), 103; Eugene Zamiatan, *We* (1924; repr., New York: Dutton, 1952), 89, 205–7; Aldous Huxley, *Brave New World* (1932; repr., New York: Harper, 1950), 23, 134.

9. Walter Tevis, *Mockingbird* (Garden City, N.Y.: Doubleday, 1980), 70.

10. James Dickey, *Deliverance* (Boston: Houghton Mifflin, 1970), 87–89 (hereafter cited in the text as *Deliverance*). One of Dickey's poems, "The Owl King" (*Poems: 1957–1967* [Middletown, Conn.: Wesleyan University Press], 1967), has to do with a boy's encounter with an owl:

> In my hand I feel
> A talon, a grandfather's claw
> Bone cold and straining
> To keep from breaking my skin.

The "grandfather's claw" is reminiscent of the last scene of William Faulkner's *The Bear*, in which Ike McCaslin visits the wilderness for the last time and uses the word *grandfather* to greet a snake.

11. Ogburn, *Adventure of Birds*, 66.

12. Jane Harrison, *Epilegomena to the Study of Greek Religion* (1921; repr., (New Hyde Park, N.Y.: University Books, 1921), 113; Denise Levertov, "Come into Animal Presence," in *Poems: 1960–1967* (New York: New Directions, 1983).

13. John James Audubon, *The 1826 Journal of John James Audubon*, ed. Alice Ford (Norman: University of Oklahoma Press, 1967), 285.

selected bibliography

Allen, Gay Wilson, Walter B. Rideout, and James K. Robinson, eds. *American Poetry*. New York: Harper & Row, 1965.

Aristotle. *Historia Animalium*. Vol. 4, *The Works of Aristotle*. Translated by D'Arcy Wentworth Thompson. Oxford: Clarendon, 1962.

Armstrong, Edward A. *The Folklore of Birds*. New York: Dover, 1970.

Arnold, Matthew. *The Poems of Matthew Arnold*. Edited by Kenneth Allott and Miriam Allott. London: Longmans, 1979.

Barnes, Julian. *Flaubert's Parrot*. New York: Knopf, 1985.

Bishop, Elizabeth. *The Complete Poems: 1927–1979*. New York: Farrar Straus, 1983.

Blake, William. *Blake: Complete Writings*. Edited by Geoffrey Keynes. London: Oxford University Press, 1971.

Browne, Sir Thomas. *The Works of Sir Thomas Browne*. Edited by Geoffrey Keynes. 2 vols. Chicago: University of Chicago Press, 1964.

Burroughs, John. *The Writings of John Burroughs*. 14 vols. Boston: Houghton Mifflin, 1904–5.

Ciardi, John. *Selected Poems*. Fayetteville: University of Arkansas Press, 1984.

Coleridge, Samuel Taylor. *The Poems of Samuel Taylor Coleridge*. Edited by Ernest Hartley Coleridge. London: Oxford University Press, 1960.

Cook, Arthur Stanburrough, ed. *A Literary Middle English Reader*. Boston: Ginn, 1915.

Current-Garcia, Eugene, and Walton R. Patrick, eds. *American Short Stories*. Chicago: Scott Foresman, 1952.

Dickinson, Emily. *The Complete Poems of Emily Dickinson.* Edited by Thomas H. Johnson. Boston: Little, Brown, 1960.

Donne, John. *The Complete Poetry and Selected Prose of John Donne.* Edited by Charles M. Coffin. New York: Modern Library, 1952.

Eliot, T. S. *The Complete Poems and Plays.* New York: Harcourt Brace, 1952.

Emerson, Ralph Waldo. *Poems.* Vol. 9, *Emerson's Complete Works.* Boston: Houghton Mifflin, 1890.

Euripides. *Greek Tragedies.* Edited by David Greene and Richmond Lattimore. Translated by Witter Bynner. Chicago: University of Chicago Press, 1960.

Everson, William. *The Veritable Years.* Santa Barbara, California: Black Sparrow, 1978.

Frost, Robert. *Complete Poems of Robert Frost.* New York: Holt, Rinehart, 1965.

Gimbutas, Marija. *The Gods and Goddesses of Old Europe.* Berkeley: University of California Press, 1974.

Goethe, Johann Wolfgang. *Goethe's Faust.* Translated by Louis MacNeice. New York: Oxford University Press, 1961.

Gubernatis, Angelo de. *Zoological Mythology.* 2 vols. 1872. Reprint. Chicago: Singing Tree, 1968.

Hardy, Thomas. *The Complete Poems of Thomas Hardy.* Edited by James Gibson. New York: Macmillan, 1979.

———. *Tess of the D'Urbervilles.* 1891. Reprint. New York: Modern Library, 1951.

Hebel, J. William, and Hoyt H. Hudson, eds. *Poetry of the English Renaissance.* New York: Crofts, 1936.

Hopkins, Gerard Manley. *The Poems of Gerard Manley Hopkins.* Edited by W. H. Gardner and N. H. Mackenzie. 4th ed. London: Oxford University Press, 1967.

Houlihan, Patrick F. *The Birds of Ancient Egypt.* Warminster, England: Aris and Phillips, 1986.

Hudson, W. H. *The Book of a Naturalist.* London: Thomas Nelson & Sons, 1919.

Hughes, Ted. *Crow.* New York: Harper & Row, 1971.

Ingersoll, Ernest. *Birds in Legend and Folklore.* Detroit: Singing Tree, 1968.

Jeffers, Robinson. *Rock and Hawk.* Edited by Robert Haas. New York: Random House, 1987.

Joyce, James. *A Portrait of the Artist as a Young Man.* Edited by Richard Ellmann. New York: Viking, 1966.

Kennedy, Charles W., trans. *An Anthology of Old English Poetry.* New York: Oxford University Press, 1960.

Lawrence, D. H. *The Complete Poems of D. H. Lawrence*. Edited by Vivian de Sola Pinto and F. Warren Roberts. New York: Viking, 1971.

————. *Phoenix: The Posthumous Papers of D. H. Lawrence*. Edited by Edward D. McDonald. New York: Viking, 1974.

————. *The Plumed Serpent*. Edited by L. D. Clark. Cambridge: Cambridge University Press, 1987.

————. *St. Mawr and the Man Who Died*. 1928. Reprint. New York: Vintage, 1953.

————. *The White Peacock*. Edited by Andrew Robertson. Cambridge: Cambridge University Press, 1983.

Lind, L. R., ed. *Latin Poetry in Verse Translation*. Boston: Houghton Mifflin, 1957.

Lorenz, Konrad Z. *King Solomon's Ring*. New York: Crowell, 1952.

Mandeville, Sir John. *Mandeville's Travels*. Edited by M. C. Seymour. Oxford: Oxford University Press, 1967.

Melville, Herman. *Moby-Dick*. Edited by Charles Feidelson, Jr. Indianapolis: Bobbs-Merrill, 1964.

————. *The Great Short Works of Herman Melville*. Edited by Jerry Allen. New York: Harper & Row, 1966.

Meredith, George. *The Poetical Works of George Meredith*. Edited by G. M. Trevelyan. New York: Scribner, 1930.

Merwin, W. S. *Green with Beasts.* New York: Knopf, 1956.

Moore, Marianne. *The Complete Poems of Marianne Moore*. New York: Macmillan, 1967.

Nietzsche, Friedrich. *Thus Spake Zarathustra*. Translated by Thomas Common. New York: Modern Library, n.d.

Ogburn, Charlton. *The Adventure of Birds*. New York: Morrow, 1980.

Pasternak, Boris. *Doctor Zhivago*. 1958. Translated by Max Hayward and Manya Harari. Reprint. New York: New American Library, 1960.

Paton, Alan. *Too Late the Phalarope*. New York: Scribner, 1953.

Perse, Saint-John. *Collected Poems*. Translated by Robert Fitzgerald. Bollingen Series No. 87. Princeton: Princeton University Press, 1971.

Plath, Sylvia. *The Collected Poems*. Edited by Ted Hughes. New York: Harper & Row, 1981.

Plato. *The Dialogues of Plato*. Translated by B[enjamin] Jowett. 4th ed. 4 vols. Oxford: Oxford University Press, 1969.

Pliny. *Natural History*. Vol 3. Translated by H. Rackham. Loeb Classical Library. Cambridge, Mass.: Harvard University Press, 1967.

Roethke, Theodore. *The Collected Poems of Theodore Roethke*. New York: Doubleday, 1966.

Rowland, Beryl. *Birds with Human Souls: A Guide to Bird Symbolism*. Knoxville: University of Tennessee Press, 1978.

Rushdie, Salman. *The Satanic Verses*. New York: Viking, 1988.

Ruskin, John. *The Works of John Ruskin.* Edited by E. T. Cook and Alexander Wedderburn. London: George Allen, 1906.

Scollard, Clinton, and Jessie B. Rittenhouse, comps. *The Bird-Lovers' Anthology.* Boston: Houghton Mifflin, 1930.

Sidney, Sir Philip. *The Poems of Sir Philip Sidney.* Edited by William A. Ringler, Jr. Oxford: Oxford University Press, 1962.

Skelton, John. *The Complete Poems of John Skelton.* Edited by Philip Henderson. London: Dent, 1966.

Spenser, Edmund. *The Poetical Works of Edmund Spenser.* Edited by J. C. Smith and E. De Selincourt. London: Oxford University Press, 1935.

Stanford, Ann, ed. *The Women Poets in English.* New York: McGraw-Hill, 1972.

Stevens, Wallace. *The Collected Poems of Wallace Stevens.* New York: Knopf, 1978.

Thomson, James. *Poetical Works.* Edited by J. Logie Robertson. London: Oxford University Press, 1971.

Thoreau, Henry David. *Collected Poems of Henry Thoreau.* Edited by Carl Bode. Baltimore: Johns Hopkins University Press, 1965.

———. *The Journal of Henry D. Thoreau.* Edited by Bradford Torrey and Francis H. Allen. Boston: Houghton Mifflin, 1949.

———. *The Selected Works of Henry D. Thoreau.* Edited by Walter Harding. Boston: Houghton Mifflin, 1975.

Walton, Izaak. *The Compleat Angler.* Introduction by Margaret Bottrall. Everyman's Library. London: Dent, 1965.

Warren, Robert Penn. *New and Selected Poems, 1923–1985.* New York: Random House, 1985.

White, T. H., ed. *The Bestiary: A Book of Beasts.* New York: Putnam, 1960.

Whitman, Walt. *Walt Whitman: Complete Poetry and Collected Prose.* Edited by Justin Kaplan. New York: Library of America, 1982.

Whitney, Geffrey. *A Choice of Emblemes.* Edited by Henry Green. New York: Benjamin Blum, 1967.

Wilbur, Richard. *New and Collected Poems.* New York: Harcourt Brace, 1988.

Wilde, Oscar. *The Letters of Oscar Wilde.* Edited by Rupert Hart-Davis. New York: Harcourt, 1962.

Williams, Oscar, ed. *A Little Treasury of Modern Poetry.* New York: Scribner, 1946.

Wordsworth, William. *Wordsworth: Poetical Works.* Edited by Thomas Hutchinson and revised by Ernest De Selincourt. London: Oxford University Press, 1974.

Yeats, William Butler. *The Collected Plays of W. B. Yeats.* New York: Macmillan, 1953.

———. *The Collected Poems of W. B. Yeats.* New York: Macmillan, 1951.